MAKE YOUR OWN DOLLHOUSES AND DOLLHOUSE MINIATURES

MAKE YOUR OWN DOLLHOUSES AND DOLLHOUSE MINIATURES

Marian Maeve O'Brien

Drawings by Eileen Kramer

HAWTHORN BOOKS, INC.
Publishers/NEW YORK

MAKE YOUR OWN DOLLHOUSES AND DOLLHOUSE MINIATURES

Library of Congress Catalog Card Number: 74-20297
ISBN: 0-8015-4801-2
1 2 3 4 5 6 7 8 9 10

To miniaturists everywhere,
whose joy in their art
keeps them happy,
retains their youth,
and perpetuates their talents.

Contents

Introduction

It is by no mere coincidence that two of the three greatest dollhouses in the world, Queen Mary's, Colleen Moore's, and Titania's Palace, are fairy castles. We all know that when we immerse ourselves in the little world encompassed by our collections, we take leave of mundane problems completely. Major Sir Nevile Wilkinson, soldier, artist, and craftsman, who conceived and constructed Titania's Palace, assures us in his autobiography that the idea for the palace actually came to him from a fairy.

One hears a dozen different versions, but the gist of the matter is that Titania, the fairy queen, worried about people's turning from pleasures of the soul to shallower realistic pleasures, and she was searching for a way to revive interest in fairies. Alighting on the back of Sir Nevile's armchair one evening, she whispered, "I want your help. I want you to build me a palace."

"Want me to build you a palace!" Sir Nevile repeated, hardly believing his ears. "But I am not an architect!"

"It's not the least good your making excuses," Titania went on.

"But you haven't a notion, ma'am, what a lot of different craftsmen it takes to make a palace! You want somebody who is a carpenter and a decorator and a builder and a stonemason and a wood-carver, and a plumber and a potter and a silversmith and a needlewoman and a—you just haven't a notion, ma'am, what a lot of different craftsmen it takes to build a palace!"

"I leave the details to you," she said, and winging upward, she touched the tip of his nose with her foot, which woke him up.

While this seems an unlikely tale and while, as we said, there are dozens of different versions, we must remember that Sir Nevile was an Irishman, an Ulster King of Arms, and that he was visited by the fairy queen in Ireland, where such things are not unknown at all. And we must remember, too, that in the world of Lilliput anything is possible. But even for fairies, building a dollhouse and furnishing it does require the work of many, many craftsmen, and that is the reason for this book.

It is a fine thing to be able to hire other artisans to make the small items that the collectors want so badly, but it is my firm conviction that any of us can become a composite craftsman. The people who can hold in their palms a tiny chair, an exquisite piece of needlepoint, or a minuscule set of curtains that sprang from their own fingers, enjoy a sense of achievement that can be found in no other way. Thus we hope to show in this book that the collector and builder can carry out the details just as Titania commanded Sir Nevile to do—and will enter a new and fulfilling world.

It goes without saying, of course, that few of us are so talented that we are masters of every craft; you may be an expert at crochet but never develop into a wood-carver, which happens to be my own weak spot. I suffered many a slashed finger and was made unhappy by many a crude piece of small furniture before I admitted that this was not my milieu.

However, the great thing about dollhouses, their making and furnishing, is that almost every craft is represented in the final result. If you can crochet life-sized objects, you can create in miniature merely by using a smaller needle and finer thread, and if you can't crochet at all, it is fun to learn. If you love the relaxation of carving or whittling, you can create lovely $\frac{1}{12}$-scale pieces, starting with only a block of wood, an X-Acto knife, and a little patience. And even though you're not much of a seamstress, you need have no hesitation about trying miniature curtains for your dollhouses, since if you don't achieve the effect you want on the first try, it's not a matter of having spoiled yards and yards of fine material; you've simply had fun with a little scrap you found in your sewing box, and you can try again.

In this small world it is simple and inexpensive to correct an error; one needs only a button to start a dish garden. And, as one artist pointed out, in painting a full-sized portrait, an ear that is out of proportion is truly a catastrophe, but on a 2 x 3-inch miniature and using the new acrylic paints, it's a simple matter to scrape off the little offending ear and do it over—or scrap the whole portrait and try for something better.

As a beginner, you must reconcile yourself to the fact that some things you attempt will be short of perfection. Even Mrs. Thorne, the inspired creator of the Thorne rooms, which are the bible of all miniaturists, once confided to a reporter that she resolved to make all the furnishings herself. She purchased the necessary tools and supplies, withdrew from her active life, and proceeded to go to work on a $\frac{1}{12}$-scale chair. When she finished some two months and many split thumbs later, what she had produced was so poor that she put everything away—the designs, the tools, and the supplies—and never again tried to make a small object.

I would hope that you won't be so easily discouraged. After all, even Leonardo da Vinci made 150 miniature models of a flying apparatus before he had one that he thought would work (it didn't though), and we read in many places of the troubles that Messrs. Chippendale and Phyffe had before they reached the perfection that we now see in their pieces.

With practice will come skill, I promise you. And with skill will come the deep satisfaction and pleasure of creating, one of the happiest emotions a person can ever know. With the directions outlined in this book, you can set yourself on the path—for if I could do it, I know that you can. At any rate, it's a thrill I'd like to share, and I hope you'll join me.

We hope that every dollhouse builder, every miniaturist will sign and date their work, so there will never be any lack of information to identify it. Some craftspeople build a little shallow box on the back of a dollhouse and in it secure the story, the dates, the photographs of work in progress, any other information that will be of help for the miniature lovers who will come after them.

Others keep a journal of their work. Sketches, daily reports of progress, bibliographies are all treasured in a spot perhaps underneath the house, perhaps in the attic.

The thing to remember is that you must have a hallmark, some unmistakable signature that will mark this work as your own in the years to come. Only in this way can we keep pace with the craftsmen of the past; only in this way can we be identified by the craftsmen of the future.

MAKE YOUR OWN DOLLHOUSES AND DOLLHOUSE MINIATURES

1 The Tools of Your Trade

That "s" on the word "trades" in the chapter title is not a typographical error; when you begin your work on miniatures you will find that you're into more trades than the handyman who comes around on Friday to sharpen the knives. Carpentry will probably be the first of them. And for carpentry you will need, first, a knife or knives. You will find one on the workbench down in the basement, but you'll do better work with less aggravation if you'll get to a hobby or hardware shop and buy yourself a good one to start with.

A workman is known by his tools, someone has said. His work is known by the tools used for it, too. You need good tools. If you are starting from scratch, we would recommend one of the complete sets offered at your hobby shop under the X-Acto label: handsomely arranged on a plastic bed is the deluxe set, which includes 2 knives, 2 packages blades, a ball-peen hammer, a coping saw, a small screwdriver, 3 jeweler's screwdrivers, a hot cutting tip and a soldering iron that you won't need immediately, a mini-vise, pliers, tinsnips, sander, awl, files, block plane, tweezers, gouges, and chisel. The smaller set is just as handsome but doesn't contain the soldering iron and cutting tip, and offers only one screwdriver. Plenty for a beginner. Both sets cost less than the items would if purchased individually. We might add that there are two other deluxe sets at $49.50 and $70.00, but these are for more advanced craft projects.

As a starter, let's buy the No. 1 knife, which is for light-to-medium work, and the No. 2 knife for heavy work, shown on the next page. The aluminum handle on the No. 1 (*far left*) is $\frac{5}{16}$ inch in diameter; the one on the No. 2 is $\frac{7}{16}$ inch. The handles shown below will accommodate any of the X-Acto blades you might need, plus the razor-saw blades shown above, the top blade being $\frac{3}{4}$ inch wide, the second 1 inch wide, and the bottom $1\frac{1}{4}$ inches wide. Notice the angled handle, which fits into the handles shown at left. You'll never know how many scraped knuckles this angle will save you, until you start

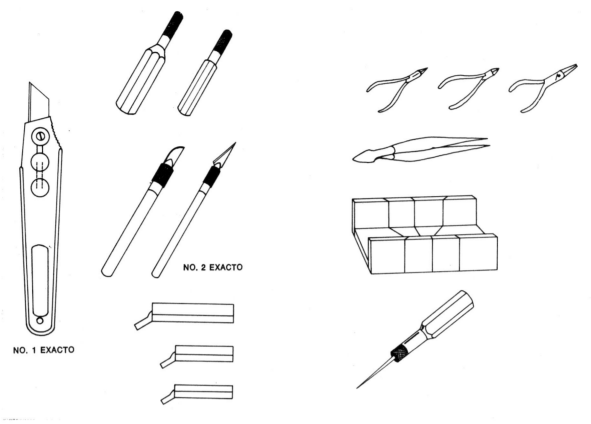

NO. 2 EXACTO

NO. 1 EXACTO

X-Acto knives

Pliers, tweezers, miter box, and awl

to work. A utility knife is useful but not really necessary. It has a blade that is reversible, giving double service, retractable, in case you are working on small pieces, and replaceable. It costs about 39 cents with extra blades.

You will most certainly need at least two pliers, the so-called needle-nose shown at right above, and the diagonal cutting type (*center*) or the flat nose shown at left. They will cost about $3.00 each. A good tweezer is indispensable and costs around $1.00. A miter box, shown next, can be purchased in a small size for around $4.00, and is also indispensable; it will give you sharp, true corners on door and window moldings and picture frames. The little awl shown in an X-Acto handle is also indispensable for starting nail or screw holes, marking lines on wood, and such details. If you have the X-Acto handle, all you need buy is the point.

Companion to the awl used in a detachable handle is the Pocket Scriber made on the same principle with tempered-steel points. This is helpful in marking woods where you want a fine line, more delicate than a pencil line. It costs around $1.20; and one with a carbide point, which will even scribe hard metals, costs $1.95 or thereabouts. There are several models available.

And right up at the top of the list, if you're thinking of tools in the order of their importance, is perhaps the least expensive of all—a metal-edged ruler. For scribing or cutting it is indispensable.

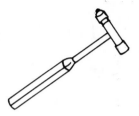

You will need, of course, a small hammer, and you might very well find one on the family workbench which will do, although it must have a rather short handle to fit into dollhouse rooms. Because good tools mean a great deal to me, I prefer to buy a ball-peen hammer, which is exactly suited to my purpose. Again, there are several brands, but I like the X-Acto with interchangeable heads. With such a tool, the craftsperson is ready for anything.

Later on you'll need a quartet of small hand C-clamps, such as we show here. They cost around 90 cents each and usually are offered in sets of four different sizes, all small enough for dollhouse furniture.

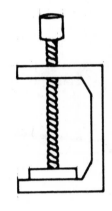

Another clamp, which I find myself using most on furniture, is the Boston, or Hunt, clip, which is on almost every office desk and available at all stationery houses. These come in sizes from 1 to 4 inches, and are invaluable for dollhouse work. They're especially great to secure trim around doors and windows, where even the smallest C-clamp won't fit.

And about the time you need the clamp, you'll begin to need a small hand drill for making holes, such as are needed in our roped bed (p. oo) and many other pieces. A small one costs about $3.00, and works exactly like a rotary egg beater. You will now have ample tools for beginning your exciting woodworking career.

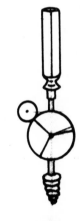

The above-mentioned tools are of professional caliber. If you would like to begin at less expense, two sets of tools are made of the types shown above, one in Austria and one in West Germany. Both adults and children can use these tools with ease, and they come in attractive leather cases lined in red which zipper closed when not in use and measure 4 x 6¾ inches in size. They contain pliers, a small wrench, a 4½-inch screwdriver with bakelite handle, and a bakelite socket handle which is used with two sizes of screwdriver, a tack hammer, an awl, and a drill. They sell (see various gift-house catalogues) at $9.00 or $10.00, and are immensely practical. I have built two dollhouses using only these tools plus a miter box and a small saw.

Ball-peen hammer, C-clamp, and hand drill

In justice to yourself, you should provide a little work space, so you don't have to clean up every time you stop working. Allegra Mott, of the Mott Miniatures clan, used to tell the story of making her miniatures, in the very beginning, in a small closet off the kitchen. In the first issue of the useful *Mott Miniature Workshop* paper, her daughter Elizabeth remembers her saying, "You'll never know how much I accomplished while waiting for the potatoes to boil!" If your children have married and you have an unused guest room, that can be your

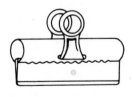

Boston, or Hunt, clip

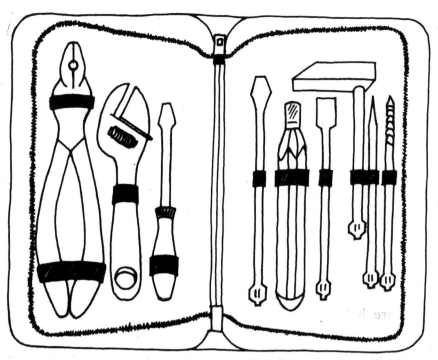

Tool set in case

workshop. An attic is ideal if you can have a telephone installed there so you won't have to run up and down the stairs—or you might prefer doing without the telephone so you can get away from its incessant demands while you are working. In my house, since I don't like working in the rather dark basement workshop, I've taken over an unused sunporch.

If you can't find an unused working space, don't despair. Keep all your tools and supplies in a large corrugated box, and use the piano bench in the living room as a workbench, as I did when I was building a little log cabin. Handy to both front door and telephone and kitchen, this takes only moments for getting ready to work and cleaning up afterward.

One other point that many makers of life-sized furniture will bring up; they'll tell you that you must have a sander or sanding block for finishing the wood. This is fine for life-sized pieces, but not true for the tiny things we are making; a sander would never get into the little crevices and corners on a ¹⁄₁₂-scale job, nor would a folded piece of sandpaper. We'll discuss sandpaper in the next chapter, but you'll find that an emery board, which has coarse grit on one side and fine on the other, is ideal for miniature-making and finishing. I sometimes even cut one in half lengthwise for a further reduction in the width, for sanding in chip-carved pieces and around turned or carved legs.

One last tool that can be handled by amateur and expert alike and will produce astounding results (once mastered, it will produce work that will compare with that of the most accomplished woodworker) is the Dremel Moto-Shop jigsaw-workshop combination, which is advertised as five power tools in one and really lives up to its billing. You may find this at your hobby shop or lumber supply house, or it may be ordered directly from Craftsman Wood Service Company, 2727 South Mary Street, Chicago, Illinois 60608. This rugged jigsaw has a power takeoff for all the accessories that you will eventually need, and costs around $50.00. It is about the size of a portable sewing machine, and can be used on a card table and stored in a closet; it is truly wonderful for the beginner. It will cut up to 2 x 4-inch wood, plastic, light-gauge metals, and practically anything else, and it comes with a rubber backing pad, adapter, an assortment of sanding discs and saw blades; the deluxe model (around $54.00) includes a twelve-piece accessory set.

A number of smaller tools that are helpful but not absolutely necessary may be picked up one at a time as you have a bit of spare change: a few jeweler's files for spool turnings; a jeweler's saw, which is a coping saw with very fine blades and can be used for scroll work; a triangle, compass, and T-square; a stone for sharpening your knives.

Dremel Moto-Shop (*Photograph courtesy of Dremel Mfg. Company*).

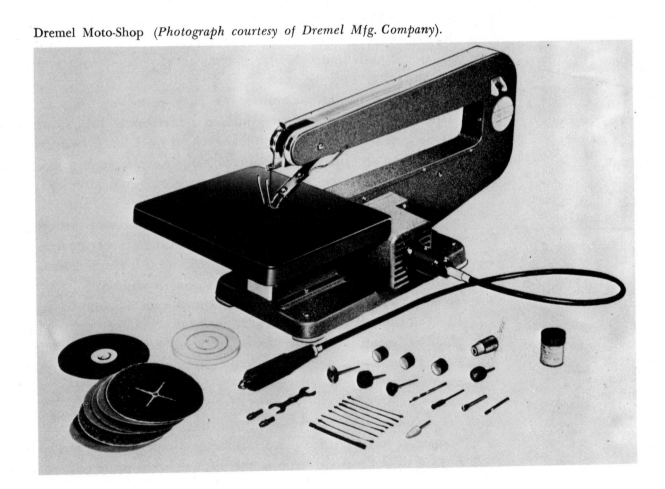

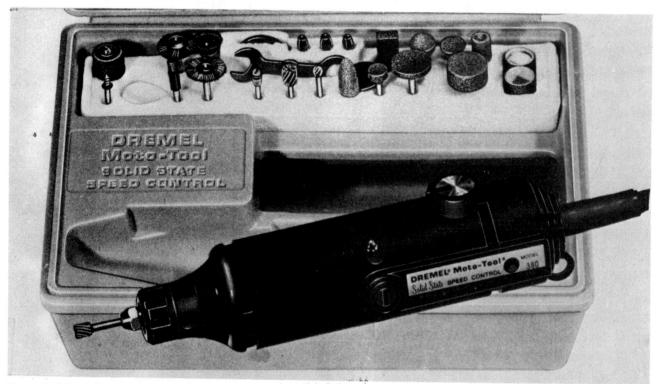

Dremel Moto-Tool (*Photograph courtesy of Dremel Mfg. Company*).

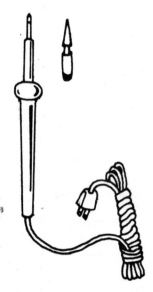

X-Acto soldering iron
and hot knife

The X-Acto soldering iron and hot knife is nice to have and useful in many places (note the instructions for the hammock frame on p. 192); we find it particularly useful in cutting plastic, when the hot knife blade is used with the heating handle. It makes windows, doors, and plastic mirrors simple to do. It is held and used like a pencil with a narrow diameter tip, perfect for getting into tiny places. It costs around $4.50. Heat sinks are available with the iron.

You will find, however, as you succumb to the fascination of working with wood that there are any number of simple tools that you can make yourself. Consider, for example, this simple miter box dreamed up by Suzanne Ash, a working miniaturist who is also a ceramist and a dealer in small things. The box is made from scraps of wood. We prefer a piece 1 x 4 x 12 inches long. A piece of 1 x 2 (any basic woods that you have are fine for this, from pine to the tougher woods) is then glued to the top of the longer piece—this one should be about 10 inches long. When completely dry, use a protractor from the dime store to make the right and left 45-degree angles on the top piece. Ninety-degree angles may also be marked. And if a protractor isn't handy, simply fold a square of paper in half diagonally and use that; it is a perfect 90 degrees. Cut through the lines with a saw, and you're ready to go with any corners you may be called upon to make.

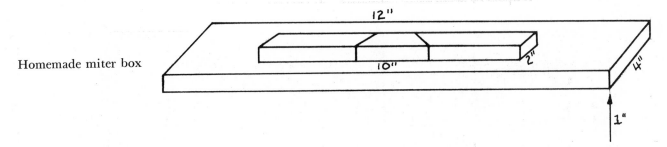

Homemade miter box

We must warn you, however, that angles on thin baseboards and moldings can be sanded to the 45-degree angle easier than cutting, which tends to splinter the thin wood.

To cut a mitered corner, simply hold the end of the wood firmly against the cut, leaving room to take off the corner, and firmly against the top board. Then fit your saw into the cuts and saw away.

While making the miter box, you might want to make a small loom on which a stair tread, a rug, a bedspread, or a tablecloth might be woven. The size of the loom will be determined by the size of your project. These are so easy to make that you can make one to accommodate any piece of weaving. For the stairs, make it the length needed to cover the stairs plus about 1 inch if the tread is to go into the second-floor landing.

For ease in handling, use 1-inch wood the length of the piece you wish to loom, and the width you want to work on. At each end, glue a piece of ½-inch wood the width of the loom, as shown in the sketch. Into this, tap some 1-inch wire nails across the width of the loom, about ⅛ inch apart, or with enough space to accommodate the wool or yarn you are going to use. Set them into the wood enough to hold them very firm—they need to stick up above the wood only enough to hold the yarn.

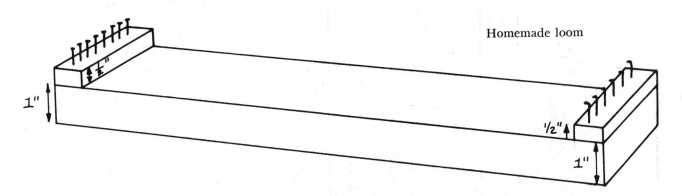

Homemade loom

Probably the most important tool for the craftsperson who is constructing things to a ¹⁄₁₂ scale is the measure developed by William B. Wright of Wildwood Crest, New Jersey who, under the trademark Little Old Man, produces some fine metal miniatures. Wright starts

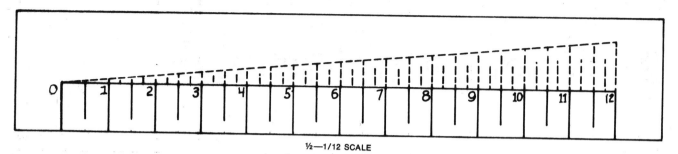

½—1/12 SCALE

Rule for a scale measure

with a piece of hard wood, ⅛ inch thick and about 14 inches long and 2½ inches wide. Buy one of the very thin plastic rulers 12 inches long —or make a paper ruler by dividing an inch-wide strip of paper, 12 inches long, into 1-inch spaces, which are then divided into quarters. Glue the plastic or paper ruler onto the wood strip at the very bottom.

Now measure at the 12-inch mark, 1 inch up on the board from the top of the ruler. With another ruler, draw a diagonal from this point down to the ruler at the first mark. Extend the ¼-inch markings on the ruler up to the diagonal. Whatever you wish to measure, lay it on the ruler and, for example, if it is 3 inches long, measure the distance from the top of the ruler to the diagonal, and that will be the length of the piece you're measuring, in ¹⁄₁₂ scale.

Remember, the rule shown in the drawing is half the ¹⁄₁₂ scale; in other words, it is 6 inches long instead of 12 inches. When you make yours, you will use a regulation 12-inch rule.

Remember, also, that in measuring something of this sort where exact measurements are necessary, a pencil mark simply won't do; a pencil mark has width, and no matter how minute the width, it will throw off your other measurements. Make all of these markings with your awl, then go over them with a fine-point drawing pen.

2 A Review of Materials

The beginning craftsperson must know a little about the materials he is going to work with, and there are so many new products on the market today in the way of glues, varnishes, and sandpapers that even the most experienced worker will benefit from a review of what is available.

Woods

Probably the biggest change is in the woods that are obtainable now. Even as little as five years ago, the miniature-maker was forced to fit his plans to a most restricted market. His hobby shop carried balsa wood cut especially for airplane models and the local lumber yard offered a very limited supply in moldings and thicknesses that could be worked, but beyond that he was thrown on his own resources.

There were always the old reliables, such as Albert Constantine and Son of 2050 Eastchester Road, Bronx, New York 10461, who has been supplying exotic woods to artists working in this material since 1812. Constantine's lists more than one hundred various woods and grains from ash, aspen, and avodire to teak and zebrawood. A study of their catalogue (send $1.00 and it is sent by return mail) is almost equal to a cram course in woods that are exciting to work with. The other large supplier is Craftsman Wood Service Co., 2727 South Mary Street, Chicago, Illinois 60608, and they too offer a wide variety of woods for every purpose and will ship as little as 3 square feet. This is all cabinet-grade lumber, kiln dried, and is obtainable from $\frac{1}{8}$-inch thickness on up. The veneers are truly beautiful, and may be obtained in $\frac{1}{28}$-inch thickness; they serve beautifully for floors and paneling, never cracking or splitting.

Start with common woods. For example, the best wood for carving projects is a clear-grained soft wood such as sugar, or white pine. Bass, cottonwood, and poplar are also good carving woods. Each of these has particular advantages; naturally it's easier and faster to work the softer woods, but you can do a cleaner, smoother job with the hard varieties. I myself started with balsa wood, simply because that was what I found in the hobby shop. This soft and light wood is strong enough for most miniature work and not nearly as "splitty" as some other woods, and even the hardest grades are easily shaped and worked, making it a good wood for beginners. It has a naturally lustrous surface and despite its softness, it is easy to smooth with sandpaper. Constantine's offers feather-weight balsa in pieces 36 inches long and 3 inches wide, in every thickness from $\frac{1}{32}$ inch to $\frac{1}{2}$ inch, which cost from 36 cents to $1.10. Tiny strips for use on paneling run from $\frac{1}{16}$-inch square to $\frac{1}{2}$-inch square, in price from five for 20 cents to 27 cents each, but it may be bought in almost any size from your local hobby shop too, so there seems little to gain by mail-ordering it. It sands well (see Chapter 5 on finishing the inside of the house, where we discuss beveled planks for floors). About the only thing the builder must remember in using it is that stain, when used, brings up the grain of the wood; it will always need a careful sanding to correct this. I would not recommend it for furniture, but for moldings, fireplaces, floors, and outside trim it is perfectly satisfactory.

Sugar, or white pine, is another soft, easily worked wood, easy to obtain and relatively cheap. It has enough body and strength to produce clean sharp edges and stand considerable undercutting. If your knife is good, this wood lends itself to such accurate and clean cuts that little sandpapering is necessary. However, it does split easily.

Poplar is noted for its light color and even density, and for the beautiful finish it will take. It is used where a relatively hard wood is needed, and can hold a wealth of fine detail which will not chip easily or shred.

There are many other soft woods which are easily worked. California redwood cuts easily and cleanly if your knife is properly sharp, and doesn't split too readily. Another possibility is cypress, which is usually straight-grained and easily worked to clean sharp edges.

In the hard woods—oak, beech, hickory, and all the nut woods—the beginner may run into difficulty because it is a problem to get fine light cuts and clean sharp notches and angles. And yet, two of the leading miniaturists in the country will work with nothing but walnut, maple, and mahogany, which proves our original contention—that there really are no rules; you will make your own as you go along.

There is little wood at your lumber company that can be used for miniature work, but both the large suppliers carry an unbelievable assortment ranging from veneers at $\frac{1}{28}$-inch thickness (one even carries a veneer at $\frac{1}{64}$ inch that may be bent around corners) on up to 1 inch. All are priced most reasonably. Craftsman, for example, offers first-quality basswood, a lovely wood to work with, $\frac{1}{8}$ inch thick at 39 cents per foot, finished on both sides. Constantine's offers a somewhat larger assortment at prices that couldn't fail to please you, again beginning with the $\frac{1}{28}$-inch thickness (a veneer) and going on up. You can have some very special fun with a "treasure chest of woods" which Constantine's offers at $5.95—fifty pieces of fifty different woods, in 4 x 9-inch specimens. We've made some fascinating little tables from these small pieces of rare woods.

And speaking of tables, both these firms also offer a wide assortment of what they call "wood inlay borders," which include some as tiny as $\frac{1}{8}$ inch wide; they are beautiful for use on furniture or floors, and they are fascinating to work with.

Another thing offered by these companies is an assortment of embossed and machine-carved moldings; these are much more beautiful than even the most professional of carvers could turn out, and while some run close to 1 inch in width, there are many as small as $\frac{5}{16}$ and $\frac{7}{16}$, which are beautiful when used as finishes where walls meet floors and ceilings, and such specialized details.

A number of people who deal exclusively in mini-woods offer moldings which the amateur might not want to tackle until he has more experience; for example, the Lilliput Shop in Beaverton, Oregon, offers a complete service on millwork, done by what you might call a resident artist, and offers to make to order anything you have in mind. Lilliput also offers cabinet woods in mini-sizes; prices are a bit higher than those at the larger suppliers, but they may be ordered in smaller quantities, too, which is sometimes more convenient. They have available in pieces $\frac{3}{32}$ inch thick and 2 x 12 inches, cherry, cedar, oak, maple, pine, birch, and mahogany at 50 cents per piece. If you can use their choice of woods, the pieces are 40 cents each. We show a sampling of their production, drawn at 4 times actual size; the top row is great for baseboards (called "mopboards" in England) and those in the second row are picture-frame moldings. The molding at left, bottom, is shown twice actual size; I have used this in the angle between wall and ceiling and on the outside of a house, up under the eaves, in the Victorian style. The spindles shown are beautifully turned and come with either a round or a square at each end. They trim nicely and may be used for banisters, bedposts, chairs, etc.

The moldings shown on page 15 are from Howard K. Pierce of The Workshop in Wichita, Kansas. These, too, are beautifully executed and are shown 4 times actual size, so you can easily see how tiny they are when viewed with the naked eye. These are suitable for door and window trim, baseboards, panel molding, crown molding, and chair and plate rails, and all are unfinished. They cost from 30 cents to 60 cents per lineal foot (prices start with the molding at right and increase to the left) and come in 1- or 2-foot lengths.

In the photograph on page 16, we show an assortment of mold-

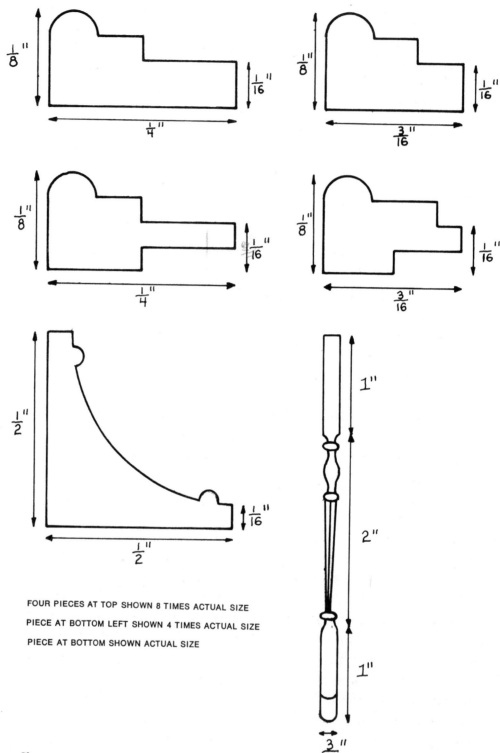

FOUR PIECES AT TOP SHOWN 8 TIMES ACTUAL SIZE

PIECE AT BOTTOM LEFT SHOWN 4 TIMES ACTUAL SIZE

PIECE AT BOTTOM SHOWN ACTUAL SIZE

Milling from the Lilliput Shop

14

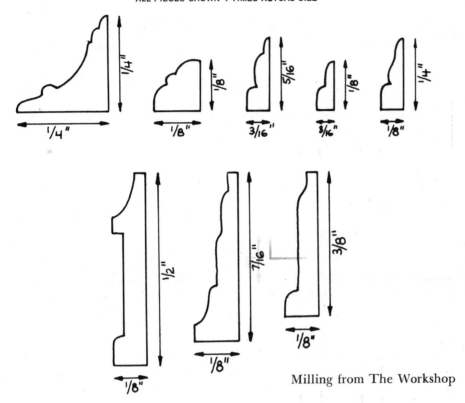

Milling from The Workshop

ings and trims, which were available at three separate lumber yards. The wide molding at top, shown actual size, we have used as door and window molding—it is ½ inch wide at top, decreasing to nothing at the bottom, and makes a majestic crown for door or window. The tiny molding at bottom is of basswood and is available from the Peddler Shop in San Francisco. The next two above the basswood are merely dowels, available anywhere. Above the dowels, however, are five little moldings which we created ourselves from basswood strips. The one second from top is ⁵⁄₁₆ inch wide and we merely glued a ¹⁄₁₆-inch strip down the middle. Very easy, very inexpensive, and very pretty. Next, we used the same strip and glued the ¹⁄₁₆-inch strips down each side. Fourth from the top is a piece of ¼-inch quarter molding, available anywhere, and the next is another molding made for a special spot where everything else seemed too big. It is merely a ⅛-inch strip of balsa with a ¹⁄₁₆-inch strip glued down the center These are interesting to make, and come in handy in many places. Also, they give the craftsperson an opportunity to make really nice moldings, door and window frames, etc., without paying the price for the similar pieces which are turned out on a lathe by the person who has the equipment to do such work.

In addition to all this, Northeastern Scale Models, Inc., of Methuen, Massachusetts, is now offering an extensive assortment of

Milling from Northeastern
Scale Models

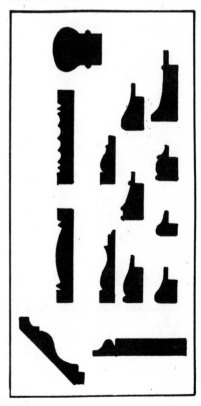

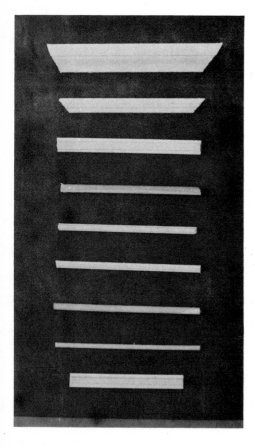

Assortment of moldings available either in finished form or made by the craftsman (*Photograph by Elinor Coyle*).

moldings for houses and picture frames. For $10.00, they will ship an assortment of door and window casings, baseboards, and picture-frame moldings, for two or three rooms. We have used them and they are of fine quality.

C. E. Bergeron of Bradford, Massachusetts, makes much the same offer of moldings for picture frames and various supplies of wood for dollhouses.

Sandpapers

There are many sandpapers for many uses, and you should know all of them. There are, however, a few basic rules which will help you turn out your pretty things.

First, we must keep in mind that in miniature work, one rarely uses the coarser papers, unless it is for the basic shaping of a large piece of wood. Coarse grits are always backed with coarse heavy papers which are too stiff to be bent and used on small pieces. About the only use of coarse papers in miniature work that I can think of is for paths outside the house. They are marvelous for this; especially in the darker grits, they are exactly the right scale for gravel, and when cut into curves and outlined with real gravel to simulate rocks, they produce a marvelous effect. I have seen coarse papers used on the body of a house, too, to simulate a stucco finish, but it never seemed particularly effective to me. One way in which it does well is to cut the sandpaper into pieces about 1 inch wide and 2 inches long, and glue these against the base of the house to simulate stone. This can be very effective.

Second, remember that for actual sanding, coarse papers will only scratch, not polish, so they should never be used. A very fine pad of steel wool is preferable to the coarse papers.

Third, sanding must always be done *with* the grain of the wood, not across the grain. Sanding across the grain will produce scratches that may be impossible to eliminate.

Fourth, never tear sandpaper; tearing will only produce ragged edges that may mar your fine work. Cut it by scoring against a metal ruler, on the back of the paper, using your awl to do the scoring. Then simply pull the pieces apart.

We're not even going to consider flint sandpapers; these are cheap and not particularly satisfactory for fine work. They aren't sharp enough for what we want, and they cut slowly. Ask your supplier for garnet papers, the paper with the reddish grit (this is the one we use for the outside paths). It is sharp, hard, and easy to work with. It will seem a bit expensive, but remember that it will do more than twice the work that flint sandpaper will, so it is worth your consideration. Garnet will cost around 18 cents per sheet, and is worth every penny of it. The ones marked "cabinet paper" are on heavy paper in grades from No. 50 (coarse) to No. 150 (fine, numbered 4/0). These are on a fairly heavy backing paper, usually used for work on large surfaces. Papers marked "finishing" are on a light backing and are better for our use; these come in grades from No. 100 (fine, No. 2/0) to No. 280 (extra fine, No. 8/0). For example, No. 220 (6/0, very fine) is right for miniature furniture and other work to be finished clear or with fine enamel. For coarser work such as beveling the planks for floors and wainscoting, or any preparatory sanding, use No. 100 or No. 120 (2/0 or 3/0).

For most of this work, you won't want a sanding block. Merely make a pad by folding one piece of paper in half with the sand side out. As one surface fills up, you need only flip the other side over.

We haven't mentioned aluminum oxide papers here, although this is what you will find in most stores. Not quite of the fine quality of the garnet papers, these cost around 12 cents per sheet and are graded just as the garnet papers are. I would imagine that more aluminum oxide papers is used in wood finishing than any other, although I personally prefer the garnet for my own work. An interesting development in sandpapers is a new one called Screen-Bak, which is made of open-mesh cloth, coated on both sides, and can be used dry or with water. It is of silicon carbide, and comes in fine (320), medium (240), and coarse (180). It costs twice as much as ordinary sandpapers (about 49 cents per sheet), but it seems to last twice as long, and the grit doesn't fill up as you work, so it is well worth trying.

Glues

Next to the wood itself and sandpaper, glue is probably one of the most important supplies you will need and, like sandpaper, there are so many types available that I would suggest your working with several until you decide which suits your method of work best. As with the sandpapers, there are a few basic rules that must be followed if you expect to achieve success:

First, always let glue dry thoroughly before going ahead with work on the item you are making. Give it the amount of drying time that is specified on the label, and then perhaps another hour or so for extra strength.

Second, always stain every piece you are working before attempting to glue. If you don't, there will be tiny spots where the glue has come up around the wood, and stain will never penetrate these. You will end up with a spotty finish.

Third, if you are gluing wallpaper, no matter which glue is used, try to do the gluing so that it can dry with a weight such as a book on it. For me, regular wallpaper paste doesn't work well; it inevitably produces wrinkles. Rubber cement adheres very well, and permits moving the paper a bit if you don't happen to get it on right with the first try. Actually, since the paper will shrink a bit in drying, you will get a better joint by cutting a piece of paper about 1½ inches wide and in length equal to the height of the room, and gluing this into the corner, allowing it to dry, then pasting the wallpaper over it right up to the corner. J. Hermes of El Monte, California, who specializes in dollhouse wallpaper, offers a very fine wallpaper paste at a reasonable price or you can make your own by stirring about ¾ cup water into 1 cup all-purpose flour in a saucepan and stirring until smooth, then cooking over very low heat, stirring constantly, until the mixture is an opaque white. You will have to add a little water as the paste cooks, and this should always be at boiling temperature. When finished, the paste should be the consistency of very thick sauce, thick enough to spread easily.

As we said, you will find your own favorite and use it successfully. For example, I found a relatively unknown glue labeled Masterpiece Decoupage, made by the Morris Mfg. Company of Garland, Texas, which is white in the bottle but dries perfectly clear. It doesn't stain or "bleed through" fine prints, and on wood it forms such a perfect bond when dry that if you want to open the joint, you must cut it open. We have used it for wallpaper, too, with great success.

Walthers Specialties, makes a fine product labeled Goo, but it dries a brick red, and so I use it only for fastening down carpets, moldings, and such jobs. Touch 'N Glue, on the other hand, is great for almost any purpose. This is made by the Weldwood people, who also make Rub 'N Buff and Stain 'N Buff, and it is great. The Weldwood people also make a plastic resin glue which is exceedingly strong, but it is one of the powder glues that must be mixed with water before using. I personally don't like them, since it seems to me that I always mix too little, in which case I must mix more, or too much, in which case I have wasted the excess. Elmer's Glue-All, which is available in a handy squeeze bottle, is easier to use, I believe, and makes an equally strong joint. In addition, it dries perfectly clear.

There is another whole category of glues which have come into being in the last year or so—the spray glues. These resin glues, which are sprayed out of cans, are exceedingly strong. While they're not practicable, of course, for small work or the gluing of joints, they are a fantastic help when gluing large surfaces. I used one while gluing cedar shingles to the roof of my Tara house and found it perfect. It is tacky by the time you get the shingle onto it, and holds well after a very short drying period. Also, spray glues are less messy than gluing with brushes and as we experiment with it, we may uncover other uses. For example, John Blauer of San Francisco has told me that he was able to make his most successful draperies for a dollhouse by spraying light-weight aluminum foil with the spray glue and then pressing the material to the foil. When dry, the material may be trimmed, the hems pressed in, and the folds pressed exactly the way you want them; they hang perfectly.

Even newer is a preparation from Technology Associates, Inc., of Dedham, Massachusetts, called Quick Stick Glue, which I find to be the most helpful of all while working on small pieces. This is a quick-setting, strong, flexible, hot-melt adhesive in the form of a white 8-inch stick which the craftsperson lights with a match. The melted glue is then dripped onto the joint area and the surfaces are held together for only one minute. Handling it will remind you of handling sealing wax, but once you are accustomed to it, it is very simple. The spot or puddle of melted glue on the joint may be manipulated by slightly touching and moving the end of the Quick Stick over the area to be bonded. The glue stick may be extinguished by blowing on it, as with punk or sealing wax, but be careful of this; some of the molten glue may splatter. Be certain, too, that when you lay the stick down it is resting on something other than your work board, or it will leave a mound of glue. I find it best to press the two parts together for about twenty seconds to a minute, then allow fifteen to twenty minutes for a complete curing. Curing (hardening) actually starts within five minutes. It works on any surface other than painted or nylon.

Sobo, billed on the bottle as "The King of Adhesives" and "The Original Arts and Craft Glue," will work on anything and dries crystal clear; in writing about it Robert Bernhard of Philadelphia, a master of miniaturia who specializes in wickerware and upholstered pieces, calls it the greatest adhesive. "Coat both parts," he adds. "Let dry, then lightly coat one surface and you'll have a really good bond. It is water soluble so that when I make a mistake, wetting the pieces makes it simple to separate and correct the error.*

"When I want to cut a fabric and avoid fraying at the edges," Bernhard instructs, "I coat the back of the fabric with a light coat of Elmer's, Sobo, or other white glue, let it dry, then cut with embroidery scissors. This way there is no double thickness of fabric to add ugly bulk to a piece of furniture, especially the wing of a wing chair."

One last suggestion on glues. There also has lately appeared a glue which does an excellent job, but we must caution that it must not be used unless you are willing to use great caution and follow the directions exactly. This applies to any glue in which the ingredients listed on the label include cyanoacrylate; the ones we found are marketed under the names of Perma Bond and Krazy Glue. It is especially effective for use on metal, but one must be very careful of it, for it can also bond the skin instantly, and could cause a need for medical attention if not used properly. It must be used in a tiny droplet, the less the better in most cases. It does make a fantastic union of nonporous materials, however, and Bill Wright, the "Little Old Man," reports that he has used it for some time with complete satisfaction. Keep nail-polish remover handy just in case some of it gets onto your skin.

The Tack Rag

One other absolutely indispensable tool is the so-called tack rag, usually termed "tacky" rag. For the perfect finish on any fine work a tack rag is essential, for its use removes any dirt, dust, or lint, much of which is too tiny to be seen by the naked eye, although it will show up in formidable proportions if stain or varnish is applied over it.

Any good soft cloth that will not leave lint will make a good tack rag, but you will be much better off if you buy a commercially treated one; they run about 25 cents and are made of a special cloth, soft, smooth, and flexible, which has been saturated with a solution that will pick up any loose particles. On these, the "tack" will last indefinitely, and you will bless the day you invested in one. Whichever kind you choose, remember that a good tack rag is the most important tool in the miniaturist's kit, particularly if you are trying for fine finishes.

* Author's Note: This is an important point since I know of no other glue which has this quality.

3 Building Dollhouses

Anyone who has the money can buy a dollhouse to suit his requirements, or can commission a builder to construct one for him, as the case may be, but we hope to show in this chapter that anyone who will take the time can build his house, and that house when completed will be considerably dearer to him than one that was conceived and executed by someone else. In the following pages, complete instructions are given for building five different types of dollhouses, which vary from a cigar box to a multiroom dwelling.

Dollhouses have been made from everything imaginable: bookcases, cupboards, shelves on the backs of doors, little cabinets to fit atop a mantel; clock cases, television cabinets, corrugated cartons. The first law of the miniaturist is *use what you have*—and that brings us to cigar boxes.

A Cigar-Box House

With the growing interest in smaller dollhouses because of smaller living space, many craftspersons are turning to shadowboxes, miniature rooms such as Mrs. Thorne's and, finally, back to that interest of the 1920s—cigar-box houses. But cigar boxes today aren't what they used to be, so the first step in this area is somewhat reminiscent of Mrs. Beeton's classic recipe for jugged hare: "First, catch your hare."

Your first concern is to find a cigar box. Today, some are made of cardboard. Others have wooden sides and cardboard bottoms. Acquire whatever comes to hand; every single one can be used for a dollhouse, as Charlotte Pack of Santa Barbara has demonstrated (she has made fourteen). If you have worked in the HO scale ($\frac{1}{8}$ inch to 1 inch), you will have no trouble coming up to the $\frac{1}{4}$-inch scale, which is what you'll need for cigar boxes. However, if you've worked only in the 1-inch scale, it will take some patience to come down to $\frac{1}{4}$ inch, but you will be rewarded. These miniature gems are a stimulus to your imagination, and working in them hones your expertise to

Front and side views of Charlotte Pack's Pink Cottage, a cigar-box house that measures 14″ x 11″ x 5½″. The depth was achieved by gluing two similar boxes back to back, thus giving the side opening. Trim around the porches is mostly tatting in ¼″ loops. Lace in the archways was cut from a paper doily. Both are given several coats of lacquer paint. Railings on the porches are German embossed gold paper with white soutache braid as an edging. The exterior of the house was covered with pink paper, hand-ruled 8 spaces by the inch in pencil. There is a spire at the top of the front gable (not visible in photographs) that was made from a metal end off one of those cord ties cowboys wear (*Photographs by Charlotte Pack*).

a fine edge. Mrs. Pack suggests that any box, cigar or otherwise, that is about 2½ inches or more deep, 8½ to 9 inches long, and 5 to 6 inches wide will make a great house. A box 5 to 6 inches wide stood on end will make a three-room house; if the box is about 9 inches long, mark 3 inches down from the top and 3 inches up from the bottom, and you're ready to go. *Note:* 3 inches on the ¼-inch scale would correspond to 12-inch ceilings on the 1-inch scale, which is just about right.

Mrs. Pack is considered one of the finest artists in these little houses, and our instructions here are based on material written by her in N.A.M.E.'s* *Miniature Gazette.*

Cut the two partitions that will be floors from ⅛-inch wood to exactly the right length. Sand the sides until you have a snug fit so they will stay in place without glue. They will be glued eventually, but in order to work inside the house, the partitions must be movable. If you have a box large enough to justify upright partitions, now is the time to cut them also.

Wallpapering comes first; plain, rough papers will make a nice stucco exterior. Tiny striped ones can be used as wainscoting. Some of the Con-Tact papers are very good, too, but each wall should be prepared separately so as not to leave air in corners that will later make the paper peel off. And there is also, as Mrs. Pack reminds us, our friend Joe Hermes, who has a special line of paper for cigar-box walls. Cut a strip of paper as high as you intend to go—all the way to the ceiling, only up to a plate rail, or the part above a wainscoting. Try your strip in the box and crease the corners well. Pull out the strip and crease again. Remove the floor pieces.

Spread white glue or wallpaper paste all over the back wall rather thinly; the paper will stick almost immediately. Press well into the corners. Then spread glue on each side and bring the paper into place. If your box is very small, you can spread all of the glue at once, but be sure to hold the paper for the side walls away from the box until you are ready for it. Paint or paper the ceilings.

Chandeliers are the next consideration. Old earrings, large beads —the possibilities here are endless. Mark two lines on the floor pieces diagonally as shown below, then drill a tiny hole (use your awl if you

Measuring for electric entry in cigar-box ceiling

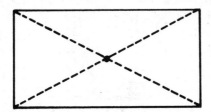 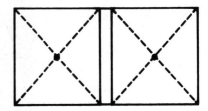

* National Association of Miniature Enthusiasts.

don't have a fine drill) where the lines intersect. Clip off the screw part of earrings and straighten out the curved part. On the floor side of the partition, make a little groove with the end of your hack-saw blade. Push the earring piece through the hole and bend down into the groove. If you are using, say, a large white pearl bead for the chandelier, use a very thin wire through a tiny bead first, then spread the ends into the groove. Fasten with a dot of glue. Glue the finished partitions in place on the floor pieces, just as you would in a larger house. Cover the floor (and wires) with wood-patterned Con-Tact paper or velveteen for wall-to-wall carpeting. You're ready for interior decorating.

Most roofs will have an overhang or pediment of some sort, so cut pieces of wood ¼ inch wide and the widths of the front and sides, and glue to the top of the house, to permit the door to open after the roof is on. You will need some ⅜-inch quarter-round or concave molding to finish the pediment. With your miter box at hand and your house upside down, measure from back to front. Place your molding upside down in the miter box and miter the corner. Recut the corner on your next piece for the long front piece, then recut the corner for the third side. Mrs. Pack doesn't bother with the back. (Be sure not to turn the molding in the miter box, she cautions. You will end up with unmatched corners if you do.) If there are little gaps at the corners after careful fitting, fill in with surfacing putty, then paint.

Out of ¼-inch or ⅜-inch plywood, cut a 4 x 8-inch piece for the base of your house—or any measurement which will give the house a setting. Again using the miter box, cut some molding to go around the four sides of this piece; glue it on flush with the top of the base.

For the roof, cut two pieces of ¼-inch balsa the same length as the depth of your house. Glue these at each side 1¼ inches from the edge. Cut two triangles of the ¼-inch balsa to fit the side walls of your house not counting the molding, with the apex 1¼ inches high. Glue these against the strips, to serve as gables. Cut the roof from heavy cardboard and color, then mark tiles or shingles with a ball-point pen. Be sure to measure your own box before cutting; the measurements given below may not be those of your box.

Cigar-box construction

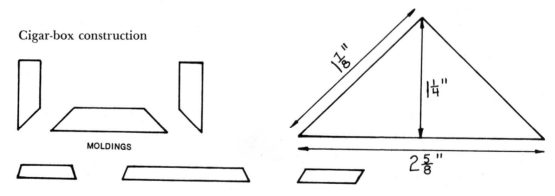

MOLDINGS

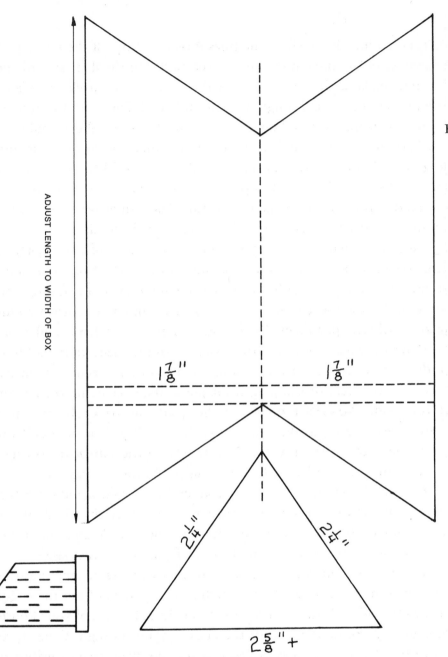

Roof and gable with chimney

ADJUST LENGTH TO WIDTH OF BOX

$1\frac{7}{8}''$ $1\frac{7}{8}''$

$2\frac{1}{4}''$ $2\frac{1}{4}''$

$2\frac{5}{8}''+$

If you have a fireplace, you will need a chimney. Using 1 x ½-inch balsa, cut off a 1⅜-inch piece. Sand or cut at an angle equal to the slope of your roof. Cover with brick paper, then glue on a ¼-inch wide piece of balsa ⅛ inch thick, making butt joints at the corners. Paint it white. Add beads or rectangles painted black for chimney pots.

The outside of the house may be finished with paint marked into bricks, brick-printed paper, or a stucco effect (stir 1 tablespoon breadcrumbs into 1 cup of thin acrylic paint) or, Mrs. Pack suggests that on her first house (the tiny Bliss-type house shown in the color section) she covered the outside with a mustard-colored marbelized cardboard that was the cover of an old sketch book found in her mother's desk. The columns on the porch are an assortment of beads on a fairly heavy wire

Cigar-box fittings for doors and windows (*Courtesy of N.A.M.E.*)

that is anchored in top and bottom pieces of the porch. The whole was then painted with flat cream-colored paint. The flagstones drawn on the base took only a Sunday evening to do.

Mrs. Pack's instructions for furniture in this tiny scale will be found on p. 183. Patterns for doors and windows may be traced from the patterns given on the previous page, then colored and pasted onto the cigar boxes.

A Tudor House

Our little Tudor House, copied from an English design by Hobby-trends of Dereham, Norfolk, England, will be a delight for the builder because it has such a professional appearance when put together. The lower half of the outer walls is covered with red-brick paper and the top half is finished in white acrylic paint into which a few breadcrumbs have been stirred to give a stucco appearance. The timber effect, which is the hallmark of Tudor houses, is achieved by gluing on irregularly cut strips of $\frac{1}{16}$-inch basswood, stained, or strips of woodgrain Con-Tact paper.

Tudor house, front elevation.
(*Photograph by Elinor Coyle*).

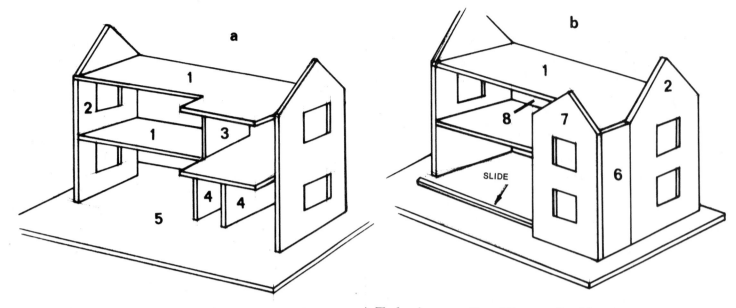

A Tudor house, 24" x 18" x 17½", with construction drawings

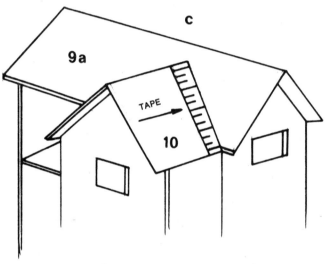

Materials Needed for Constructing Tudor House

1 piece ³⁄₁₆" plywood, 4' x 2'
1 piece ¼" plywood or balsa, 24" x 20"
1 piece ⅛" balsa or plywood, 36" x 14"
1 package ½" wire nails
Plenty of good glue for wood, such as Tacky or Sobo.
Imitation grass to cover base for garden
Various materials for finishing, including paint, wallpaper, molding inside and outside, tape for roof joins, etc.
Wood grain Con-Tact paper or 2 36" strips (¹⁄₁₆" wide) basswood for timbering

The house opens front and back on a sliding principle, which is a blessing if you are short of room. Study the plan first. Study the actual measurements of the pieces, and mark them onto your wood. We used either balsa wood or plywood, since it will all be covered with paper. Notice that some pieces are cut from $\frac{1}{4}$-inch wood, some from $\frac{1}{8}$-inch, and a few from $\frac{3}{16}$-inch. It is necessary to use these thicknesses if your pieces are to go together without adjustment. Cut a pattern by enlarging our drawings 8 times, then trace the pattern onto wood of the proper thickness, then cut out. We used a Dremel saw throughout the project, with a Dremel Moto-Tool for some of the finishing.

When all pieces are measured and cut, set the house up on the base (5) to make sure that everything fits snugly; when enlarging patterns 8 times, there might just possibly be some difference in measurements that will prevent your house being strong and square.

When you are certain that all pieces fit properly, get busy with the inside finishing. Install door and window moldings and windows and doors. Hang wallpaper if you are going to use it. Paint walls if you are going to paint. Finish the floors according to your plan. Finish the outside, also, with red-brick paper at the bottom and a rough white finish on the second floor, consisting of the acrylic paint into which 1 tablespoon of fine breadcrumbs is stirred per cup of paint. Add the timber trimming as described in chapter 5.

When this exterior work is completed, glue the floors (*1*) between the end walls (*2*). The floors may be strengthened by driving in two $\frac{1}{2}$-inch wire nails on each end after the glue has set. Fit in inner walls (*3*) and (*4*)—no nails are required here. Now position the whole house on the base (5) and if you wish to reinforce again, drive a few of the $\frac{1}{2}$-inch nails up from the bottom of the base (5) into the ends and walls.

Finish the roof pieces (*9* and *9a*) with shingles, paper, paint, or whatever you have decided to use, then glue or tack into place according to chart 3. Note that the roof (*9a*) with the cutout piece comes at the front of the house to admit the gable. Finish the gable roofs also, then add as shown in chart 3, on piece (*7*). Don't attempt to use the wire nails here because of the angle; simply glue, then reinforce with wide pieces of masking or Mystik tape. This can also be used to strengthen the ridgepole of the house. This is the time to complete your inside finishing.

The strips which form the guide for the sliding back (*11*) and front (*12*) are now tacked to the base (5). Make certain that the sliding walls will run easily between the slide pieces. Do any necessary finishing on the outside, such as shutters. Place windows in position and secure with small tabs at the back. Add a small roof over the door and glue on·your shutters. Place two fireplaces in the proper places on the

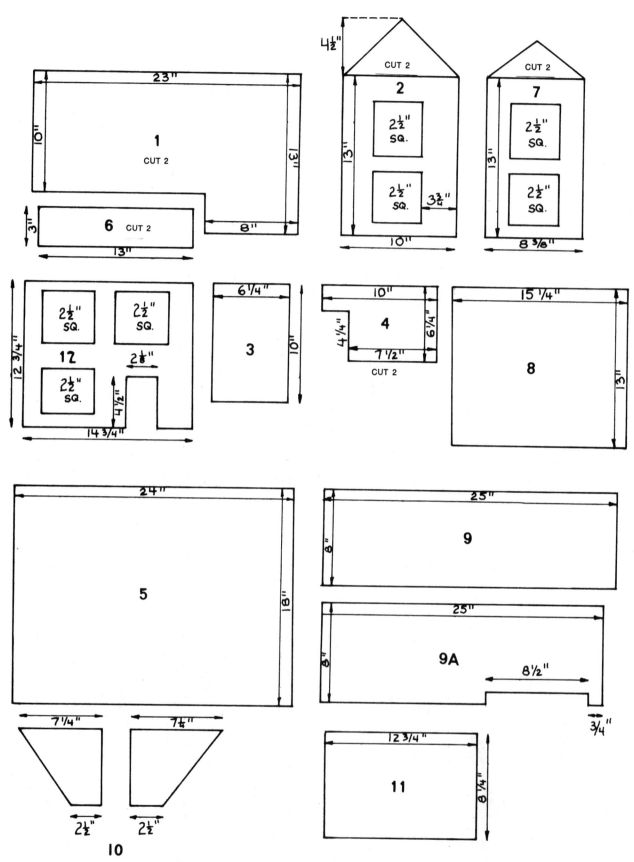

Patterns for Tudor house. Enlarge 8 times for 1/12 scale.

first floor, others on the inside walls of the second floor if you wish, then add a chimney covered with the red-brick paper. You're ready to move in.

A Victorian House

One of the finest Victorian dollhouses we have ever seen is the one pictured on this page, made from scratch by a father-daughter team with no previous knowledge of woodworking and no tools except a Dremel Moto-Saw and Moto-Tool plus various hand tools.

Overall measurements of the house are 60 inches in length including both sets of porch stairs, 28½ inches in width including the tower, and 38 inches in height to the top of the tower roof. Width of the house proper is 24½ inches. It is open on both sides, where strips of aluminum storm-window channels were attached to carry sheets of Plexiglas, ¼

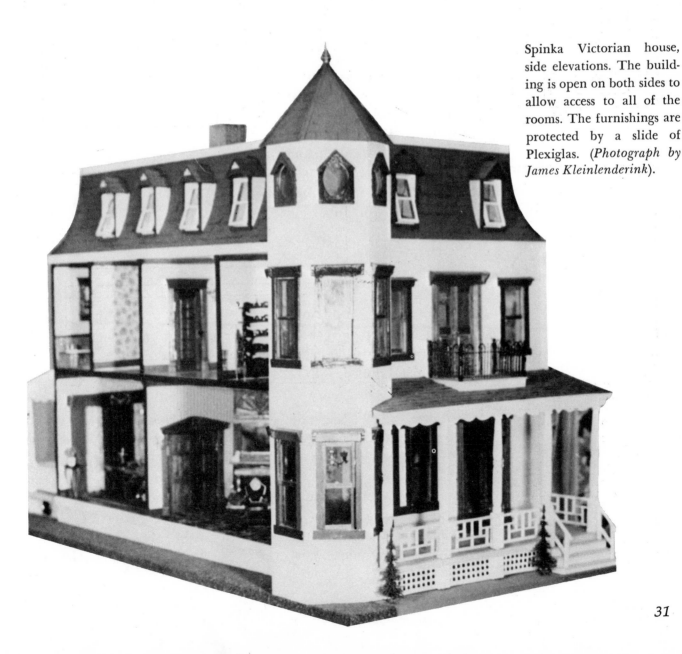

Spinka Victorian house, side elevations. The building is open on both sides to allow access to all of the rooms. The furnishings are protected by a slide of Plexiglas. (*Photograph by James Kleinlenderink*).

inch. The front and back porches are removable for easier moving of the main structure and better access to the house itself.

Materials Needed for Constructing Victorian House

1 sheet ⅜" particle board (Masonite), 24" x 56"
1 sheet ½" particle board (Masonite), 24" x 56"
   Pine strips, 1" x 2" x 20'
   Mahogany for cove moldings, ½" x ½" x 10'
   Mahogany for baseboards, ⅛" x 1" x 10'
2 sheets ⅟₂₈" mahogany veneer, 24" x 56"
2 sheets maple veneer, 24" x 56" ⅟₂₈"
1 sheet basswood for porches, 15" x 2'
   Teak boards for upstairs hall, ⅛" x ¼"
   Basswood for clapboard siding (or buy ready-made siding)
1 sheet birch plywood, ¼" x 24" x 56", for attic floor
2 pieces ¼" plywood, 24" x 36"
   Contact cement
   Finishing nails, ¾"
   Garnet papers No. 220 and No. 400 for finishing
1 piece sheet aluminum, 8" x 15'
8 inches steel bar stock, ¼"
4 sheets No. 60 sandpaper
2 sheets Plexiglas, ¼" x 22" x 30½"
   Gloss Defthane for finishing
   Various paints and stains
   Dremel Moto-Shop
   Dremel Moto-Tool

The subfloor consists of a sheet of particle board (Masonite) ½ inch thick by 24 x 56 inches. This is reinforced on the bottom with 1 x 2-inch pine strips glued on edge parallel to the sides and ends to ½ inches from the edges. Three more 1 x 2-inch strips are glued in, equally spaced across the width. The hexagon subfloor for the tower is cut to size from the same material, mounted on 1 x 2-inch strips on the six edges (mitered) to within ½ inch of the edges. With the base and subfloor assembly lying flat with its length to the worker, mark the lower-right corner of the subfloor using the tower subfloor as a template so that one side of the hexagon will cut across the corner of the main subfloor at an angle. That will place an adjoining side of the hexagon at right angles to the end of the main subfloor. Cut this triangular corner off and glue to the tower floor. A few finishing nails should be used on all the 1 x 2-inch reinforcing strips to clamp the glued parts together.

The porch subfloors are made of ½-inch particle board mounted on 1 x 2-inch pine strips the same way as the main floor and glued to it. Porch floors and main floors along with the tower floor should be on the same level.

The ceiling height of the main-floor rooms is 12 inches. The walls are cut to size from ⅜-inch particle board, and door and window openings are cut. All trim except baseboards is finished before gluing the walls in place.

All doors, windows, and trim in the house are of mahogany. The doors, with their frames, should be made and finished before installing. The frames should be ⅜ inch wide so that upon installation when the trim is glued in, the frames with their doors will lock in and a perfect fit will result. The living room and upstairs-hall arches are treated the same way. The kitchen has a pair of swinging doors to the dining room with a pantry under the kitchen stairs.

Cove moldings were "milled" from mahogany, ½ x ½ x 36 inches, using a Dremel Moto-Tool mounted under a 14 x 18-inch tabletop with the cutter protruding from the surface of the tabletop. By guiding the stock along an adjustable guide the unit was able to turn out shaper work. By changing the various cutters any pattern was possible to cut into the material. The baseboard was shaped the same way, and for this ⅛-inch mahogany strips were used. All items, such as window trim, door trim, and curved parts of furniture, are formed on this miniature shaper.

All floors are individually laid boards ¼ x ¹⁄₂₈ inch thick on a base of ¹⁄₂₈-inch veneer laid cross-grain. Contact cement was used for laying the boards. When thoroughly dry they were sanded with No. 220 garnet paper and finished with No. 400, then thoroughly cleaned with a good tack rag. Two coats of gloss Defthane were then applied, they were lightly sanded with No. 400 paper, cleaned again, and given three more coats of the Defthane, sanding lightly between coats. They were given a final finish of Old English Wax and then glued in place using again contact cement. The baseboard was then installed.

Both the entrance hall and the upstairs ballroom have parquet floors; the former combines mahogany and maple in a Louis (cube) pattern, while the latter combines mahogany and birch in a checkerboard pattern.

All windows have glass panes and double-hung sashes. They do not use sash weights but have a slat spring glued to one edge which holds the sash at any position. The doors have wooden enameled knobs and brass escutcheon plates with keyholes, except for the front and

33

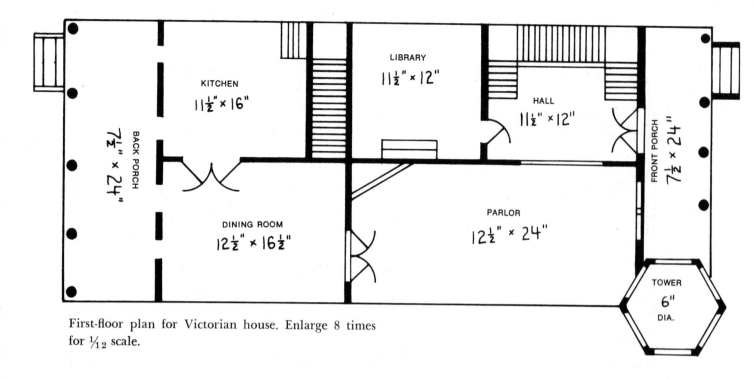

First-floor plan for Victorian house. Enlarge 8 times for $\frac{1}{12}$ scale.

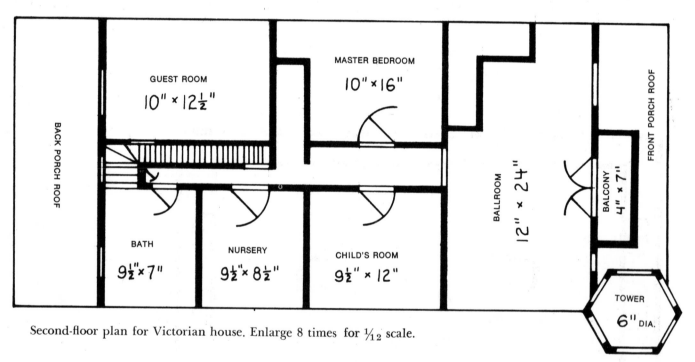

Second-floor plan for Victorian house. Enlarge 8 times for $\frac{1}{12}$ scale.

balcony doors which have latch-type pulls. The windows have brass lifts and locks.

The two fireplaces are assembled and finished completely and glued in place before the walls are installed, as are the bookshelves in the library. All stairways and landings are also completely finished

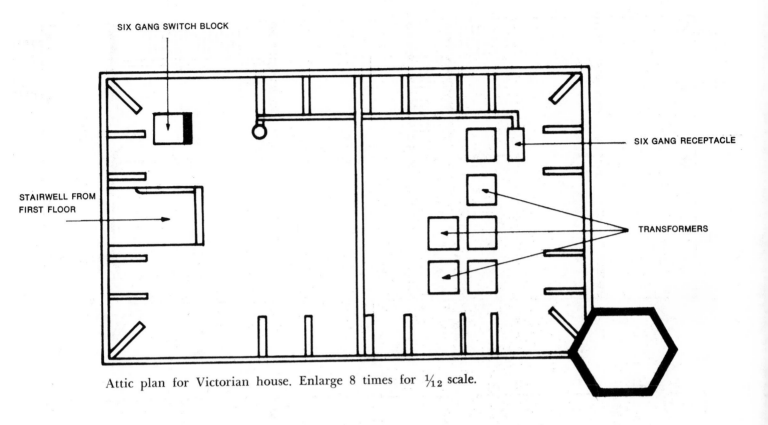

SIX GANG SWITCH BLOCK

STAIRWELL FROM
FIRST FLOOR

SIX GANG RECEPTACLE

TRANSFORMERS

Attic plan for Victorian house. Enlarge 8 times for $\frac{1}{12}$ scale.

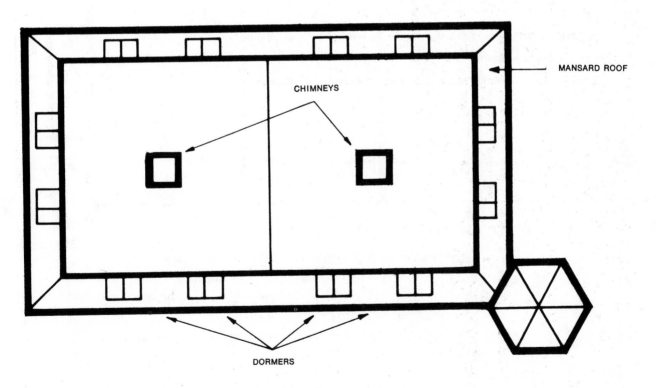

MANSARD ROOF

CHIMNEYS

DORMERS

Roof plan for Victorian house. Enlarge 8 times for $\frac{1}{12}$ scale.

before installation. Entrance-hall stairs and upstairs-hall stairs, which lead to the attic, are of mahogany with lathe-turned spindles and posts. Most were turned with a 1/4-inch electric drill with a homemade "tailstock." The kitchen stairs are of painted basswood.

All second-floor rooms have 10-inch ceilings. All bedroom floors are made of individually laid strips of maple. In the front of the ballroom a pair of doors open onto the 4 x 7-inch balcony on the front-porch roof, which has painted basswood flooring and a wrought-iron fence. Corner posts are made from 1/4-inch square steel bar stock with portions lathe-turned for decoration. This is painted gloss black.

The upstairs-hall floor consists of teak boards laid lengthwise, as do the other upstairs floors. Near the rear end of the hall a stairway with a balustrade runs up into the attic. This connects with the kitchen stairway at the lower end.

The attic floor is made of a sheet of the 1/2-inch particle board into which are routed raceways to carry the wiring to the transformers, switches, and second-floor lights. This is covered with 1/8-inch birch plywood to give a finished appearance. A dividing wall runs across the attic to separate the transformer area from servants' quarters planned for a later date.

Sides of the mansard-style roof are formed of sheet aluminum curved so that the lower portion has an 8-inch radius and the upper 2 inches are perpendicular. Before these sections are installed the dormers must be cut and finished, with their windows that tilt, and the holes for them cut in the roof sides. Then curved studs are made and fitted to the subfloor so that the curved side of each stud will conform to the shape of the sides of the roof. Glue these in and string "rafters" across and glue in. The roof proper is made of two pieces of 1/4-inch plywood, one for each section of the attic. These merely rest on the rafters; they are painted flat black to simulate a tarred roof.

The chimneys are made from 1/2-inch pine and scored, using an X-Acto knife and a razor saw. They are then painted brick color and Spackle is laid into the mortar lines and quickly wiped off with a damp cloth. The resulting chimneys look just like old brick.

The sides of the roof, the roofs of each dormer, the hexagonal tower roof, and the two porch roofs are covered with No. 60 sandpaper cut to scale in the shape and size of old-fashioned asphalt shingles. These are then given three coats of latex paint because of absorbency.

Cover the supports for the foundation with a simulated fieldstone linoleum, lightly sanded and painted to give it a dull finish. Glue with contact cement. Cover small blocks of wood the same way and use for porch supports. Lattice work (to keep out miniature stray dogs and cats) is made of 1/4-inch strips of 1/28-inch maple and painted white.

The house is completed by the addition of basswood clapboard siding (p. 56) available from many dealers, painted with soft semi-gloss off-white paint.

Light fixtures are wired with electric bulbs through six switches to six 14-volt transformers located in the attic so that each transformer and switch controls eight to twelve light bulbs. A single 120-volt standard receptacle is mounted in the side of the rear-porch foundation into which an extension cord from a 120-volt outlet may be plugged. Two 14-gauge wires are then run under the first floor, up through the floor in a corner of the pantry where they are out of sight, through the second-floor stairwell and straight up through the attic floor.

A groove is routed out in the attic subfloor to the front of the house where the transformers are located and connected to a six-receptacle block. Each of the transformers is plugged into this block.

Another raceway is routed in the subfloor which carriers six pairs of wires to the hole in the floor through which the power supply is led. At this point one leg of each pair of wires goes to a switch in the switch panel and another wire from each switch returns to the same opening. The wires are paired here and three branch circuits are laid the same way, through raceways routed in the floor and led to the various pre-drilled openings to supply the second-floor light fixtures. These three circuits are divided in such a way that from eight to twelve bulbs will be on each circuit.

The other three sets of wires are fed down through the stairwell and, using the same procedure as on the first floor, the fixtures are wired. All of the wiring must be done before the floors are laid and before the walls are in place. This procedure precludes the possibility of pinching or crimping any of the wiring. It does a better, neater job than tracing wires along moldings and baseboards.

The kitchen-stair fixture was wired by drilling a ⅛-inch hole straight down through the wall from the second floor and meeting it with a horizontal hole at the mounting point of the fixture and tapping into the kitchen light circuit. This plan could be used in any dollhouse, but also see Chapter 6, "Electrifying the Dollhouse." Dollhouse builder George F. Ober demonstrates the procedure for finishing inside walls and floors before inserting them in the house.

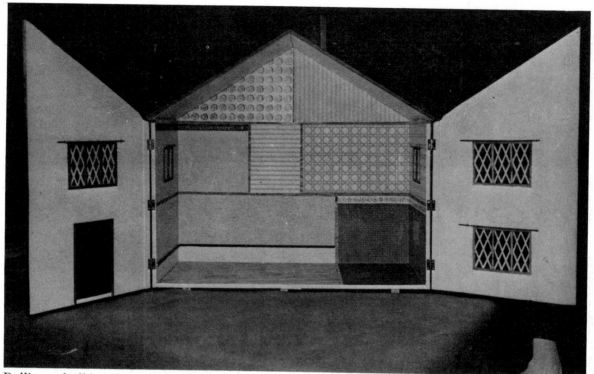

Dollhouse-builder George Ober shows a house with
interior walls and floors decorated.

Dividing walls and floors are slid into the completed
frame.

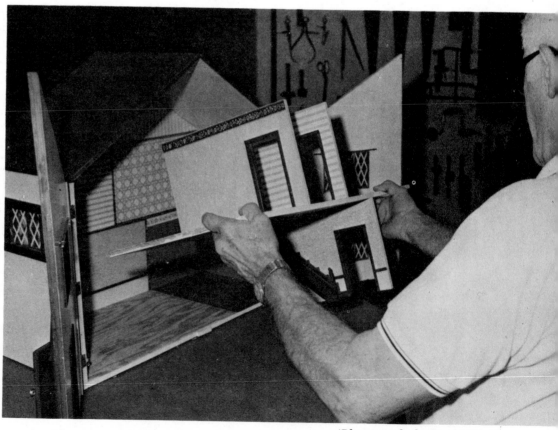

(Photographs by David Ober)

All finishing is completed, even the stairs are mounted on the wall.

Because of careful measuring and cutting, everything fits exactly.

The Beretta Display House

One of the most fabulous of American dollhouses is that owned by Jackie Beretta of San Antonio, Texas, which her parents had built for her to accommodate her collection of miniatures gathered from all over the world. The exterior is a copy of the Nostell Priory house in England's Yorkshire, and one is struck by its similarity to the Uppark Baby House, built in 1730. Everything on the Uppark house is here; the tiny figures on the railing on the roof, the family crest (in this case the actual ancient crest of the Beretta family), and a host of other details filling twelve rooms.

Mrs. Beretta and her two daughters sketched the room arrangements they wanted and an employee on the Beretta ranch, Keith Williamson, made the building. To quote Mr. Beretta, Mr. Williamson's spirit and interest in his work duplicates the zeal and pride of the craftsmen of yesteryear who also built beautiful miniatures and dollhouses.

Materials Needed for a Beretta Display House

1 sheet ¾" plywood, 7' x 6', for back
2 sheets ¾" plywood, 6½' x 24', for sides
3 pieces ¾" pine, one 14" x 6", two 14" x 24"
5 sheets ½" plywood, 5½' x 24', for floors and roof
1 piece 1" pine, 5½' x 2', for base

These are the basic requirements. Statuettes on the roof were purchased. Railing on the roof was made with a Dremel Moto-Tool. Roof itself is flat, surfaced with sandpaper to simulate a tarred roof. Peak in the front is faced with handmade shingles. All moldings must be ordered according to the individual's requirements.

The house is 64¼ inches long, 23½ inches wide, and is built on a 14-inch stand similar to that of the Uppark house, where the stables were housed. Outside walls are of ¾-inch plywood, inside walls and floors are of ½-inch plywood, and all the floors are overlaid with ⅛-inch veneer. Notice in the floor plans how the three floors run the length of the house and the dividing walls are fitted between them. Thus there is really no need for specific directions on the building of the house; the secret of its perfection is the time and pride put into it by people such as Keith Williamson. Centuries from now miniature lovers will no doubt be pointing to it with pride.

Beth Martin of San Antonio provided many of the fine finishings. Mary Dudley Cowles of Chestnut Hill Studio made all the curtains

The Beretta Display House, exterior (*Photograph by Billo Matthews Smith*).

The Beretta Display House, interior (*Photograph by Billo Matthews Smith*).

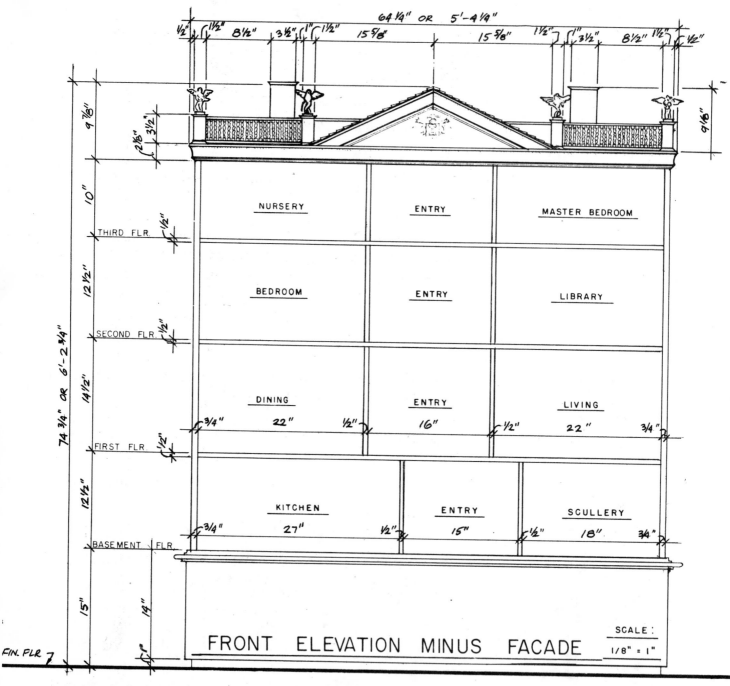

64 1/4" OR 5'-4 1/4"

1/2" | 1/2" | 8 1/2" | 3 1/2" | 1" | 1 1/2" | 15 5/8" | 15 5/8" | 1 1/2" | 1" | 3 1/2" | 8 1/2" | 1/2" | 1/2"

9 7/8"

9 1/8"

2 1/8" | 3 1/2"

10"

| NURSERY | ENTRY | MASTER BEDROOM |

THIRD FLR. | 1/2"

12 1/2"

| BEDROOM | ENTRY | LIBRARY |

SECOND FLR. | 1/2"

14 1/2"

74 3/4" OR 6'-2 3/4"

| DINING | ENTRY | LIVING |
| 3/4" 22" 1/2" | 16" | 1/2" 22" 3/4" |

FIRST FLR. | 1/2"

12 1/2"

| KITCHEN | ENTRY | SCULLERY |
| 3/4" 27" 1/2" | 15" | 1/2" 18" 3/4" |

BASEMENT FLR.

15"

19"

1"

FIN. FLR

FRONT ELEVATION MINUS FACADE

SCALE:
1/8" = 1"

Front elevation, Beretta Display House

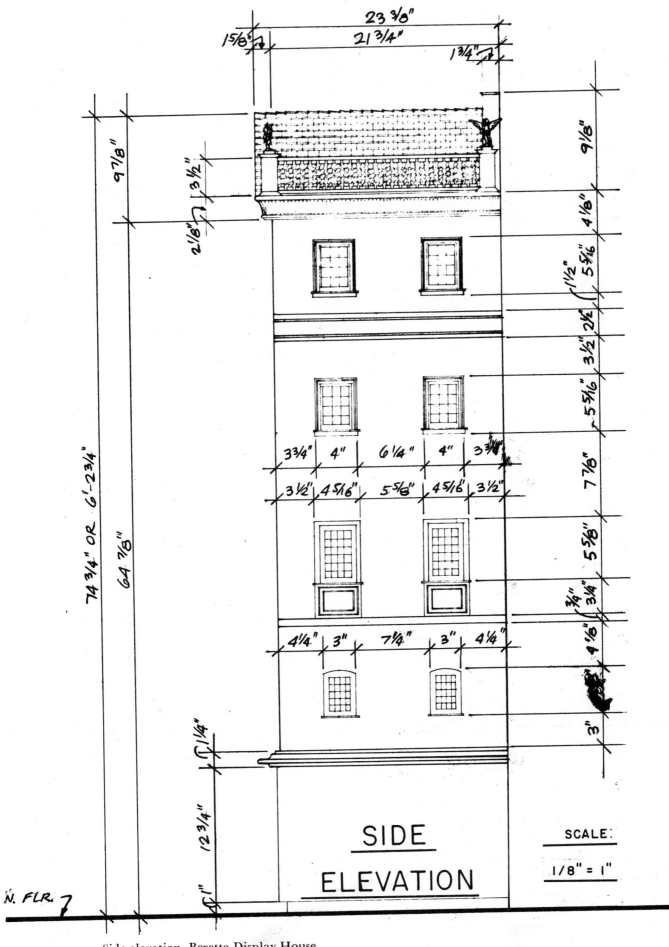

23 3/8"

21 3/4"

1 5/8"

1 3/4"

9 7/8"

3 1/2"

2 1/8"

9 1/8"

4 1/8"

5 5/16"

1 1/2"

2 1/4"

3 1/2"

5 5/16"

7 8/8"

5 5/8"

3/4"

3/4"

4 1/8"

3"

3 3/4"   4"   6 1/4"   4"   3 3/4"

3 1/2" 4 5/16"   5 5/8"   4 5/16" 3 1/2"

4 1/4"   3"   7 1/4"   3"   4 1/4"

74 3/4" OR 6'-2 3/4"

64 7/8"

1 1/4"

12 3/4"

4"

N. FLR.

SIDE
ELEVATION

SCALE:

1/8" = 1"

Side elevation, Beretta Display House

as well as the tiny tea set, each piece of which is marked "J. Beretta" on the bottom. Chestnut Hill furnished the wallpaper in the dining room, which is a hand-painted mural. The decanters on the Chestnut Hill mantel are carved of emerald and the one on the table is carved topaz; the dining table is by Jonathan Bateman, but nearly everything else in this room is old.

The chest against the back wall of the fourth-floor hall is from Titania's Palace, where two pieces were once bought at auction. The small embroidery in the master bedroom is late eighteenth- or early nineteenth-century English. Mrs. Beretta made most of the needlepoint rugs, 24 stitches to the inch. All in all, a treasure for generations to come.

While the fittings may be beyond the reach of most of us, the house itself is a possibility for any talented, diligent builder using the sketches and materials list provided.

A Turn-About House, ca. 1870 and 1920

The Turn-About House in the author's collection was built in 1940 and was recently acquired. Originally it was a single-family dwelling consisting of twenty-three rooms, open front and back. However, since we invite Girl Scouts and other groups over to see our dollhouses several times per week, we decided to redesign the Turn-About House so that it would provide the groups with an educational experience as well. Now this house has two different sides, each a different period. The "front" side of the Turn-About House is a complete house furnished in authentic Victorian style, *ca.* 1870, and includes an art gallery as well as a private theater. Instructions are provided throughout this book for many of the furnishings in the rooms. The "back" side is a complete fourteen-room house, plus a two-room attic, furnished in the 1920s Golden-Oak style. Directions for the French doors in the second-floor guest bedroom at left are given in this book. The entire house is based on a sturdy table of proper dimensions on free-swinging casters, so that it may be turned about for viewing of both sides.

The Victorian side of the Turn-About House consists of nine rooms exclusive of the attic (*Photograph by Sam Taylor*).

The back side of the Turn-About House shows thirteen rooms, exclusive of attic, that are furnished in a 1920s, or Golden-Oak, style (*Photograph by Sam Taylor*).

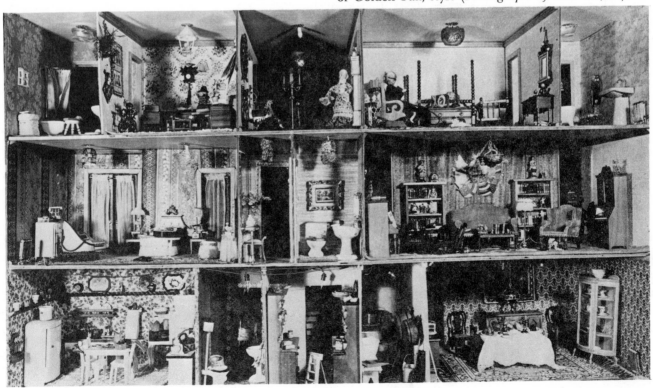

Materials Needed for the Turn-About House

1 sheet plywood 54" x 36" x ¾" for base
3 sheets plywood ¼" thick for floors, ends, and dividing walls
1 piece pine 48" x 1" for ridgepole
   Shingles for roof
1 sheet veneer ½₈" for finishing floors
   Various moldings, baseboards, and facings for trim
   About 500 bricks for chimneys
   Dremel Moto-Shop and Moto-Tool for cutting
   Various stains, varnishes, etc.
   Various sandpapers, brushes, and wallpapers
   Imitation grass finish for the base around the house

The house is built on a sheet of plywood, 54 x 36 x ¾ inches. Notice that it is divided by a piece of ¼-inch plywood the length of the house, in which all doors and moldings are installed before the divider is placed. Once the ¼-inch plywood outside walls (on the ends only) are installed, this divider is secured and a 1-inch-square piece of pine 48 inches long is nailed between the side peaks to serve as a ridgepole. Then the dividing walls, each 9 inches high, are finished and installed. The roof pieces are swung on hinges, finished with shingles, and merely hang over the ridgepole. If the wood is cut from the patterns, nearly all crafting and lighting can be handled from the instructions with the Victorian house.

With the two long sides open, there is no space for windows in such a house. However, this gives much more wall space for arranging furniture, and the plan is to have two façades built, one in each period, complete with bay windows and 1920 windows and doors, thus providing the window interest which is so sadly missed.

This is a fine house for a beginner, since it provides ample room for displaying miniatures and at the same time avoids the more difficult areas of house building. We are building a theater and art gallery in the attic (both copies from a lavish Victorian mansion in St. Louis), which is a test for our imagination and a joy to do.

We built a small extension on the house (see patterns for patio pieces, p. 51) with a flat roof on the top of which we arranged a patio. This is even with the second floor; this houses all electrical equipment and will eventually be a garage with a folding door. Outside walls are covered with used brick paper. Remember, however, that this necessitates making your ¾-inch plywood base at least 18 inches longer to accommodate the extension.

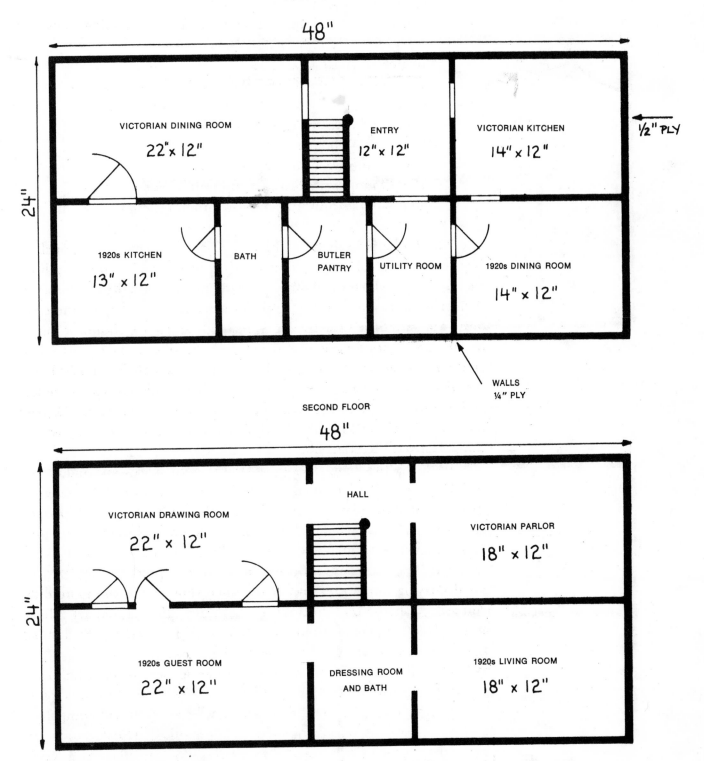

FIRST FLOOR

48"

24"

VICTORIAN DINING ROOM
22" x 12"

ENTRY
12" x 12"

VICTORIAN KITCHEN
14" x 12"

1920s KITCHEN
13" x 12"

BATH

BUTLER
PANTRY

UTILITY ROOM

1920s DINING ROOM
14" x 12"

½" PLY

WALLS
¼" PLY

SECOND FLOOR

48"

24"

HALL

VICTORIAN DRAWING ROOM
22" x 12"

VICTORIAN PARLOR
18" x 12"

1920s GUEST ROOM
22" x 12"

DRESSING ROOM
AND BATH

1920s LIVING ROOM
18" x 12"

Floor plans, Turn-About House

47

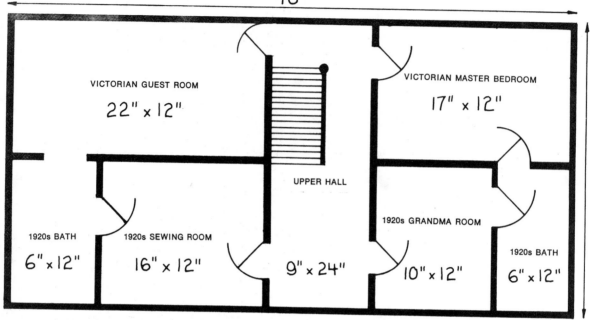

THIRD FLOOR
48"

VICTORIAN GUEST ROOM
22" x 12"

VICTORIAN MASTER BEDROOM
17" x 12"

UPPER HALL

1920s BATH
6" x 12"

1920s SEWING ROOM
16" x 12"

9" x 24"

1920s GRANDMA ROOM
10" x 12"

1920s BATH
6" x 12"

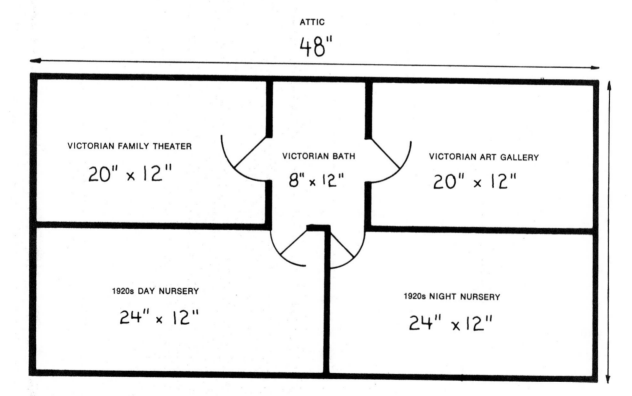

ATTIC
48"

VICTORIAN FAMILY THEATER
20" x 12"

VICTORIAN BATH
8" x 12"

VICTORIAN ART GALLERY
20" x 12"

1920s DAY NURSERY
24" x 12"

1920s NIGHT NURSERY
24" x 12"

Third-floor, attic plan, Turn-About House

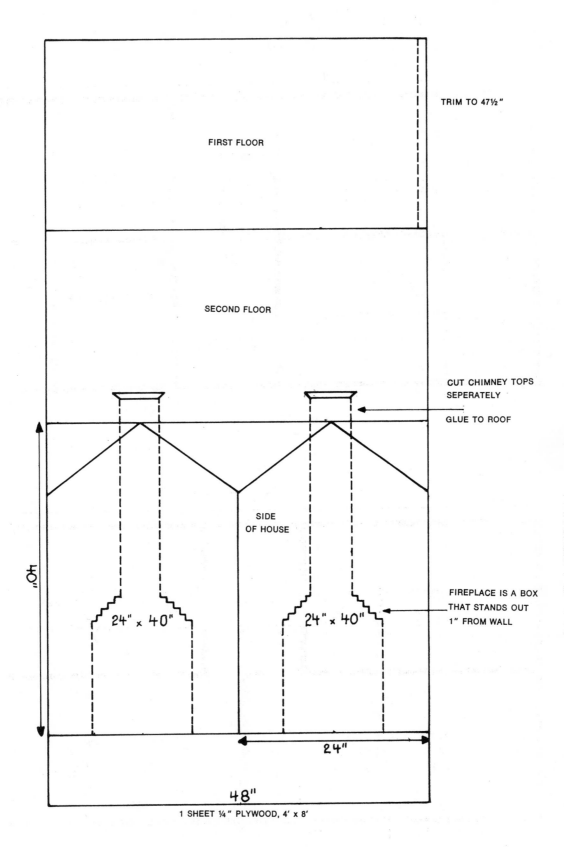

FIRST FLOOR

TRIM TO 47½"

SECOND FLOOR

CUT CHIMNEY TOPS
SEPERATELY

GLUE TO ROOF

SIDE
OF HOUSE

FIREPLACE IS A BOX
THAT STANDS OUT
1" FROM WALL

24" x 40"

24" x 40"

40"

24"

48"

1 SHEET ¼" PLYWOOD, 4' x 8'

Patterns, Turn-About House

1 SHEET ¼" PLYWOOD, 4' x 8'

16 PIECES, 10" x 12" FOR ROOM DIVIDERS

ATTIC FLOOR

THIRD FLOOR

Patterns, Turn-About House

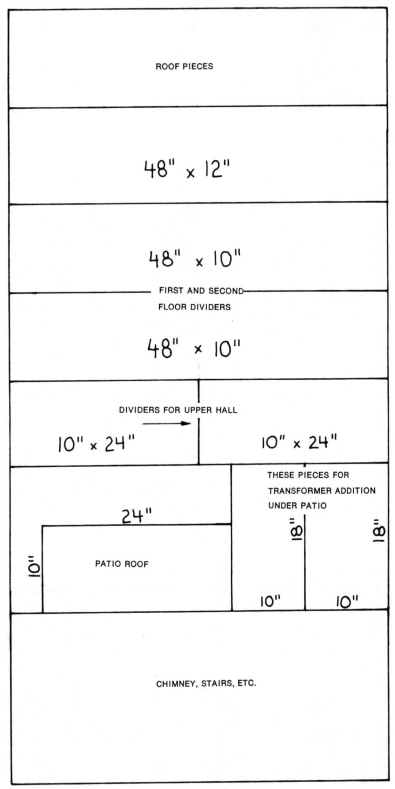

ROOF PIECES

48" x 12"

48" x 10"

FIRST AND SECOND
FLOOR DIVIDERS

48" x 10"

DIVIDERS FOR UPPER HALL

10" x 24"   10" x 24"

THESE PIECES FOR
TRANSFORMER ADDITION
UNDER PATIO

24"

10"

PATIO ROOF

18"   18"

10"   10"

CHIMNEY, STAIRS, ETC.

1 SHEET ¼" PLYWOOD, 4' x 8'

Patterns, Turn-About House

4 Finishing the Outside

When building our own dollhouses, we have a tendency to push forward with work on the inside so that we have a place in which to put our miniatures.

Resist that urge. From the past experience of this author and many others interviewed, I can tell you that if you slight the exterior part of your house, it is extremely unlikely that you will ever get around to it. The things we must do on the inside are simply so fascinating that we soon become accustomed to an unfinished look to the outside, and are are apt to excuse it.

Exterior Finishes

One need not go to extreme lengths to finish the outside; consider the photographs opposite, which show a large house (7½ feet long) that belongs to Jean Schroeder of Euclid, Ohio. Imposing because of its size, the builder of this house advertised it as "a huge rare old Dutch Colonial circa 1900." He was wise indeed to use a thin coat of white enamel on the outside, which Ms. Schroeder cherishes because it is so easy to keep clean—something we have never heard from other dollhouse owners. She reports that it resembles any oil-base paint on a people-sized house. The trim on the exterior of the house is dark green, including on the window sashes. The double front door, however, is painted brown. The fence and double gate which surround the house are engaging; obviously, someone went to a lot of trouble to build them.

This is the only dollhouse we have ever come across that has a basement as well as three floors. The brick facing at the base of the house is wood, scored and painted and applied to look like very realistic brick. And we might mention here, although roofs are discussed elsewhere, that the roof is made entirely of cardboard shingles individually placed, not formed in strips. The roof was then painted the same dark green as the trim. This detailing may have taken many hours but now it looks absolutely perfect.

Exterior of a Dutch Colonial house owned by Jean
Schroeder. The house measures 7½″ x 3½″ x 2½″
(*Photograph by Ric Hampton and Associates*).

Interior of the Schroeder house, showing attic opening
so that space may be better utilized (*Photograph by
Ric Hampton and Associates*).

Exterior of a house owned by Nan Webster. The Victorian carved moldings over the windows and doors are ornamental and lighten the exterior of the house. The columns lend prominence to the door (*Photograph by Nan Webster*).

Interior of the Webster house. The staircase, which is described on p. 91, and the wallpapers are especially interesting (*Photograph by Nan Webster*).

The next house, which belongs to Nan Webster of Plainwell, Michigan, has a basic exterior finish of paint over wood. Notice that little adornments have been added to the house including carved copings over the windows and door, columns flanking the entrance, brick stairs, and stained woodwork. These are all little details which should be remembered when you are finishing the outside of your house, for they all add to your satisfaction with the finished job. We have included photographs of the interior of both houses because of their great interest; the Schroeder house contains pieces from all of the greats of the miniature field—Betty Valentine, Willoughby's 18th Century, John and Ellen Blauer, Chestnut Hill, and so on.

Another finish for exteriors of houses is that used by Mary Jane Hubers in her handmade dollhouse that was illustrated in *The Collector's Guide to Dollhouses and Dollhouse Miniatures*. This is Liquitex modeling paste, an artist's product that is available at hobby and artists' supply stores. It consists of a mixture of gesso and marble dust and is marvelous for finishes, such as stucco, but it is very difficult to work with, since it hardens almost immediately.

Ms. Hubers reports that she tried to produce the impression of stones by marking with a painting knife, but the modeling paste dried so fast that one could work with only a small area at a time, and where different areas met there was a difference in appearance. Neither she nor other builders advise using the paste, although if one has the expertise, the effect is perfect.

Clapboarding is another method of finishing exteriors, depending upon the period of your house. The ⅜-inch-spaced clapboard is a good size for a dollhouse, and for this the builder would specify ¾-inch strips of poplar, pine, or balsa, ¹⁄₁₆ inch thick. Sand these a bit on one side, the side which will be covered, so it will be thinner and the covering boarding will glue over it.

Measure and cut the clapboarding to fit the outside of the house as shown in the photograph on page 56. Be sure that the horizontal lines of the boards are even all the way across the front and sides, then paint each piece and allow to dry before gluing. As sections of the clapboarding are glued, hold them in place with a small C-clamp, but remember to use a buffer board to prevent clamp from marring the clapboards.

Northeast Scale Models, Inc., of Methuen, Massachusetts, makes a simulated siding that comes in 3½-inch-wide strips on which the clapboards are cut from a single piece of veneer-type wood. It is a bit more expensive than doing the work yourself, but it does save a great deal of time.

Greatest ideas for time-saving, however, are the houses already built of pressed wood but unfurnished. Talents Unlimited, of Anchor-

Accurate measuring and marking are necessities for clapboarding dollhouses if they are to have a professional look. Note that the boards are first laid over the house shell and then the window and door trims are fastened over the boards for a truly finished look (*Photographs by Lorraine Yeats*).

Detail of C-clamp shown slightly enlarged to remind the dollhouse builder that whenever clamps are used, a piece of "buffer" wood must be used between the object being glued and the clamp, to prevent marring of the surfaces. This is especially true of soft woods, such as pine and balsa (*Photograph by Lorraine Yeats*).

age, Kentucky, sells various sizes of these so that builders can add both outside and inside finish themselves. You should check into this carefully; many dealers carry such houses both assembled and unassembled, wired or not wired for electricity.

Probably the quickest outside finish of all is the gluing of simulated-brick paper to the outside walls, as R. Bliss did with his wooden dollhouses.

Holgate and Reynolds of Evanston, Illinois, offer a number of plastic surfaces to be used on the outsides of dollhouses. These range from flooring and trim to patio-stone or pebble-stone walls and are made of a special vinyl plastic that can be easily colored with any paint found in a hobby shop. Regular acrylic, lucite, or latex paints sold in any hardware store are also excellent for achieving flat softer tones, and these materials may be bent, scored, or cut accurately with a pair of scissors to produce neat corners. They are rigid enough to stand alone, and develop great strength when glued to balsa wood or cardboard backings. Try to find them in your hobby shop before ordering, however, since many of the plastic surfaces are intended for HO-gauge trains and are too small for dollhouses.

USED BRICK

NEW BRICK

CLASSIC BRICK

Papers for outside finishes

Roofs

There are several ways in which builders can finish their roofs. Tongue depressors or cardboard have been cut and used as shingles as in the Schroeder house on p. 53, with fine effect. J. Hermes offers a paper covering of about the weight of wallpaper in a "fishtail" pattern that is also very effective. The Dollhouse Factory in Lebanon, New Jersey, offers real hand-hewn cedar shingles, which can be glued to the roof base. We have at various times used asphalt shingles, people-sized, cut to fit dollhouses, for a fine effect. Construction paper of heavy quality or light cardboard such as is used as backing on pads of paper also make fine shingles, especially the cardboard, since it can be painted and after painting the edges curl up a bit just as real shingles do.

Once I made a thatched roof of dried pampas grass from our back meadow, which upon drying turns a fine golden color that looks like straw. (Just gather a handful of the grass in your left hand, cut off at the end with a sharp knife to get even edges, then tie firmly at intervals of 2 inches, the length of a stalk, using only enough stalks to make a bundle about the size of your little finger in width.)

These little bundles are then glued to the shell of the roof—in the case of my log cabin, they were glued against corrugated cardboard,

Thatched roof for a log cabin was made on a base of corrugated board; the thatches were stalks of dried grass tied into bundles just as the early ones were. The privy and well at left (without roof), as well as the other furnishings in this photograph, are described elsewhere. Author's collection (*Photograph by Elinor Coyle*).

58

starting at the bottom and overlapping about every ½ inch. To properly finish the roof, a strip of ¼-inch balsa wood or basswood may be stained and glued to the front edge of the corrugated cardboard which shows beneath the thatch.

Other papers available for roof coverings (these from J. Hermes) are shown here. All provide nice effects and are easily applied on a plywood or Masonite roof if it is given a coat of varnish first. But they do not, of course, supply the effect of depth that results from a material that actually has depth.

Gardens

While the garden itself has little to do with finishing the outside of your house, it is an important component, since it provides a setting for the house. I am always distressed at the sight of a dollhouse set smack on its base on a table or shelf, since with just a little extra effort it could have been mounted on a piece of plywood or heavy cardboard (if the house is not too heavy) large enough to allow a foot of space on each side so that a garden could be prepared. After all, this is the way that most people-sized houses are planned, and this is what we are trying to reproduce.

A fairly good effect for lawns is produced by green-lawn substitute which is available in hobby shops that carry miniature railroad supplies. It is easily cut and glued down and makes a nice background. You'll find there is another one with the "grass" about ⅜ inch deep, which looks more like grass, but gives the definite impression that the people who live in this house aren't very responsible about cutting their lawns.

For paths, we believe that sandpaper in its various weights is unequaled. The coarsest type of sandpaper simulates gravel very well and the finest serves as a background for mounting stones, as shown at the bottom of the photograph on p. 60. The stones here and the bricks at the top of the photograph were all modeled from Liquitex modeling paste in a process perfected by Virginia Updegraff of Des Moines, Iowa. Mrs. Updegraff shapes the bricks on small oblongs of cardboard in scale sizes, then when dry paints them with red acrylic paints. She antiques the bricks by brushing with brown acrylic, put on very thin and then wiped off immediately. When dry, a thin coat of white modeling paste is spread on the path surface and the bricks are pressed into this; the paste rises around the bricks to give a mortared effect.

The small pattern of stones directly beneath the bricks is made in the same way, except that it is glazed with one coat of Deep Flex Decoupage Glaze (or papier-mâché glaze), then sunk in the modeling

Papers for roof finishes

TILE ROOF

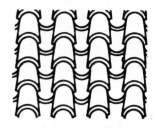

FISH SCALE ROOF

SHINGLE ROOF

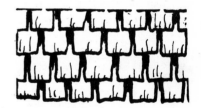

paste in the same way. Notice, in this photograph, the patterns for making this sort of stones; made in the proper shapes these could be fitted together to make a perfect slate floor. In that case, the mortar is watercolored a deep green.

The large section of path at the bottom shows stones in a "natural" shape; the pattern for these is given at center left and they should be traced, then cut from light cardboard and along with the paste shaped on the cardboard. The stones at center right are in a "cut-stone" pattern. Both are fine for outside paths or foundations. Stones for paths should be made in shades of brown, gray, and off-white, all with an antiquing effect gained by brushing with brown acrylic. Be sure to wipe off the brown wash quickly. These, too, can be sunk in acrylic-stained paste "mortar," but the ones shown at bottom were glued onto a base of very fine sandpaper which was the exact color of sand.

Sobo glue and Deep Flex brush cleaner and thinner are Mrs. Updegraff's favorites. For the watercolors, use brushes numbered OOO and one medium brush. The acrylic paints come in various shades. When either bricks or stones are shaped but not dry, any irregularities may be brushed out with a brush and water. However, we found the irregular effect infinitely better.

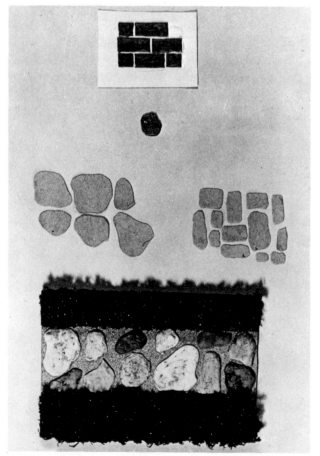

Bricks (*top*), stones for paths or floors (*center*), and stones with a natural finish may be made from Liquitex modeling clay on a base of thin cardboard. At bottom, a path laid on sandpaper is bordered with artificial grass (*Photograph by Sam Taylor*).

60

One last idea for paths. In the miniature-railroad department of your hobby shop, you will find small bags of tiny chips which are labeled "ballast," for use, we suppose, in constructing tracks or loading freight cars. This "ballast" is exactly right for dollhouse paths; simply cut your path base to scale in the shape you want, then spread lightly with glue and sprinkle heavily with the stone chips. These paths make lovely additions to gardens.

Fences

It is strange, when we consider how much a fence does for tying a dollhouse to the ground and giving it a generally "homey" appearance, that we don't see more fences used. They are simple to make and easy to install. Paige Thornton of Atlanta has some beautiful fences around her houses, one an authentic antique iron one, and Jean Schroeder of the Cleveland Minaturia Society made a beautiful picket fence for her large mansion. In my own collection there is a white picket fence around one house and a dark green fence of plastic around another, and both make valuable additions to the general effects.

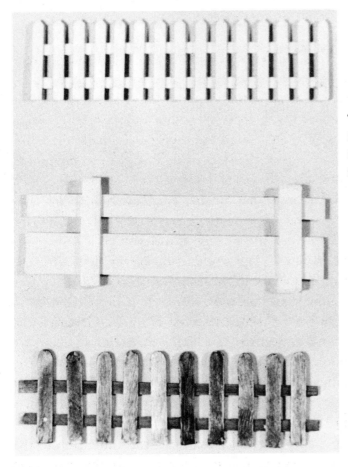

Three easy-to-make fences for beginners. The picket fence (*top*) is cut from ¼″ balsa; Shaker fence (*center*) is cut from ⅛″ wood; country fence (*bottom*) is made from tongue depressors (*Photograph by Sam Taylor*).

Shown on p. 61 are three fences of wood which are fun to make. At top, the picket fence, constructed of 1/4-inch balsa wood which you can buy in 1/2-inch strips at most hobby stores or from either of the wood supply houses that we've mentioned before.

Paint all wood strips first. Use 1/4 x 1/8-inch wood for the pickets. Use 1/4-inch strips for the crosspieces, and the pickets may be glued or tacked. Tacking them gives a more realistic effect, but in this case you must use 1/4-inch wood for the pickets, since a 1/2-inch wire nail is the smallest available and these make 1/4-inch pickets and crosspieces a necessity.

Figure the height you want your fence, and cut the wood for the pickets to this size. With your X-Acto knife, slant off one end of each piece so it comes to a point. Mark the point where you want to affix the pickets to the crosspieces, since they must be very even to look professional. Glue or tack the pickets. You will find that it is easier to make the fences in 12-inch strips rather than to tackle larger pieces. Strips can always be cut to fit at the corners.

The next fence shown is known as the Shaker fence, since this was first used by the Shakers because of its simplicity. Use 1/2-inch wood for the uprights, then a 1-inch strip of 1/8-inch wood at the bottom, and a 1/2-inch strip at the top. Uprights about 4 inches long are are just right. Make this in 12-inch pieces too, with an upright at each end and one in the middle.

The crude but engaging fence at the bottom is made of tongue depressors glued or tacked to crosspieces cut from 1/4-inch balsa or basswood. Notice that we have cut these unevenly, to carry out the feeling of a handmade country fence. Tongue depressors are available in varied lengths; a 6-inch one might be cut in half for a low fence, but they're so inexpensive that you could cut them to the length you desire. You will find, also, that they have a rather hard finish, which indicates that some sort of filler has already been used on them; thus they don't take well to stain, but we used Stain 'N Buff on the one photographed, and found that the uneven finish was very realistic.

For a more modern house, one couldn't do better than with the two fences shown next. These are made from a material called Gutter Cover, which is available at all hardware stores. It is properly used to cover the gutters on a house, to keep out leaves. It comes 6 inches wide, a nice height for a chain-link security fence on a modern house and we used it with 1/2-inch-square uprights. The black one is used for the same purpose but is made of plastic. Cutting off the top cross-thread of the plastic makes a very presentable finish for the top of the fence, rather like some iron fences.

And last but not least, we would like to call your attention to the possibilities in man-made materials, just to demonstrate that you must

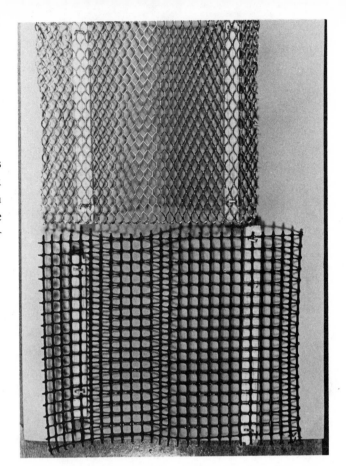

Two possibilities for fences are the 6″ Gutter-Gards shown here, which make exact replicas of chain-link fences. The top one is made of aluminum, the bottom of black plastic. They are easily erected on ¼″-square fence posts, and may be cut to any height the builder wishes (*Photograph by Sam Taylor*).

look at *everything* as a possibility for the dollhouse. At left in this photograph is a fence or railing cut from a piece of wood-filled composition which is used architecturally for divisions in rooms, balustrades on staircases, and such details. It comes in 4 x 8-foot sheets but is easily cut with a saw, and your dealer may have some scraps that he will be glad to give you and which will suit your purpose perfectly. It takes paint nicely and holds well with glue. At right is a piece of metal stripping found in a junk shop; it makes a pretty fence used "as is," and can be cut off at different levels to vary the design.

Shown at left is a piece of pressed wood, or Masonite, that makes a very nice fence, and one or two rows make most impressive stair railings or balustrades for an outside porch. This comes in 4′ x 8′ sheets, but may be cut to order at any point. The metal railing at right, recovered from a junk shop, may also be cut at any point to get the desired height or design (*Photograph by Sam Taylor*).

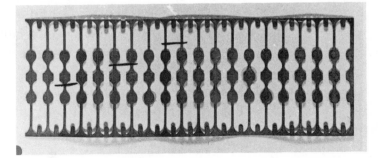

Windows

Windows are without a doubt one of the most important details in the finished appearance of a house whether life-sized or mini-sized, so it is a blessing that they are so relatively simple to make. I use balsa wood for the frames and muntins (muntins are the little dividing pieces that form the panes) because it is so easy to work and holds the glue well. For the "glass" I can see no objection at all to using triple-weight celluloid or a plastic heavy enough to stand in the frame; either of these may be cut with scissors.

Ordinary glass is too thick to laminate between the wood frames, but for those who are sticklers for detail, Louis and Barbara Kummerow, who under the firm name Dollhouses make both houses and miniatures, offer both glass and mirrors that can be cut to order in what they call "micro-glass" and "micro-mirror," which is only $\frac{1}{40}$ inch thick. Another item that the Kummerows offer is etched glass for windows and door frames. One glass pattern even carries the initial of your choice in the center of the etching, just as they were made at the turn of the century. The Kummerows also offer Tiffany-style windows in brass frames which are simulated glass but with unbelievably realistic hand-painted designs.

Now to begin. If you are using the micro-glass, order it in a size to fit your window opening. If you are using celluloid, cut a piece to fit. Butt joints are used on windows; cut lengths of $\frac{1}{4}$-inch-wide and $\frac{1}{16}$-inch-thick balsa wood to fit your opening, and end pieces to fit between them. Paint these and all other wood; you will probably want the outside white, and the inside a stain or other color. Form the window on your cutting surface, check the measurements, then lay the celluloid or glass over it, with tiny droplets of glue to hold the glass. Over the glass or celluloid, using again tiny droplets of glue, place the second set of lengths and widths and set aside to dry.

I like to dry these under a weight; a better bond seems to result. When the frame is dry, cut two pieces of the $\frac{1}{16}$-inch balsa $\frac{1}{8}$ inch wide. This forms the crosspiece between the windows; if your upper and lower panes are to be equal, glue it in the center of the frame. If you are constructing what is called an 8-over-12 window like the one in the drawing, glue the crosspiece at that point.

Many possibilities exist; we have mentioned the 6-over-6 window before, and some elaborate houses even had a 9-over-12 arrangement. Use whichever you prefer or whichever is appropriate for your house. When the crosspiece is thoroughly dry, use the $\frac{1}{16}$-inch-thick balsa strips to cut the muntins; your measuring must be very accurate here, for while on the up and down of the window you will be dealing with

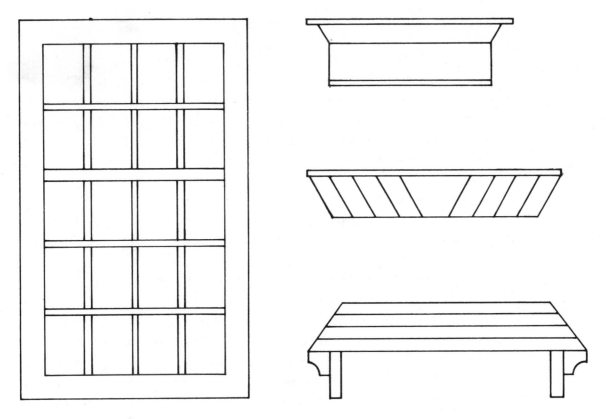

Window with sample cornices

a fairly large piece of wood, on the cross muntins, which must fit between the up-and-down muntins, the pieces are very small.

Most important to consider is the amount of glue used. If you use enough glue here so that it comes out over the "glass," you can never get it off. In making windows, glue must be used so sparingly that it never bulges outside the frames.

Dry under a weight again, then turn over and install the muntins on the other side of the glass, using wood stained or painted to match the inside of the house.

Small Gothic window by George Ober showing adhesive tape strips used as muntins (dividers) (*Photograph by David Ober*).

On some dollhouses, the window frames are left very plain on the outside, as with the Schroeder house on p. 53. On others such as the Webster house on p. 54, all sorts of ornamental cornices may be used. A few more are shown on the previous page; these are simply cut from the wood and glued against the house at the top of the window.

A much simpler way to finish the window is to use tape or adhesive paper instead of wood for the muntins in the manner shown in the photograph opposite, a detail from one of George Ober's houses. Here adhesive tape may be cut into 1/8-inch strips and applied to the windows, or an architectural tape now on the market may be bought in many narrow widths. For the inside muntins, one of the brown, stained-effect adhesive papers may be used after cutting into the 1/8-inch strips.

Many ideas can be found by the discerning craftsperson in this charming little mini-shop discovered in Bath, England, by Paige Thornton. The glass of the windowpanes is actually leaded.

Needlework booth at a country fair, a print reproduced from an 1883 women's magazine. Notice the rolls of canvas and partly worked pieces used as decorations. Width, 15"; depth, 12"; height, 15". A memento of the United Federation of Doll Clubs meeting at Louisville in 1973 (*Courtesy of Marjorie Brandt*).

5 Finishing the Inside

As we come to the finishing of the inside of our house, we begin to realize that there are, indeed, as we mentioned in *The Collector's Guide to Dollhouses and Dollhouse Miniatures*, three types of collectors: the antiquers, the builders, and those who just love everything that's miniature.

We—those who are using this book—are builders, but even within our group there are divisions: for example, there are those who are dedicated to building every single item, and others who enjoy accepting a bit of help from the outside, so that they can take time to have fun working out the details.

Interior Woodwork

For those who are happy to accept (and pay for!) a little help, there are a number of people who make the woodwork for finishing mini-interiors. We illustrate opposite a few of the things available from Howard Pierce of The Workshop in Wichita, Kansas.

At top left is his 6-over-6 window with a raised outer trim, next a Dutch door and, at right, a Pennsylvania window with plain trim and an arched top. This arched top, incidentally, might well be copied for a finish for outside windows; it is most impressive when so used. At bottom, we show his so-called double-cross door (the effect made by the paneling is of a cross at top and another at the bottom), a larger 6-over-6 window, and the plank door, which is great for schoolhouses, ranch houses, and log cabins.

Chestnut Hill offers no less than six doors, with two windows and a number of panels. John Blauer of the Miniature Mart offers woodwork in sets: the top set, an authentic Victorian design, is complete with roundels and wainscoting for walls and for under windows. His Georgian woodwork, which is illustrated below, includes a door, win-

Inside millwork from Howard Pierce's Workshop (*Photograph by Rorabaugh and Millsap Studio*).

Chestnut Hill Studio's magnificent doors, windows, and paneling are exact copies of those of the period they work in; door *8* is a copy of the windows in the living room (a double room with two matching fireplaces) of the Cowles family's post-Colonial house, an early stagecoach tavern, western New York landmark built around 1811. The double-cross door (*4*) is also an exact copy of the doors in their house.

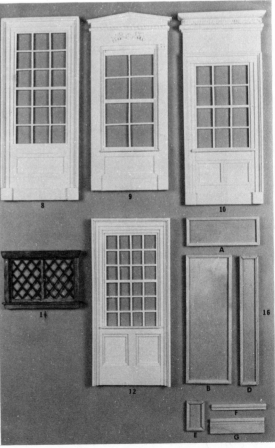

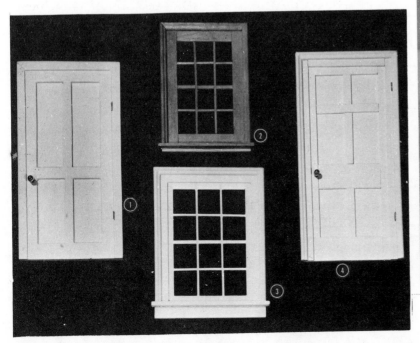

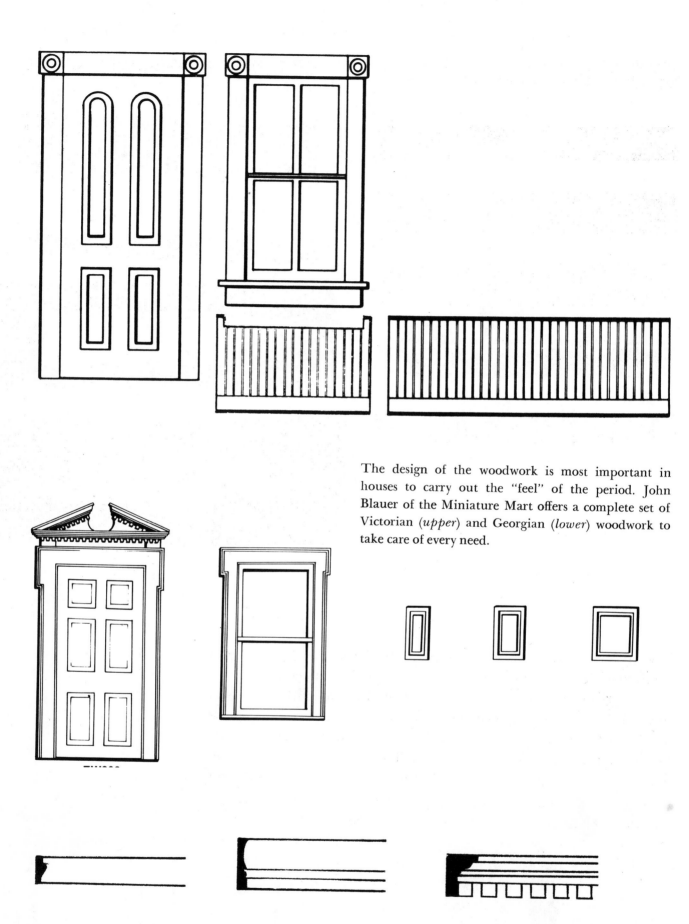

The design of the woodwork is most important in houses to carry out the "feel" of the period. John Blauer of the Miniature Mart offers a complete set of Victorian (*upper*) and Georgian (*lower*) woodwork to take care of every need.

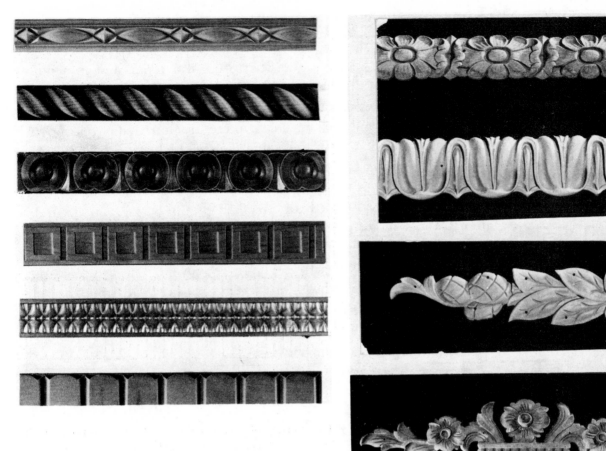

Moldings from Constantine's.

dow, and paneling, plus a chair-rail molding, baseboard, and a most
impressive dentil molding which we've never seen elsewhere.

A series of ornamental moldings offered by Constantine's are pictured above. Notice that some of these are narrow enough to be used as
woodwork trimming as they are, but several of the wider ones, especially
the ones at the right, could be cut in half. The flower and the rope moldings, second and third from top, are beautifully ornamental when cut
in half, and the halves make lovely ceiling moldings or plate rails.
The smaller designs are actually carved from wood, but the larger ones
are molded from a wood-filled composition. Where the design is not
repeated, parts may be cut to use as smaller decorations, such as the
pineapple at the bottom of the spray carving, and the various flowers
and leaves from the basket design.

Floors

Any interior decorator will tell you that it is better to start at the bottom when planning the decoration of a room, and in a dollhouse this is especially true because in working upward, one has more leeway for covering mistakes—and, after all, we all make them.

When starting with the floors, there are four paths one might follow: First, one can stain the actual base of the house, on the inside, and use this as the background for the rooms. The perfectionist will never be satisfied with this step, however, for an open-pored wood, such as pine, was probably used for the shell of the house, and it rarely absorbs the stain of the finish wanted. Second, one might cover the floors with paper. There is a variety of papers designed for just this purpose; all are most attractive. The three shown below, as well as the parquet pattern at left above on the next page, are all from the collection of J. Hermes of El Monte, California, and all come in nice

WOOD SQUARES	RANDOM BOARD	WAINSCOTING
	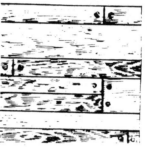	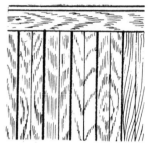

Paper coverings for floors

shades of brown. They will take a little care in laying, but make most satisfactory floor finishes. See below (pp. 76–77) for the directions on how to apply the papers. These, even the wainscoting, must be applied, you should remember, before the baseboard or quarter-round is in place; then, if the paper doesn't truly meet the wall, or the wainscot is a fraction of an inch short, the wood trim, stained before applying, will cover everything. In one house we even applied a wooden chair rail at the top of the wainscoting and found that this added greatly to the effectiveness of the paper.

The papers at top right and bottom right (p. 73) are also from the Hermes catalogue and both are true copies of old floor coverings; both make a floor astonishingly like old tile. The one at left bottom is from the Miniature Mart and comes in a selection of blue, brown, or red.

A paper which was actually a people-sized wallpaper but with a smaller pattern is shown on the next page at upper left; this could

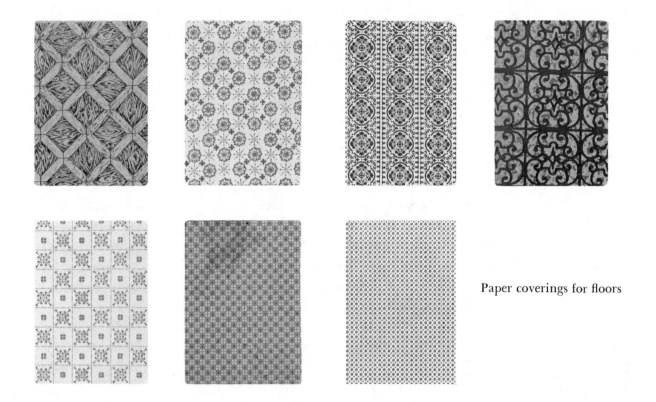

Paper coverings for floors

have been used in the dollhouse on either walls or floor, and we used it in a small breakfast room and then sprayed with plastic, for a beautiful effect. This, of course, is a heavy paper and will wear well even though the dollhouse family is an active one. It occurred to us that it would be effective as flooring for a porch or patio, since it gives the effect of a metal grid over concrete. One of the interesting things about these floor papers is that they may be varnished or sprayed with clear plastic, which gives them a waxed finish that makes them look exactly like the old-time linoleum used in kitchens and bathrooms. It is tremendously effective.

The next idea we might consider for finishing the floors is actually laying a wooden floor over the base rough floor, just as is done in a house. For this a good choice is $\frac{1}{16}$-inch strips, 1 inch wide, of basswood, balsa, or spruce. If you want random-width floors, use strips 1 inch wide and cut some strips in half to give a $\frac{1}{2}$-inch width. It is very effective, too, to cut some shorter than others, so that the planks meet at random points. A floor expert will tell you that the planks should be laid tight against one another, but for some reason this doesn't give much of an effect; you will find it much more pleasing to cut your planks into the lengths wanted and then, some quiet evening, sit down with an emery board and sand off the edges and ends at an angle. Then proceed with staining and varnishing after carefully wiping each plank free of any sawdust, and when dry, glue to the floor. You'll find that the slanting edges give a pretty pattern.

The possibilities of tile for dollhouse floors are tremendous; asphalt and rubber tile are thin enough so that they don't appear to be out of proportion, and they are easily cut so that almost any space can be readily fitted. The range of patterns will leave you so excited that you'll feel almost as though you were decorating your own people-sized house. In the 9-inch squares which this material usually comes in, you'll find marbleized patterns from pink and gold to slate color; wood patterns; copies of old linoleum; and so many others that you'll be at a loss to know what to use, unless you have some pretty definite ideas. There is one catch to this unbelievable find, however; the tiles are usually sold in boxes or packs, and the dealer won't break a box. Your best bet in this case is to find someone who is building a people-sized house, and beg a few squares from him. At our house, we religiously save every tile left from remodeling jobs and find that eventually they are just what we need. For example, my daughter's kitchen was paved with a lovely vinyl tile made to look like slate; the design showed little irregular pieces from 1 to 2 inches in diameter, deeply recessed so that they actually looked like imbedded rock. Eventually, I decided to build a separate Colonial kitchen and wanted a paved floor for it; we simply used this slate tile and sprayed it lightly with a brick-colored, quick-drying paint, a flat finish. If the spraying is done carefully, there is enough variation in the color to give a perfect rock look. It made a lovely floor.

In this connection, you might be leaning toward a brick floor, either in a Colonial kitchen or for such specialized purposes as the Victorian conservatory in the color section. You probably won't find brick tile, but don't despair. Jean Kirkwood and Elizabeth Zorn, who operate the Ginger Jar, in Sylvania, Ohio, make perfect bricks to scale, a lovely soft red, at about $1.00 for a bag of fifty. And just to show you that it really pays to shop around even in the miniature world, when I learned this I had just finished paying $5.00 per hundred for bricks from another miniaturist, which really weren't half as nice. The Ginger Jar's brick are 3″ x ⅓″ x ⅙″.

One of the finest finishes for dollhouse floors now available is porcelain tile. Until a few years ago, these were made so thick and the tiles so large that using them as miniatures was out of the question, but today we have an enormous choice of tiles as small as ⅜ inch square, and ⅛ inch in thickness. You will find these at your nearby handcraft store or hobby shop, and you may find some at a tile store for life-sized houses; wherever they are, you will be in a whirl of delight. They are fascinatingly easy to handle, since they usually come already assembled in the various colors on a net backing, in 12-inch-square sheets. One has only to cut the net to the size and shape one wants, and glue it directly to the floor. Used this way, there is about a $\frac{1}{16}$-inch space between the tiles, which I personally don't mind at all, but if you want the tiles to butt up against each other exactly, they can be taken from the net one by one and pressed against the floor which has been spread with glue. Laid the first way, on the net backing, one can always go between the tiles with the grout which is used to fill the joints on ashtrays and such handcraft projects. However, it's a nerve-testing job, unless you elect to spread the grout between the tiles while they are still on the net which has been cut to fit your floor space. Then clean the tiles well before inserting in the house.

Colors in the tiles will delight you. In a mosaic tile you will have an effect that is very much alive. In gold porcelain tile, either gold flecked or with a full gold surface, you will have an exotic effect that would be great anywhere. In porcelain mosaic tile we counted some sixteen color combinations, some of them containing tiles with little blue flecks which look exactly like the "hand-painted" tiles that some miniaturists use as trim for their fireplaces.

There is even a Venetian-glass tile available in some handcraft shops, although it is growing more and more difficult to find. Costing

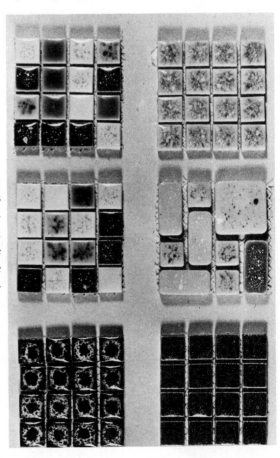

Tiny commercial ceramic tiles are shown here full size: at top right, a floral decoration of blue-on-blue looks exactly like the hand-painted tiles found on mini-fireplaces; the tile shown at center right is lovely on a bathroom or patio floor, and the two at bottom have metallic glints in black or brown grounds which are beautiful. All come attached to a net backing (*Photograph by Sam Taylor*).

about $1.50 per pound (a pound covers an 8 x 12-inch area) it also comes in ⅜-inch tiles that are very thin and easy to handle and are exactly to scale. The only drawback is that they are not evenly shaped, and thus are a bit difficult to lay.

In any event, no matter which of these floor coverings you choose, you will have only one problem: the finished floors will be so pretty that you'll hate to put rugs over them. Have fun with the work.

One of the most favored finishes for floors in Colonial or Provincial houses, and today in Contemporary houses, is the mottled finish of splatter, which to me has always been a favorite because it covers so many of the defects that the amateur craftsman finds in his completed work. All you need is the color you want to use in your scheme, and a good hard enamel-finish paint, together with a very coarse, stiff, small-sized (no larger than 1-inch) paint brush. Be sure to do the splatterdashing before you finish the side walls, or if your walls are already finished, protect the walls with paper taped to them.

First, paint the entire floor the solid color of your choice and allow it to dry thoroughly—at least twice as long as you would an ordinary paint job.

When this is completely dry, apply a second coat of the solid base color to about half the floor. Let this portion dry until it's slightly sticky; on a tacky surface, the splatter colors will hold nicely.

Dip the brush into the second color you wish to use; take care not to have it too full of paint—it must not drip. Hold the brush a couple of inches above the floor and strike it sharply with a stick. The amount of paint on the brush will control the size of the splatters. Practice first!

Cover the painted section with the first splatter coat, then add the next splatter color. Some decorators use only one splatter coat, some use two or three contrasting colors, for example, a dark blue floor with red, yellow, and white splatters, or a pale green floor with black, white, and pink splatters. When the first section is finished, you can go on to the second section, although if your rooms are not too large, the whole thing may be done at one time. After the entire floor is finished and completely dry, give it a coat of clear varnish, or wax it well.

Here are some of the combinations used both in old houses and in old dollhouses:

Light gray background, first splatter red, second splatter purple
Darker gray background, first splatter white, second splatter black
Green background, with black splatter

Yellow background, first splatter green, second splatter purple

Dark brown background, first splatter Indian red, second splatter
   olive green

Black background, dark red splatter

Dark green background, first splatter black, second splatter purple

And finally, for the builder who is willing to go to a bit of extra
trouble, there is the true parquet floor of wood. In one of our dollhouses we made such a floor using $\frac{1}{16}$-inch veneer plywood, which
comes in beautiful tones. It must be cut in 1-inch squares and the
squares must be exact, which is a bit difficult unless you have a saw
such as that on the Dremel Moto-Shop. The squares are laid on a wood
base and must butt up against each other exactly, one with the grain
going one way and the next with grain going the other way, in a
sort of checkerboard pattern. The squares may be laid and finished
afterward if you are careful to use very little glue and not let it come
close to the edges of the squares. This saves a tremendous lot of time.
Glue the squares to the floor and weight with heavy books (or with a
block and clamps if the floor is not yet in the dollhouse) until dry.

Endless variations on this theme are possible if you will study the
various woods available from suppliers. Colors vary widely, and a beautiful effect is easily achieved.

Painted Canvas Floorcloths

One of the most fascinating dresses for your floors and one of the
easiest creations for the mini-craftsman, is the painted canvas floorcloth which was used often in eighteenth-century America by the
colonist because rugs were so scarce and expensive, and the Oriental
ones took so long to import. Oddly enough, we know of no dollhouse
in which these are used except our own, but Mary Ferrari of Colling-
dale, Pennsylvania, a subscriber to *The Dollhouse News,* found mention of them in doing research on the period of a projected dollhouse,
and even worked out a method—the same used on the one that Thomas
Jefferson ordered for the White House!

Mary uses regular canvas such as is used for paintings (we use
sailcloth of a heavy variety to be found in yard-goods departments).
People-sized floorcloths are made with six layers of a base formula, but
we, like Mary, used simply a base coat of white paint. We found two
coats ample to coat the canvas and fill the pores. Allow plenty of time
for drying between coats; the longer the paint dries, the more durable
it becomes.

When this flat coat is ready, trace the design onto it with soft pencil. One rare old floorcloth was painted to match a collecion of pottery by Thomas Whieldon; here the base coat was made of cream color and small bits of brown and green acrylic paint were dabbed on with a sponge to achieve the tortoise-shell effect that was Whieldon's favorite in the middle 1700s. One can easily see the vast possibilities when considering all the sources of design. At any rate, when the design is finished, Mary then gives it one or two coats of a clear plastic spray to protect it and make it easy to clean. Even Thomas Jefferson was aware of the necessity for this—he always had his floorcloths rolled up after a banquet!

Mary Ferrari's design is similar to one in the collection of Leonard C. Crewe; both Mr. Crewe's and hers are done in alternating diamonds of Kelly green and white. We have made one which is stunning in gray and Venetian red, and the old tried-and-true black and white would be equally good.

Painted floorcloth

One thing that is very important in finishing your floorcloths is that the edges must be finished before the paint is applied to the top; otherwise you may crack the paint. With canvas, duck, or sailcloth, we found the best and easiest way was to cut the material ¼ inch larger all around than needed, then fold this over and press down with an iron and a damp cloth. Fasten with a strip of masking tape, cellophane tape, or Mystik tape, then go ahead with the painting. Here are a few more designs typical of the late seventeenth century/early eighteenth century copied from actual people-sized rugs: In the pattern at left on p. 79, the original was done on a gray background, the shaded pattern in Venetian red and the white in dead black. In the next pattern, the background was dark brown, the shaded pattern in olive green and the clear pattern in brick red. In the two next floorcloths, both copied from a pair in a museum in New England, the first design was done on a background of dark green, the dark figures are black, and the stars are purple. The design of tulips at right was done in black against a background of dark red. These small patterns, of course, may be traced from the page on tracing paper and then transferred to the painted cloth with carbon paper. Don't be too concerned if the designs are somewhat less than perfect; remember that this is folk art, and it was never meant to be like something produced by a machine.

One of the most fascinating methods for making carpeting for a dollhouse is described by Lucille Spinka, whose Victorian house we show on p. 31. The wall-to-wall carpet in this house was made by

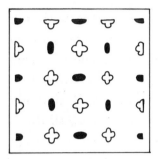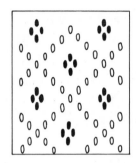

Painted floorcloths

gluing patterned velvet to light card and cutting that into shapes and again gluing it to a light-card base, rather like a fabric jigsaw puzzle. There are nineteen cutouts to each 1½-inch-square area of repeating pattern. The possibilities in such a method are endless; one might use contrasting colors of velvet in a geometric pattern, cutout flowers and leaves glued onto the base velvet, or even Oriental designs.

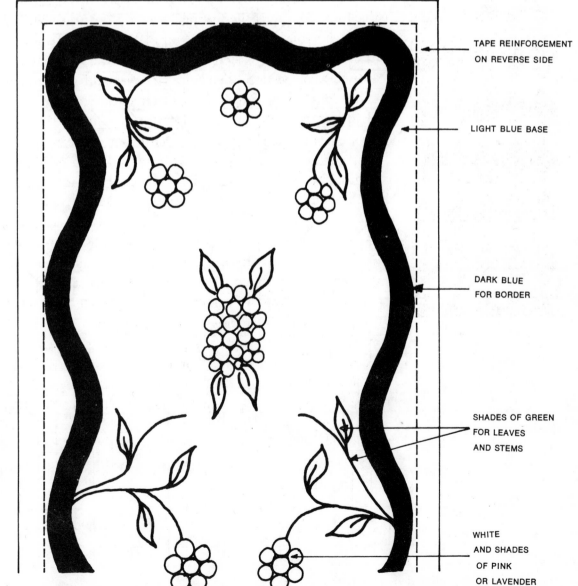

Felt rug design

TAPE REINFORCEMENT
ON REVERSE SIDE

LIGHT BLUE BASE

DARK BLUE
FOR BORDER

SHADES OF GREEN
FOR LEAVES
AND STEMS

WHITE
AND SHADES
OF PINK
OR LAVENDER

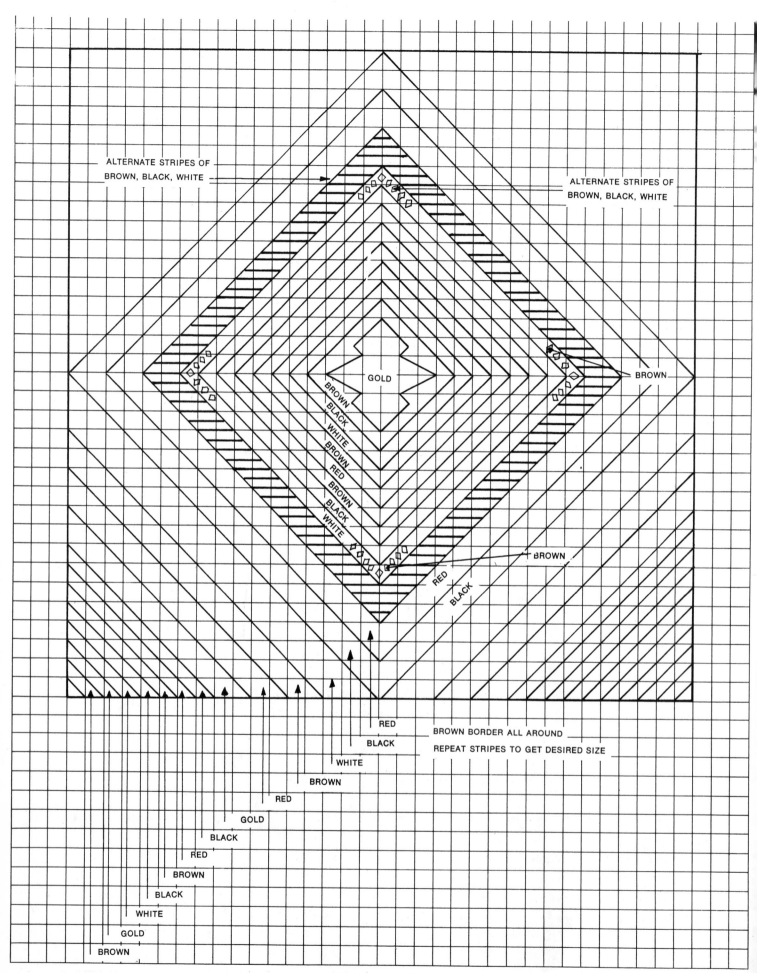

ALTERNATE STRIPES OF
BROWN, BLACK, WHITE

ALTERNATE STRIPES OF
BROWN, BLACK, WHITE

GOLD

BROWN
BLACK
WHITE
BROWN
RED
BROWN
BLACK
WHITE

BROWN

RED
BLACK

BROWN

RED
BLACK
WHITE
BROWN
RED
GOLD
BLACK
RED
BROWN
BLACK
WHITE
GOLD
BROWN

BROWN BORDER ALL AROUND

REPEAT STRIPES TO GET DESIRED SIZE

Detailed plan for Indian-design floorcloth

Another idea which I have used to great effect in many rooms starts with a felt base cut to the size needed. Strengthen the felt with Scotch tape or masking tape around all edges on the wrong side. Using a soft pencil, sketch your design on the right side, or trace from a pattern found in a book or magazine. The one drawn on p. 79, in shades of blue, I made for a bedroom. Carefully cut out the border and stems in the shades desired; in this case, the wide border was a darker blue, stems and leaves were varied shades of green, and the flowers were varying shades of pink, punched out with a hand paper punch.

Cut out the border and stems. Using the decoupage glue that dries clear, run a tiny line of glue along the border line—one side at a time. Carefully press the border strips along this line. You'll find the felt can be stretched so that you can make all sorts of lovely curves with it. Press it down or renew the glue as you go along. Do the same with the other sides, then with the design in the center. Be careful to have the strips of border felt meet at the corners, or at some point where you can cover them with another detail of the design. When all is done to your satisfaction, press it under a heavy book such as a Bible. Once you've decided upon a design and traced it on felt, you'll find that an entire 9 x 12-inch carpet can be finished in an evening.

The miniature Indian floorcloth on artist's canvas was purchased at the St. Louis World's Fair in 1904. Acrylic paint on artist's canvas was used to reproduce this cloth. See color plate and the graph opposite.

Curtains

Curtains are without a doubt the bête noir of the dollhouse decorator. In every antique dollhouse they are billowy and clumsy, and in contemporary houses they frustrate us beyond belief.

Almost all curtains in dollhouses are either held back with bands of material or left hanging straight to the floor; many students of dollhouse styles contend that these were the only styles used. However, the jabot drape (a) was much admired in Jefferson's time and the Austrian pouf curtain (b) such as Lucille Spinka used in the Victorian house (p. 31) was a great favorite in the mid-eighteenth century. Ms. Spinka, by the way, uses the pouf shades in the dining room, making them of chiffon, and they actually work by virtue of heavy thread run through channels made with very narrow strips of iron-on tape. Rosalind Arthur, a miniaturist who specializes in the pouf shades, makes hers of very old, soft, fine net, hand hemmed on either side and gathered with a thread with stitches so fine they can't be seen, from bottom to top.

Material is all-important; it must be soft and drapable. My best bedroom curtains are cut from an old French batiste nightgown which

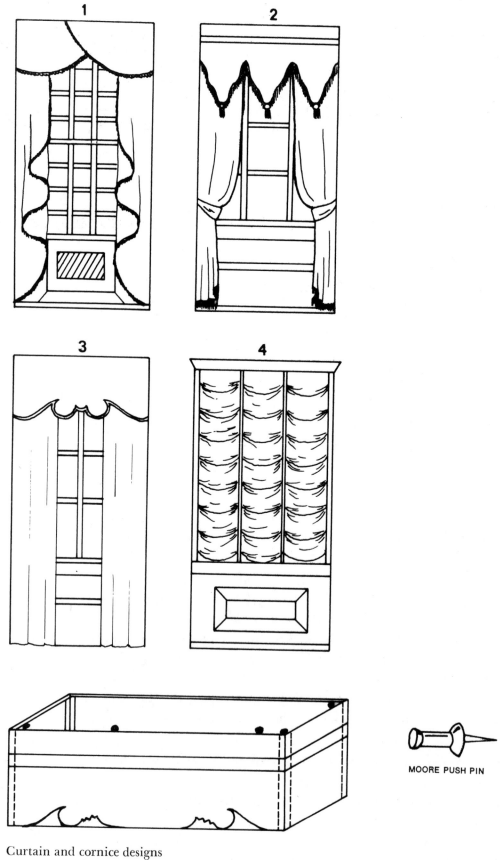

Curtain and cornice designs

MOORE PUSH PIN

82

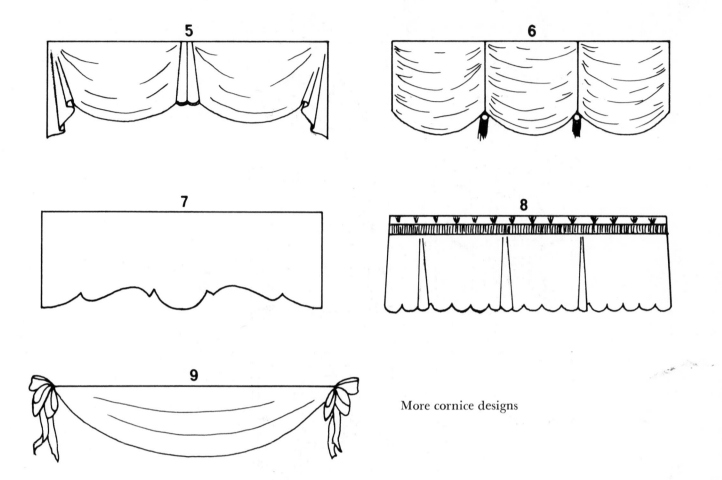

More cornice designs

has been washed a hundred times. Adelaide Mannion's draperies in her formal rooms are made from a very soft white silk, lined with sheer French voile. In spite of all one reads about using damask, I found the best material for formal draperies was a sort of china silk lining material, sheer but not transparent. The new Qiana nylon materials are perfect, and come in a wide range of colors and patterns.

There are literally hundreds of designs for valances, as witness these suggestions from the Williamsburg restoration people:

Festoon and jabot design; jabots and center pleats are laid on separately over the swag. Similar to Jefferson's design at Monticello. Soft festoons for formal rooms. This shape is influenced by French design in the eighteenth century.

A Chippendale-type design. Here the material is glued directly to the box-type valance discussed later.

Single shirred valance, suitable for any room, depending upon the material used. Simply run a casing in the material and shirr on the rod.

Victorian-type swag used mostly in bedrooms in the latter half of the nineteenth century, over lace or sheer curtains.

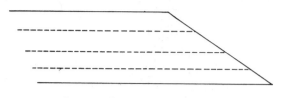

Pattern for jabot curtain

"Jabot" drapes are cut as shown in this sketch, larger or smaller as your design requires. Those on the valance in 5 on p. 83 are only 1 inch long, while those in 1 must reach to the floor at the back edge. Cut, hem, then fold over in soft pleats on the dotted lines and sew or glue to the rods.

My own preference in valances is a small box such as is shown on p. 82. This may be made from ⅛-inch balsa or from a piece of corrugated carton; cut a piece about 1 inch wide and in length the width of your window plus ¾ inch on each end. This is for a valance 1 inch deep. If you're using the corrugated, have the ribs going up and down; score at the ¾-inch mark and bend the ends back. If you're using balsa, cut the ends off at the ¾-inch mark. Now cut another piece, same depth, same width of the window. With corrugated, fit this piece onto the sides which you folded over and secure with masking tape. With balsa, glue onto the sides, then glue tiny ¼-inch strips cut 1 inch long on the inside of the corner for support. You will have a hollow box.

Moore push pins with glass heads about ½ inch long and a ½-inch pin are used to hang the valances. After the box is covered to your satisfaction, press a push pin through each end at the back. This is then pushed into the wall over the window; the push pins hold it up. You will have more than enough space to slip your completed curtains, on a rod, inside the box and onto the glass heads. Holds them perfectly.

I much prefer the metal extension rods described on p. 193. However, ⅛-inch dowels cut to fit and finished with gold leaf or brass paint will do nicely if the ends are fitted with fancy beads.

For the large jabots to fit the sides of a window, cut the material according to the pattern and twice as wide as needed (probably the width of the entire window). Cut the lining and sew with the right sides inside, then turn and press, applying edging as desired. Valances Nos. 1, 2, and 3 as well as Nos. 5, 6, and 7, may be applied directly to the valance board. No. 8 is shirred directly onto the rod and No. 9 is made with a casing at top, then slipped onto the rod. Cut twice as deep as you want the valance after draping. Fasten at the ends and decorate with bows.

Thin felt glued onto the valance box makes a fine finish; contrasting strips of ribbon or braid may be glued to the felt.

Pennsylvania Dutch punched-tin pie safe. Doors open to reveal shelves. Shown on top are pumpkins and a gingerbread house. Author's collection. (*Photo by Slawomir Dratewka*)

Butcher block table with knives, cleaver, and mallet. Author's collection. (*Photo by Slawomir Dratewka*)

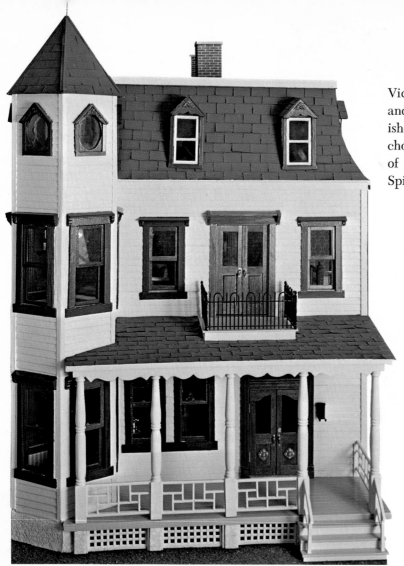

Victorian mansion, ca. 1870, made by Emil and Lucille Spinka. Both floors were finished completely before they were anchored into the shell. A perfect example of fine craftsmanship. Courtesy of Lucille Spinka. (*Photo by James Kleinlenderink*)

Front stairway of the Spinka house. Spindles in the balustrades were made by hand. Behind the ornate woodwork is the first floor hall, complete with a hatstand on which a straw "boater" may be hung. The magnificent chandeliers are made of brass and bread dough roses. Courtesy of Lucille Spinka. (*Photo by James Kleinlenderink*)

Library in the Spinka house. All of the furniture and books were made by the owners. The chandelier is especially fine. Courtesy of Lucille Spinka. (*Photo by James Kleinlenderink*)

Another staircase is located in the kitchen of the Spinka house. All of the late nineteenth-century furnishings were made by the Spinkas. Courtesy of Lucille Spinka. (*Photo by James Kleinlenderink*)

The dining room of the Beretta Display House. Notice the manner in which mirrors have been mounted on the panels above the doors. The chandeliers and sconces, made from crystal beads, are particularly fine. Courtesy of Mary Austin Beretta. (*Photo by Billo Matthews Smith*)

The library of the Beretta House. All books, which have pages, were made by hand. The rug is an antique petit point. The chaise longue (center right) was made by Elizabeth Zorn and Jean Kirkwood of The Ginger Jar. Courtesy of Mary Austin Beretta. (*Photo by Billo Matthews Smith*)

Fourth floor hall of the Beretta House. The antique chest against the back wall is from Queen Titania's Palace. The wallpaper is from Miniature Mart, and the iron fire engine and wicker doll buggy are both nineteenth-century toys. Courtesy of Mary Austin Beretta. (*Photo by Billo Matthews Smith*)

Woodwork in master bedroom is finished in a soft Williamsburg blue. The small embroidery over the desk is late eighteenth-century English. Most of the furniture is from Chestnut Hill Studio. Window and bed draperies were made by Mary Dudley Cowles, of Chestnut Hill Studio, who also made the tiny export tea set. Each piece is marked on the bottom "J. Beretta." Courtesy of Mary Austin Beretta. (*Photo by Billo Matthews Smith*)

The Victorian side of the author's Turn-About-House, ca. 1870. (*Photo by Sam Taylor*)

The author's Turn-About-House, ca. 1920. (*Photo by Sam Taylor*)

Every opulent Victorian house had a conservatory. The one shown was made by the author from a plastic container for growing herbs. (*Photo by Sam Taylor*)

Rustic dining room set created by James Sweet. The wash stand at right is from Miniature Mart, and the petit point rug in the foreground was made by Sandra Choron. Mary Schnarr made the food. Author's collection. (*Photo by Bernard Glickman*)

Floor cloth with an Indian motif. Author's collection. (*Photo by Sam Taylor*)

A group of tiny quilted pillows, none more than 1½ inches square. Author's collection. (*Photo by Elinor Coyle*)

Two quilts approximately 6 inches by 7 inches, both made by Selma Webber. The Texas Star quilt is generally considered one of the most complicated to make, especially in miniature. Author's collection. (*Photo by Elinor Coyle*)

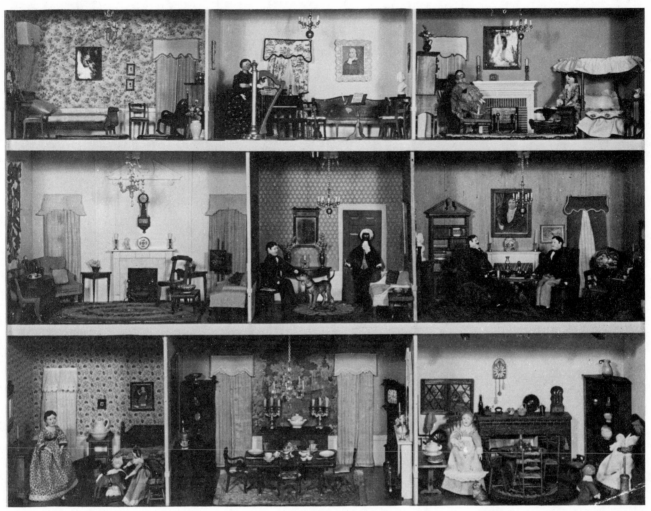

Display house in the collection of Mrs. R. B. Snyder of North Palm Beach, Florida. Notice how much the valances and curtains add to the beauty of these rooms (*Photograph by Merrill Green*).

Many ingenious methods for holding the pleats in the curtains have been devised. John Blauer glues the material to a sheet of aluminum foil, then folds foil and material into the pleats and lets it dry. Other miniaturists like to pin the material, after hemming and finishing, into pleats on a board, then spray with hair spray. I personally have the best luck with corrugated, using the ribbed side. Have the drapery pieces hemmed and finished, then coat the ribs of the corrugated lightly with glue and place the material over it, forcing it down between the ribs.

Wallpaper

As we turn to the inside of the house, we find ourselves hoping that if you have built or bought a new house, you have planned ahead of time to do the finishing—trimming, painting, wallpapering, etc.—on each floor as it is ready. It is a tricky job to hang wallpaper or paint trim if the ceiling is already in place. The invariable result is dabs of paint where they don't belong, and forearms and elbows decorated with stain and paste where you found it necessary to reach in to a back wall.

With the wallpaper we begin, as usual, at the bottom, just as we do with so many dollhouse jobs; it seems to be a miniaturist's law. Give the selection of your wallpaper some serious thought. If, after the paper is up, you decide that you would prefer something else, scraping off old paper is a trying job, and pasting over old paper almost invariably causes the old paper to come loose, so that old and new finally dangle at the ceilings and hang free altogether.

The best sources for fine miniature wallpaper that we have found are J. Hermes of El Monte, California, and Ellen Blauer of the Miniature Mart in San Francisco. These are people who have given much time and attention to finding papers that are truly miniature, and all miniaturists and collectors are deeply indebted to them. There are, however, other sources that shouldn't be overlooked. Gift wrappings, if one searches for truly small patterns, are beautiful; you will find they are of lighter weight than true wallpaper, but I have never found one to wrinkle in the pasting. The one shown lower left in the selection of wallpapers from J. Hermes originally was a Hallmark gift-wrap paper. The pattern is of Revolutionary soldiers in red, white, and blue uniforms against a gold background. I used this pattern in a room for

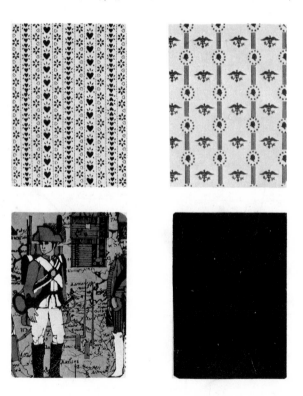

An assortment of miniature wallpapers from the J. Hermes catalogue. The heart paper (*upper left*) is from his Super Tiny group, and looks delightful in a child's room. The paper at upper right is perfect for Colonial rooms. At lower left is a gift-wrap paper, and at right, a paper from a carrying bag in a men's shop.

a little boy, covering two walls with the wallpaper and the third wall with a plain, deep blue construction paper, which matched the coats of the men. The floor was then stained a deep walnut and a rug was crocheted from red mohair wool matching the other color in the paper. The mohair gave a soft, hairy finish much like fur on a small scale.

The checkered paper next to it, lower right, was originally used as a carrying bag in a Manhattan men's store. It, too, was a bit on the thin side, but it took the paste perfectly, with never a wrinkle to annoy the paper hanger.

If you live near a book bindery or an art supply store, you may be fortunate enough to find some book-binding paper, the kind that is used for end papers. I personally don't care for the marbleized or flowing patterns which are normally used on this sort of paper (after all, you wouldn't want that in a house you lived in, would you?) but this paper is meant to be pasted, so it works beautifully, And if you search long enough, you may find some very pretty patterns.

We liked any of the four papers shown on this page for a youngster's room. The papers illustrated are intended only as indications of the wealth of selection available. The toile pattern (*lower left*) comes in rose, blue, lavender, and green, but is available in only a few places, one of them being the Country Store in Jefferson Memorial, Forest Park, St. Louis. The other pretty Victorian stripe (*top right*) is from the Miniature Mart, and the two scenics (*upper left and lower right*) are from J. Hermes and represent a whole new school of thought. These

The two shown at upper left and lower right are from J. Hermes and show the new monotone prints which the decorator may color to suit her color schemes. The Victorian stripe (*upper right*) is from the Peddler's Shop, and the Victorian toile pattern (*lower left*) comes from the Country Store in Jefferson Memorial, St. Louis.

The flocked paper (*upper right*) is from the Peddler's Shop, and the paper at upper left is a commercial Con-Tact paper. Amusingly enough, the paper shown at lower right is the backing for the flocked paper at upper left. The design is a miniature and exactly right for dollhouse rooms. The paper shown at lower left is a Victorian print and comes from the Peddler's Shop.

are printed in a monotone, and are intended to be colored with the watercolor pencils which are available today. Using these pencils, one may add one color or more, to bring out the design, or paint the whole sheet according to the directions on the pencils. These colors will run when wet, however, so the paper must not be moistened when it is applied to the wall.

In miniature wallpaper hanging, it is well to keep in mind advice gleaned from full-sized paper hangers. The glue must be of a consistency that will spread easily and absolutely without lumps. Perhaps you have watched paper hangers in your home paste one side of the paper, fold the strips paste side in, and allow the paper to stand for a few minutes. This is essential to allow the paper to "give" and be easy to handle.

Corners are terribly important in papering a dollhouse. *Never* simply bring the paper around the corner and onto the adjoining wall. One workable method is to cut a 1-inch strip of your wallpaper, fold it in half lengthwise, and paste this into the corner, then affix the paper on the walls adjoining the corner, allowing about ⅛ inch in the corner itself. Another is to paste the wallpaper around the corner and about 1 inch onto the adjoining wall, brushing well into the corner. In using this method. I sometimes use the tip of my little finger to press the

This group of papers represents copies of very old designs. The classic Blue Onion pattern (*upper right*) is available at the Country Store, Jefferson Memorial, St. Louis. Next to it is J. Hermes' Victorian. The two at lower left and right are copies of old Victorian patterns from the Peddler's Shop.

paper into the corner, so as to achieve a sharp angle. Then paper the adjoining wall and bring the paper over the joint and into the corner.

Always wipe down with a wet sponge or cloth after affixing, to work out any air bubbles, but don't work at the paper any more than necessary. If you find some wrinkles, gently pull the paper away from the wall, starting in a corner, then just as gently brush it back against the wall with your moist cloth. A little care will work out any wrinkles. The wetter you can leave the paper, the better the job will be; it will pull up as it dries and give a nice straight effect.

In the matter of glues, almost every miniaturist has his own favorite, many of these being flour concoctions which must be cooked, but our own experience has been that the very best results are achieved with the regular wallpaper paste which is available dry in paint and paper stores. It is simply mixed with a little water to a consistency of pancake batter, allowed to stand for thirty minutes, and there you are. I like to make about a pint so that it is always available when a small job must be done, and it keeps practically forever in the refrigerator. Do remember the refrigeration, however; it will sour eventually if not kept cold.

After many visits to research departments of several large glue companies, we're convinced that vinyl wallpaper adhesive is probably the best bet for keeping dollhouse wallpaper on the walls "for at least

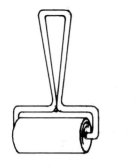

Brayer for wallpaper finishing

fifty years," as one executive promised, because it doesn't have a tendency to dry out. It is also very easy to work with.

If you plan on doing quite a bit of wallpapering, you'll want a "brayer," shown at left. This is the rubber roller with which the wallpaper hanger smooths out paper and seams after the paper is hung; if you ask around at paint or wallpaper shops, you may be able to find one, but the greatest we've seen is of real rubber, barely 4 inches long, and with a handle short enough so that you can get into dollhouse rooms with it. It costs around $2.00, and the only place we know of that offers it is Talents Unlimited, of Anchorage, Kentucky.

The most important thing to remember is that it is far simpler to get the wallpaper on first, and then glue the inside woodwork over it, than to complete your framing of doors and windows, and then have to fit the paper up against the frames. If you are renovating an old house, of course, this is necessary, although I've known many dollhouse workmen who insisted that it was easier to take off the existing door and window frames and then wallpaper than to try to fit the paper against the frames.

Miniature murals are now available commercially in several designs. The one at top is Chestnut Hill Studio's hand-painted strip, made to order. Below this is the chinoiserie pattern produced by Willoughby's 18th Century to match both a silk and a cotton fabric in the same design.

Two murals from J. Hermes may be used "as is"—the top design is printed in maroon on cream and the bottom in green on cream, or colored with watercolor or water pencil to conform with a special decorating idea.

Stairs and Staircases

In people-sized houses, staircases usually have a riser of 7 inches, but in a dollhouse this (on a $\frac{1}{12}$ scale) is a bit awkward looking. Thus, after a great deal of experimenting, we now use a riser of $\frac{1}{2}$ inch (6 inches on the $\frac{1}{12}$ scale) and it is very graceful. Oddly (or perhaps not so oddly?) enough, the $\frac{1}{2}$-inch riser makes it possible to use $\frac{1}{2}$-inch wood, which saves a lot of trimming, and this is what we used in the stairs pictured opposite.

Actually, these are not stairs. They are two or three steps which are used to finish the bottom of a staircase, bridge a difference in levels between rooms, or perhaps serve as an entrance where only these few steps are needed. They are simple to make, and give a finished look to a dollhouse. For the stair itself, use $\frac{1}{2}$-inch balsa; for the top of the stair, $\frac{1}{16}$-inch cherry, mahogany, or other hard wood.

It is impossible to give you a pattern for the so-called Greek stair, since the curve in the stair is dependent upon the width of the opening, and you may wish to fit the stair into the opening, or outside of and larger than the opening, as shown in the drawing. Decide which

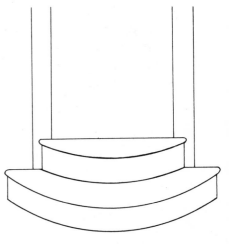

Circular stairs

you want to do, then draw a circle with the diameter equal to the width of the top stair. Cut the circle in half, and that's your top stair. The flat, or diameter, side goes against the wall.

For the next larger stair, draw a circle with a diameter 1 inch larger than the first, then cut it in half. You will find that the smaller semicircle will position itself in the center of the larger, with equal measurements all around.

Stairs or steps look very unfinished without a topping; for this, use 1/16-inch hard wood (possibly cherry or mahogany) and trace the pattern from the semicircles already drawn. Cut this hard-wood pattern 1/8 inch larger than the step itself, except for the straight side; this should be even. Sand the curved edges so they are smooth and rounded, then finish the toppings, one side only, in the stain you prefer. Remember that you must bring the stain around the edge and over the bottom just a bit, for 1/8 inch of the topping is going to stand out over the riser.

Sand the large semicircles smooth, especially on the top and around the risers. Paint the risers white if that is what you prefer; they will need two coats. If you wish the risers stained to match the toppings, do this now. When all is dry, spread the underside of the toppings with glue and carefully fasten them to the top of the stair circles, with the straight edges even at the back. The front and side edges should protrude the 1/8 inch which you allowed when cutting the topping. Dry under pressure, then spread the bottom of the smaller semicircle with glue and center it on the larger circle with the back, or straight, edges even. Let dry again under pressure, and you are ready to glue to the wall, to the opening, or to the bottom of the staircase.

Material Needed for Circular Stairs

1/2"-thick balsa wood
1/16"-thick cherry or mahogany
Any good glue, Sobo or Tacky
Fine sandpaper or emery board
Tack rag
X-Acto knife No. 2 or Dremel Moto-Tool

We came across a most interesting use for this stair recently in building a private theater on the fourth floor of our Victorian house. In a room 24 inches long which would accommodate only ten chairs, we didn't want a stage with square corners protruding into the chair space. Thus we cut this semiround on a 12- and 10-inch diameter and used the top (10-inch) level for the stage. The inch between the 12-inch semicircle and the 10-inch stage we filled with a row of potted ferns from Pickwick Miniatures. It is beautiful. For this use, we carpeted both semicircles in velvet.

An entirely different approach from that used on the preceding circular stairs is that which we use for the utilitarian stairs which carry us from one floor to another. At the top of page 94 we show a stair stringer, which is used for a basic stair. This you could cut of ⅛-inch wood from the pattern on p. 94, or if you don't want to take the time for this, C. E. Bergeron of Bradford, Massachusetts, offers stringers, ready for use, of ⁵⁄₃₂-inch wood in 22-inch lengths. The stair pieces are then cut in the width you want for the staircase and these are glued between two stringers. Risers are fitted underneath. If you are using stained wood, be sure to stain and finish before gluing. If you are painting your stairs, however, or painting the stringers and covering the steps with carpet, the whole staircase may be completed and installed in one piece.

The second procedure for a stairway is to build the steps on a base of ¹⁄₁₆-inch wood. Buy or cut a piece of ¾-inch wood and split it on a diagonal as shown in the drawing. You will find this is easier if you cut it first into lengths the width of the stairway, then split these short lengths. Now cut a piece of ³⁄₃₂-inch or ¹⁄₁₆-inch wood as wide as the width of the staircase and the length required to reach from one floor to the other at the proper slant. The split pieces are then glued, long side down, to the base, giving you a nice ¾-inch (9 inches on the ¹⁄₁₂ scale) riser and step. For a professional finish, add a top to the steps, cut from ¹⁄₁₆-inch wood on which you've gently sanded the edge that meets the riser to a rounded edge.

Any number of ideas will occur to you for making the handrails which finish off the stairs. We show in our drawing here a series of upholsterer's nails (these usually have very pretty heads) which are pushed into the wall through the links of a fine chain or the chain used for a pull on electric lights. A thin silk cord might also be used, with tassels hanging down at each end. A piece of single crochet made from six strands of mercerized D.M.C. embroidery cotton gives a very handsome effect.

Many finishes for your banisters will occur to you. The one shown at top in the drawing is simply three ⅛-inch dowels cut the length you wish to use, spread with glue, and piled two on the bottom and one over the meeting point at the top, to form a pyramid. They must, of course, be stained before gluing. When completely dry, cut the length you wish to use and mount atop the banister posts. A handsome upholstery tack stuck in the end makes a nice finish.

The second drawing shows a handrail made from three pieces of cord about the thickness of the dowels. Cut these a little longer than

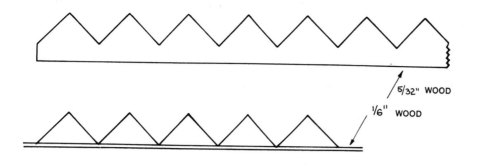

5/32" WOOD

1/6" WOOD

UPPER FLOOR

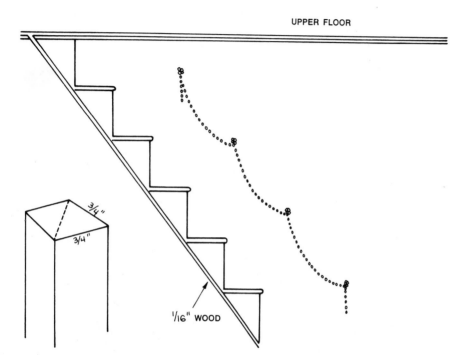

3/4"

3/4"

1/16" WOOD

Stair patterns and rails

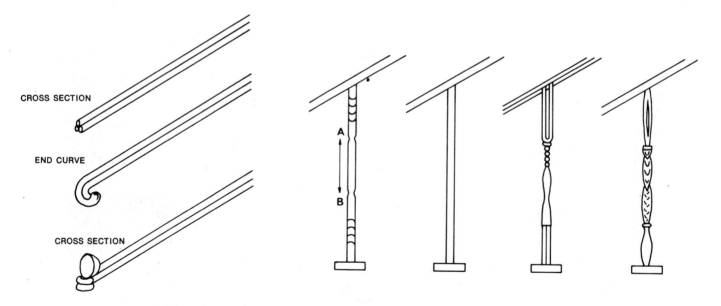

CROSS SECTION

END CURVE

A

B

CROSS SECTION

Handrails and banisters

the length you need, then glue together in a pyramid as described above. Clip a Boston or Hunt clip over them and hang up to dry with a weight attached to the bottom. When the glue is almost dry, very tacky to the touch, remove from the clip and lay on waxed paper. Then press the string pieces together tightly in the pyramid shape, but to the length you want plus 1 inch, and patiently curve the extra inch to the curve shown in the drawing.

The bottom drawing shows a handrail made from one turned out by Northeastern Scale Models, Inc., and is simply cut to fit. All of these may be stained, painted, or gilded (our preference) since they're dried.

There are many possibilities for the balustrades. The one shown here is a 1/8-inch square notched at *A* and *B*, and gently rounded with an emery board at these two points. This gives you a round post in the center, with two square ends. The square ends may be left plain or carefully carved with your X-Acto knife No. 1 into circling rings. Second from left is simply a rounded toothpick stained, then mounted by inserting in the handrail and into a 1/4-inch square of 1/8-inch wood into which you've made an opening with your awl or a small nail.

One way of handling the blank wall space below a stairway which makes a sharp turn above a landing. In the third-floor hallway of the Beretta house, an in- laid French cabinet was placed against the railing, which continues down (*Photograph by Billo Matthews Smith*).

In the Webster house, the blank space has been converted into an appealing plant nook (*Photograph by Nan Webster*).

The two balustrades on the right were made from cocktail picks, the one at right of wood and the second of plastic. In both instances the pick part was cut off to make the top of the balustrade, and the handle part was used as the bottom. These, too, are then mounted on the little blocks of wood to form the balustrade, and the handrails are put in place before the banister is put up. All are then glued.

Fireplaces

The fireplace is the heart of the dollhouse just as it is the heart of a people-sized home. Variations on the basic form are infinite, but to us one of the greatest ideas for a basic structure is that devised by Virginia Updegraff of Des Moines, Iowa, who also worked out the method for making tiles.

She begins by selecting the material and size for the hearth, usually ¼-inch wood or a ¼-inch deep frame into which tiny bricks may be laid. She then selects or makes a cardboard box which is to be the size

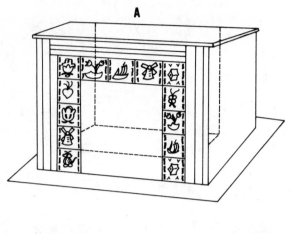

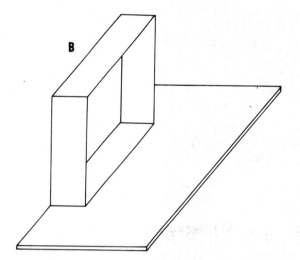

Basic box fireplaces

of the inside firebox, in this case about 1¼ inches deep and 2¾ inches square. The bottom of the box becomes the back of the fire box; the front is open. This is easily worked with; it may be papered inside with brick-effect paper or coated with acrylic paint and then marked into bricks. Or you could cut some bricks from thin cardboard, paint them, and then glue them to the inside. Remember to smear the inside back and sides with a bit of charcoal, carbon paper, or other blackening, then glue this box form to the finished hearth, as in drawing *b*.

You will then need another box about ½ inch larger from top to bottom and from side to side. This box, too, is easy to work with before it is attached to the hearth. In drawing *a* the box was painted a basic color suited to the room and tiny panels of wood were finished a harmonizing wood color and glued at sides and top of the fireplace opening. Here we cut the fireplace opening in the front of the box and the back is left open. Glue the wood molding on according to your own design; in the case of the fireplace sketched, we marked off ½ inch all around the fireplace opening and coated this heavily with Liquitex modeling paste, then sank the ½-inch tiles into the paste. This was then allowed to dry and finally glazed with a coat of Deep Flex Decoupage Glaze.

Another of these simple cardboard fireplaces made from boxes is shown on p. 98. Here a piece of heavy cording was glued against the mantel shelf to simulate wood-carving. Pieces of ⅛-inch wood, suitably stained and finished, were then used to outline the fire box and to break up the side surfaces of the fireplace, and then a very heavy crochet-type braid was glued to the fireplace. These were painted with a thin coat of Liquitex modeling paste and allowed to dry, after which they were painted either with stain or with color to match the surrounding wood.

Delft tiles actually ½″ square (shown here twice the size to bring out the detail in design) are made by Virginia Updegraff on a base of light cardboard with Liquitex modeling paste, painted in blue watercolor with a OOO brush (*Photograph by Sam Taylor*).

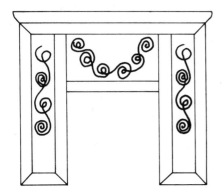

Decorated box fireplace

If you can find this very heavy-type lace, it is surprisingly effective in simulating carving. In one instance Mrs. Updegraff applied it to a 4-inch circle of cardboard, then painted with the Liquitex, then repainted with the wall or ceiling paint. This makes a most effective medallion to glue against the ceiling as a background for a chandelier.

There are times, of course, when one desperately needs a corner fireplace in a dollhouse for the same reason that we sometimes need one in a people-sized house; to conserve wall space. A corner fireplace is most attractive, too, because it does away with the corners that are so hard to fill.

A simple way of constructing one is by cutting off the corner of a box such as a shoebox so that the sides are the length you want against the walls. This leaves the front open. Form the back of the fire box by cutting a piece of cardboard to a size which will fit into the corner and still give you a satisfactory depth, then paint this black or simulated brick, with black smudges. Fit into the corner and glue into

Possibilities in fireplaces are shown (*left*) in a simple one by Shackman and (*right*), Chestnut Hill Studio's beautiful Delft tile design with handsome bolection molding (*Photograph by Sam Taylor*).

place. Cut the front of the fireplace to fit over the diagonal side of the box. Cut off box and front at the bottom so that you have the height you want. Cut an opening in the front, centered, for the fireplace opening.

We might mention here that in working with cardboard it is well to reinforce the fireplace opening so that it doesn't sag. If you are using tile around the opening, then glue pieces of ⅛-inch balsa or basswood against the tile and cardboard to make a finished opening. If you are using molding, a piece of molding will make a nice finish when glued flush with the cardboard, but the ⅛-inch strip glued underneath will have a more professional look.

With your fireplace installed, a chimney breast is essential in the corner, and most pleasing up against any wall. You might cut a pattern from the one shown in the drawing of the corner fireplace and provide a cap and pediment as shown by gluing several ⅛-inch strips atop it, from wall to wall. The curve makes a nice finish.

A small mirror in the right dimensions is another possibility, and this would, of course, be finished with very small molding around the edges. A panel of wood set into the center and finished with molding would be another possibility. In many of the great French houses of the sixteenth and seventeenth centuries, a fine piece of tapestry was stretched here. Petit point would be a great idea, as would any print on heavy paper which was the right size.

The main thing to remember in planning the chimney breasts is to have the height in proportion to the fireplace, For example, the

Corner fireplace

fireplace shown in the drawing is reduced about one-half; the original from which it was copied was 4 inches high, and the chimney breast then went on up to the ceiling, which might be another 5 inches high. Use your own judgment as to the height of the chimney breast. You want something that will *look* right, not necessarily something that is cut exactly to scale.

Third and last is our big Colonial fireplace, shown here in detail because so many confusing ideas have grown out of the making of Colonial miniature fireplaces. Not all Colonial fireplaces included cranes from which to hang pots, and we have used another method just because it is different. This and most of the other features included in this pattern were taken from one of the fireplaces in the John Whipple house in Ipswich, Massachusetts, a restored building which dates back to the late seventeenth century.

Before we embark upon so important a project as a fireplace, we must make some decisions. First, are we going to include a chimney breast and if so will it rise straight to the ceiling or taper? Secondly, if we are not to use the chimney breast, will we use a mantel that merely caps the fire opening, or one which covers the whole fireplace? Last and most important, what will be our material? In this period bricks were being made; fireplaces were made with brick, with stone, or with a metal fire box and a front of wood paneling or wood covered with clay and then whitewashed.

Materials Needed for the Colonial Fireplace
1 piece balsa 15" x 6-7" x ⅛"
1 piece balsa for hearth, 7" x 3" x ¼"
 Light cardboard for oven box
1 piece balsa for door in back, 2" x 2" x ¼"
1 strip brass, 4¾" x ¼"
4 or more S-hooks, ½"
 Dull black paint
 Glue
 Stain
1 piece balsa for mantel, ½" square
 Flat gravel for rocks, brick or whitewash paint for finish

We will make a frame of ⅛-inch balsa. Our fireplace is to be 6½ inches wide, 5 inches to the mantel, and 1½ inches deep. It will stand on a hearth 2¾ inches deep but the same width. Cut one full piece of the back from hearth to ceiling. The door in the back of the fireplace will be a fake, since we don't have sufficient space in a dollhouse to make a fireplace stand out enough to take the oven—it would look

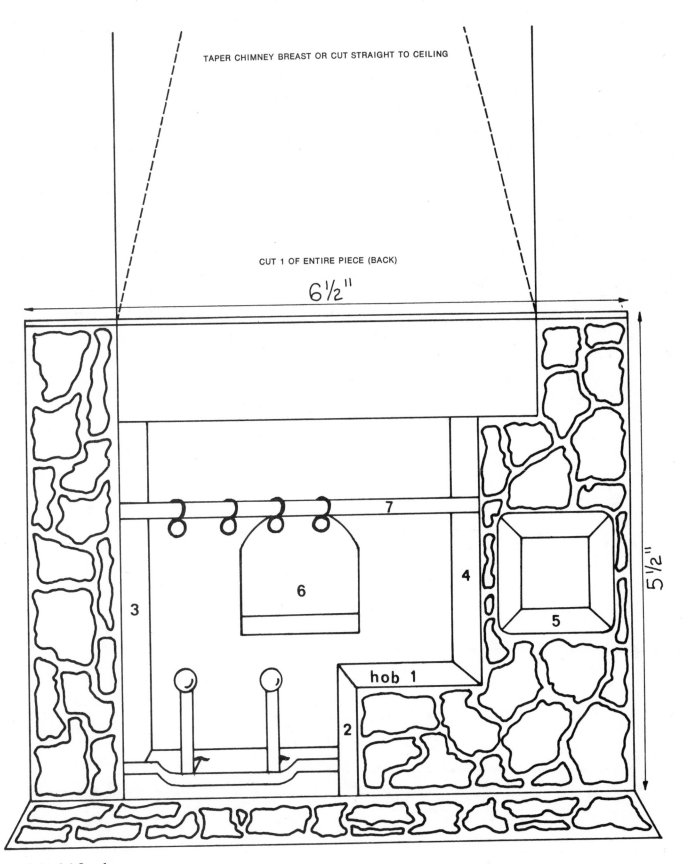

TAPER CHIMNEY BREAST OR CUT STRAIGHT TO CEILING

CUT 1 OF ENTIRE PIECE (BACK)

6½"

5½"

3

6

7

4

5

hob 1

2

Colonial fireplace

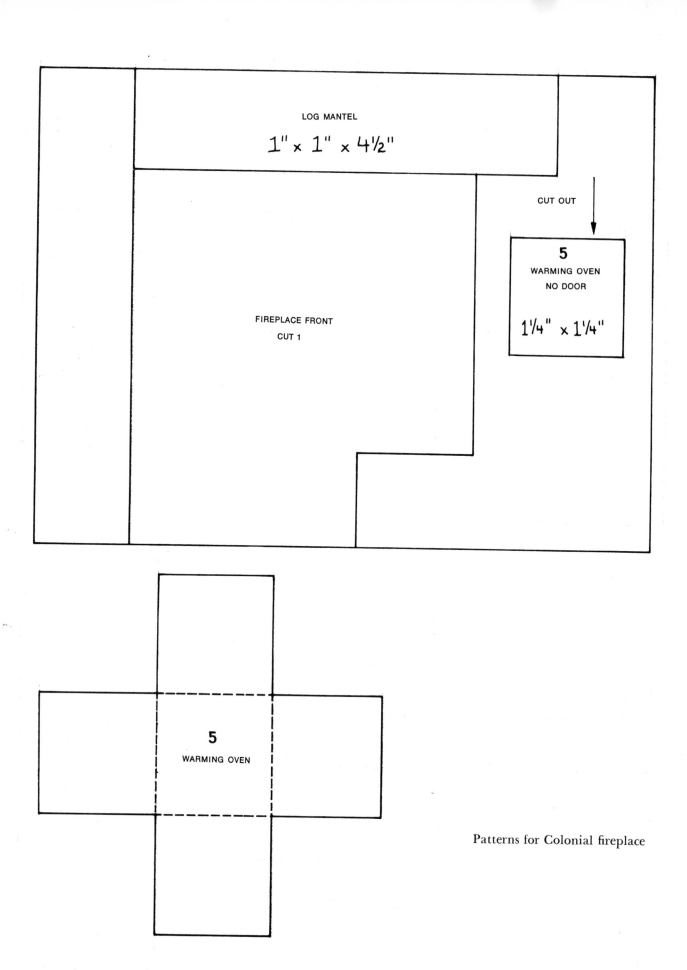

LOG MANTEL

1" × 1" × 4½"

CUT OUT

5
WARMING OVEN
NO DOOR

1¼" × 1¼"

FIREPLACE FRONT

CUT 1

5
WARMING OVEN

Patterns for Colonial fireplace

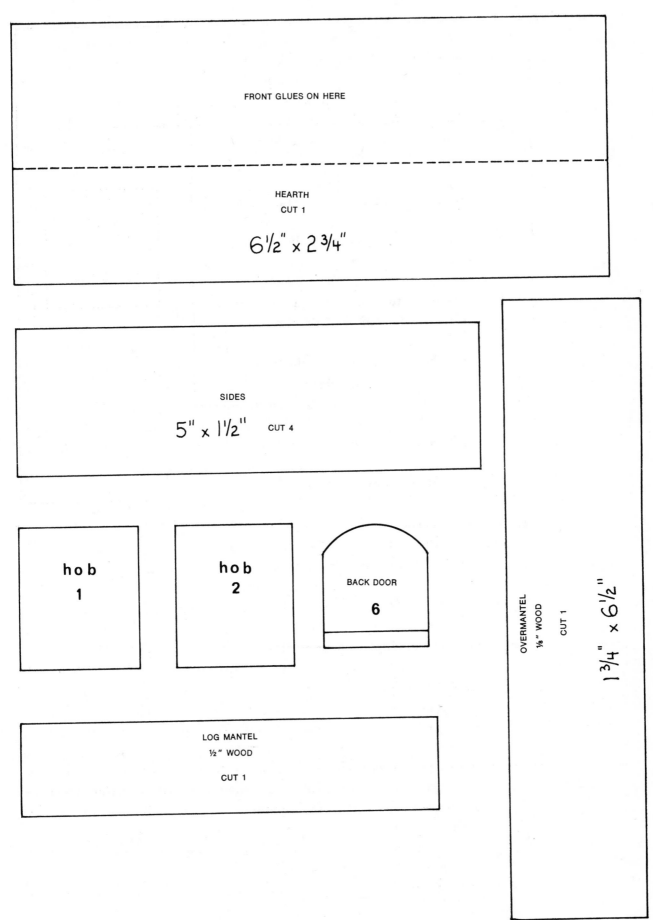

FRONT GLUES ON HERE

HEARTH
CUT 1

6½" x 2¾"

SIDES

5" x 1½"   CUT 4

h o b
1

h o b
2

BACK DOOR

6

OVERMANTEL
⅛" WOOD

CUT 1

1¾" × 6½"

LOG MANTEL
½" WOOD

CUT 1

awkward if we did this. So, trace the door from the pattern and cut it out. If you are going to have a brick-lined fireplace, mark the bricks and color. Cut a door for this back oven from 1/4-inch wood and sand the top edges so it is nicely rounded, as an iron door would be. Cut a tiny strip of tin 1/8 inch wide and about 3/4 inch long and bend the edges at a right angle to make a handle. Fasten this to the door with Krazy Glue. Spray the whole door with dull black, then glue to the back piece as shown. Now we are going to build a sort of box. Using two of the pieces marked "sides" in the pattern, paint each on one long side only with a dead-white acrylic paint into which you've stirred enough fine breadcrumbs to give a spackled effect—about 1 tablespoon crumbs to 1/2 cup paint. Allow to dry. If you want the chimney breast white-washed as well, paint this in the space above the mantel. Allow to dry.

Glue the two sides to the edge of the back piece at right angles and allow to dry. Now we will use two more of the pieces marked "sides" to box in the fireplace. First mark the bricks and color these, just as you did the back. Smudge with a little charcoal or with a piece of carbon paper. Smudge the back around the oven door, too.

Instead of a crane, use a piece of brass strip 1/4 inch wide (this will come from the miniature-railroad supply counter) and cut 1 inch longer than the fireplace opening, which is 3 1/4 inches. In other words, cut the strip 4 1/4 inches long. This is piece 7 on the drawing. Spray or paint with dull black, then cut a slit in pieces 3 and 4 about 2 inches below the top of the mantel. Make the slits very fine so the strip can just be forced into them. Paint around the strip a bit with the dull black paint.

Now you must decide whether you want brick, whitewash, or rock for the mantel facing. If you decide upon brick, spread the piece labeled "fireplace front" with white caulking compound—the best mortar for miniature bricks you'll ever find. Smooth it out about 1/16 inch deep, then gently press your bricks into the compound and around the fireplace opening and the warming-oven opening. *Do not affix bricks or rock* to the portion marked "log mantel." You could even place a row of the 1/2-inch tiles mentioned previously up the sides of the fireplace opening for a very pretty effect. Before you come around to the side marked "warming oven" with your finish, cut out the opening marked "warming oven." Cut out pattern 5 and fold the sides together to make a box with no front. Spray or paint with dull black to simulate iron, then fold up the sides and secure with masking tape. Hold this against the back of this opening and secure with black masking tape, electrician's tape (has a nice texture) or Mystik tape 1/4 inch wide, folding the tape in half lengthwise and pressing half to the front of the fireplace and half underneath to secure the oven box. At this point

I like to take two or three pieces of the tape and, on the back side of the fireplace, run the tape up the back of the oven and over to the fireplace, thus securing the oven so that it will not work loose. Continue with the finishing of this side.

Finish off the hob (this is the ledge where the Colonial homemaker kept her teakettle hot) by cutting three pieces of the balsa the same as the pattern marked "hob No. 1" and "hob No. 2" and gluing these one at the side, one at the top, and one at the back. The top piece may be finished with bricks or by whitewashing.

The log mantel is cut from a piece of ½-inch square balsa the length of the pattern, or whatever length you wish to use. Stain this first but don't finish; it should look raw. A nice touch is to groove the beam in places with your awl, to simulate the marks of the adze used by frontiersmen to shape the wood. Glue this to the fireplace front even with the top of the piece, then carefully glue the front over the back. All that remains, then, is to cut the overmantel, round off the edges, and glue this to the top of the log and fireplace.

Hooks to hold the pots and kettles are simply the smallest S-hooks you can find (we found some ½ inch in length). These are painted dull black, then slipped over the fireplace rod.

Doors

While we date our French doors about 1850, we realize that this is hardly a fair cataloguing of these airy architectural appurtenances. Everyone who has traveled in France has seen both doors and windows (the windows being merely elongated openings reaching to the floor, but of the same general design as the doors) of this type in chateaus and palaces of several centuries earlier. However, their general use in America doesn't seem to be manifest until the last half of the nineteenth century. John Maass, in his fascinating book *The Victorian Home in America*, mentions and illustrates several examples of such doors in houses which he can definitely date 1850 and for two or three decades thereafter, and in our own book *The Collector's Guide to Doll Houses and Doll House Miniatures*, p. 5, we show a charming dollhouse of Mediterranean design which has been authentically appraised as dating from about 1900, on which the whole front façade is a series of French doors. Between the early French chateaus and the Victorian homes, they seem to disappear.

Our whole reason for including them in this book, aside from the fact that they will dress up the interior of your dollhouse tremendously, is that they are fun to make. Use a single door for a regular-sized door opening. A double door such as the one shown in the sketch would

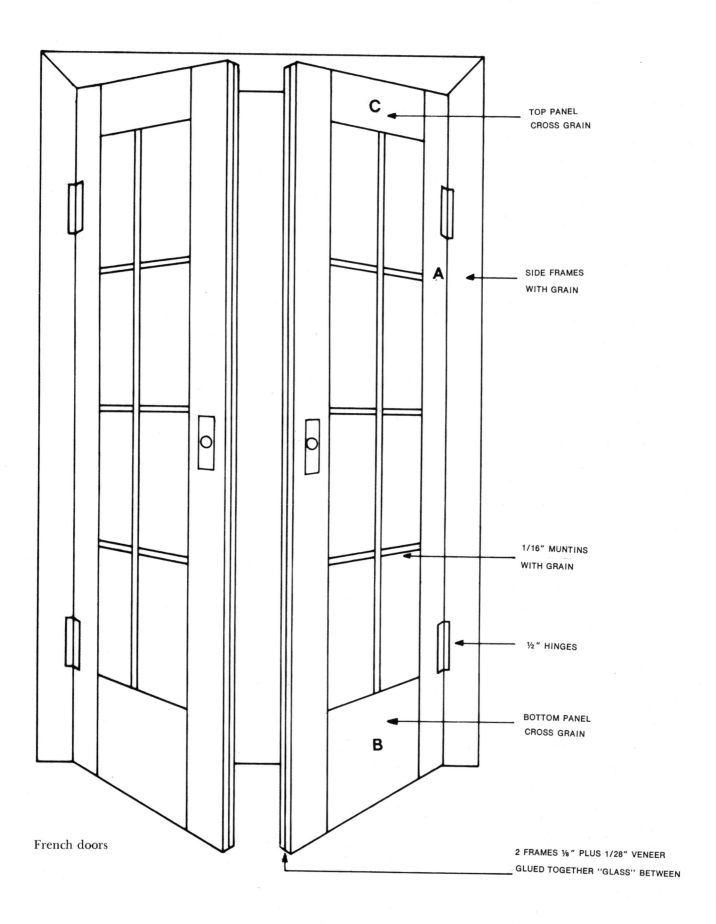

TOP PANEL
CROSS GRAIN

C

SIDE FRAMES
WITH GRAIN

A

1/16" MUNTINS
WITH GRAIN

½" HINGES

BOTTOM PANEL
CROSS GRAIN

B

French doors

2 FRAMES ⅛" PLUS 1/28" VENEER
GLUED TOGETHER "GLASS" BETWEEN

be fine for a wide opening between rooms. It was often the standard door to the conservatory in Victorian homes. Or, if the style of your dollhouse is such that long floor-length windows would be in order, use the French doors as windows, as they appear in the Mediterranean dollhouse.

We will give the standard procedure for making a door, and you will find it simple to expand this to meet your needs. We used a core of basswood or balsa for the door, covering this with the $\frac{1}{28}$-inch veneer supplied by Albert Constantine and Son, Inc. This ingenious idea does away with the tedious procedure of finishing the wood in the door and, while sturdy and nonwarping, allows one to insert knobs, curtain-rod supports, and so on with very little pressure—the fittings may be attached with the fingers.

We have made some doors with cores of two thicknesses of $\frac{1}{8}$-inch wood, plus two sides of veneer. We also made some with cores of two thicknesses of $\frac{1}{16}$-inch wood plus the veneer. The first, resulting in $\frac{1}{4}$-inch thickness, is a bit over scale for the $\frac{1}{12}$ dollhouse. The second is true to scale, but for some reason looks a bit fragile when installed. We like the two thicknesses of $\frac{1}{8}$-inch core wood better. Craftspeople will have to make their own choices.

Measure the opening and make a paper pattern the exact size. Check to make certain the opening is square at the corners. Make certain the door frame is properly installed and the framing is square, with mitered corners. Make your veneer selections. Some of the finest offerings can be found at A. Constantine and Son, who will ship their Introductory Veneering Kit, which consists of 8 square feet of fine veneer in $9 \times 9 \times \frac{1}{28}$-inch squares, plus a pint of their veneer glue, and a treatise on veneering. Another Constantine offering is what they term their "Rare Collection of the World's Fine Woods," consisting of fifty 4×9-inch samples of a simply astonishing assortment of woods mostly in $\frac{1}{28}$- or $\frac{1}{32}$-inch veneers. These samples can be used for small pieces of furniture or for doors and windows, and one learns a great deal about woods while one is choosing.

Despite the fact that I feel we'll hear shrieks of protest from miniature crafters, I found the best finish for a first coat was Masterpiece Decoupage all-purpose finish. Made by the Morris Mfg. Company of Garland, Texas, this finish is created for decoupage projects; it's an excellent sealer. Brush it on the pieces of veneer you have selected from top to bottom, using a full brush. It dries very quickly to a clear matte finish, silky dull, that is really beautiful.

Let this first coat dry thoroughly; it will seal the veneer so that a random drop of glue won't make a spot on it. Then spread a piece of the $\frac{1}{8}$-inch balsa or basswood evenly and thinly with a coat of the veneer glue. Do three pieces this way, then place under heavy books overnight or until dry.

Now stop for a moment and study the doors in your house. The two side panels run the entire length of the door. Make them ½ inch wide and as long as your opening. The panel at the bottom is set between these two sides. Make it the width of the door minus 1 inch, and ¾ inch wide. Bottom panels are invariably made wider than the top panels, to form a sort of kick plate. The center panel at top should be cut ½ inch wide and as long as the width of the door minus 1 inch. The side pieces of the door should be cut the length of the grain (see the sketch); the cross panels at top and bottom, the width of the grain. Place between the side panels at top and bottom and glue under pressure. If you have cut and measured straight, your door should be straight. You will need two such frames for each door.

Now for the "glass" in the door. We used and liked double-strength celluloid from the hobby shop. Very fine (½₂-inch) Plexiglas is practical, if you have someone handy who can cut it. (See p. 64 for instructions.) Lew Krummerow of Dollhouses (see suppliers' list) offers micro-glass ¼₀ inch thick at 35 cents per square inch. This ships well, but must be handled very carefully while installing in doors and windows. Micro-mirror glass of the same thickness is also offered, at 50 cents per square inch.

Cut your pieces of glass for each door, ¼ inch larger all around than the opening. Fasten it to the unfinished side of the frame with a few dots of glue, evenly spaced. Be very careful not to make the dots so large that they will run over onto the glass. Brush the frame from glass to edge thinly with glue. Brush the plywood side of the other side of the frame with glue and carefully affix it to the first side, over the glass. Dry under pressure. If you have been careful in applying the glue, your glass should be clear and clean.

Sand all edges lightly, check to make sure they fit snugly. Rub very clean with a tack cloth (see p. 20) so that no vestige of dust remains on the wood. With a very fine brush, finish the edges where the plywood shows with a stain to match the wood of the veneer. Allow to dry, then apply about two more coats of the decoupage clear matte finish to both sides of the door, allowing at least two hours drying time between coats. For a harder finish, you may use up to five coats of this all-purpose varnish. No sanding is needed between coats, and the finished piece will be as smooth as silk, and handsomely dull.

Last of all in the actual door construction are the muntins, those tiny strips of wood which mark the division of a window or door into panes of glass. If you are making a single door, you may want to use one muntin down the center and three across, as we show. Some doors had only cross-muntins, with no vertical divisions. Any piece of wood no more than $\frac{1}{16}$ inch thick and the length of your glass can be split to make the muntins. We like a $\frac{1}{16}$-inch square strip of balsa, which Constantine's carries, that costs only about 4 cents each. Cut to fit the opening, then sand two edges lightly to make the strip slightly rounded on two sides. A little more impressive because of the shaping is a basswood molding stocked by the Miniature Mart, $\frac{3}{16}$ inch wide but easily split lengthwise into thirds. Howard Pierce's Workshop in Wichita, Kansas, and Marge Geddes' Lilliput Shop in Beaverton, Oregon, both offer moldings and mini-lumber to your specifications. Planks, 12" x 2" x $\frac{1}{16}$", for example, are offered by the Lilliput Shop in birch, pine, maple, Luan mahogany, cherry, or walnut. Any of these are easily split into $\frac{1}{16}$-inch widths. Then cut the length to exactly fit the length of the glass panel. Be careful. Remember that even the width of the lead in a pencil can throw your measurements off, resulting in a muntin that may be a fraction of an inch too short, and thus worthless. Stain carefully. Glue the long muntins down, making certain they are absolutely straight, and allow to dry. Then measure and cut the bisecting muntins and glue them down, fitting carefully between the center muntin and the side of the frame. After they are completely dry, do the same to the other side. Two things are absolutely necessary here: first, the muntins must be straight, for appearance's sake; and second, glue must be used sparingly so that none squeezes out against the glass. The spaces are too small to permit cleaning.

We experimented extensively in an effort to make and install muntins in a more foolproof way, but the only practicable change, it seemed to us, came with using the $\frac{1}{28}$-inch veneer itself for the strips. Using a steel-edged ruler, it is no trick at all to cut $\frac{1}{8}$-inch or $\frac{1}{16}$-inch strips the length of the veneeer. Coat with the decoupage finish, or varnish, then glue to the glass. With this, the crosspieces don't have to be fitted between the vertical pieces; crosspieces can be glued right over the center muntin, because the veneer is so thin. The net result, however, is not quite so handsome as that achieved with muntins of greater thickness, but you might try this and see if the work it saves is worth the diminished effect.

Hinges for the doors are always a problem; the small ones are too small and the common type in craft stores are too large. But Suzanne Ash of Mini-Things, Englewood, Colorado, has come up with a procedure that works very well. Remember, however, that this must be used only with wooden doors. Doors cast from combination materials such as John Blauer's can't be used this way.

The basic principle is the same as attaching a cabinet door without hinges. Instead of using pins on the door, Suzanne Ash uses wooden

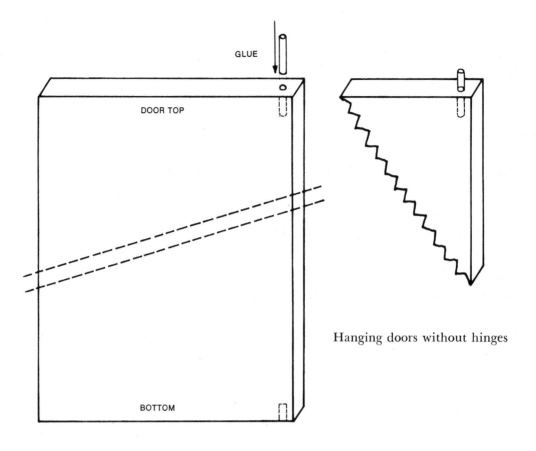

GLUE

DOOR TOP

BOTTOM

Hanging doors without hinges

These two photographs show the door being fitted into the holes at the bottom of the door jamb. Holes already drilled in the door are put there to facilitate ap-plying ornamental hinges and knob later (*Photographs by Lorraine Yeats*).

110

sticks from a cotton swab. A hole is drilled the diameter of the swab stick in the ends of the door, 1/4 inch deep. Since it is impossible to get a drill at a perpendicular angle in the door jamb, use a nail the diameter of the swab and gently tap it in about 3/8 inch top and bottom. Do this in stages and wiggle the nail gently so you can get it out with your fingers.

Glue a 1/2-inch piece of the stick in the top of the door. Let this dry. Cut another piece of the swab stick 3/8 inch long for the bottom hole in the door. Carefully put some Elmer's Glue-All in the hole at the bottom of the door and place the stick in so it protrudes only 1/8 inch at the bottom. Place the top stick in the door in the hole at the top of the door jamb. Line up the bottom of the door with a hole in the door jamb at the bottom. Now, with a tiny pair of scissors, pull the stick down into the door-jamb hole. Let it dry slightly. Then gently move the door back and forth until completely dry, so if any glue got into the bottom hole of the jamb, the door will not be glued shut.

6 Electrifying the Dollhouse

I have always been one for acknowledging my own limitations, because I find it less frustrating than trying to bull one's way through a job and end up with everyone, including oneself, realizing that the results are not entirely satisfactory. Thus, while I realize that many people are expert at electrifying their dollhouses, I asked Ed Leonard of Illinois Hobbycraft to share with us his expertise on the subject. An acknowledged leader, he explains dollhouse lighting in the following manner:

> The methods and materials which may be used for lighting a dollhouse are many and varied. The final choice of components is usually governed by the amount of money the dollhouse enthusiast can afford to spend and the amount of time he or she is willing to expend on the installation. If all the fixtures are purchased and of fine quality, the cost of the completed installation will be relatively high. If the owner makes all the fixtures himself or uses only bare bulbs, the cost will be relatively low. Many mini-electricians choose a middle road, buying the more complex decorative fixtures, such as chandeliers, and making the easier fixtures themselves.
>
> In planning a dollhouse lighting system a number of factors must be taken into consideration. Some of these are safety, service life, proper installation, and ease of maintenance. The most important of these is safety. A dollhouse should never be wired to operate directly from the 115 volts obtained from the wall outlet of your home. One constantly hears that tiny bulbs and wires may be safely connected to 115 volts if the dollhouse is wired "in series," but this is simply not true.
>
> In miniature lighting systems the most vulnerable element is the bulb used in the lamps and fixtures. Ordinary miniature bulbs are not especially designed for long life and when a bulb is operated at a voltage higher than its rated voltage, its life is short-

ened. Conversely, when it is operated at a voltage lower than its rated voltage, its life is greatly extended. For example, if a 12 volt bulb is operated at 13 volts (only 1 volt higher than its rated voltage) its life may be cut by two-thirds. But when a 12 volt bulb is operated at 11 volts, its life will be nearly three times normal. Maximum bulb life can only be obtained if the bulb is operated at a voltage that is lower than the voltage for which it is rated. To accomplish this, it is recommended that the dollhouse lighting system be equipped with sixteen volt bulbs operated from a 12 volt transformer.

We cannot over-emphasize the need to take time to carry out the installation properly, and so insist at the very beginning that these primary requirements be heeded: (1) Select components that are properly rated and adequate for the job. (2) Operate the components at something less than their full rating. (3) Solder all splices and connections at locations where connecting screws or terminal strips are not provided. (4) Be sure all splices and wires are properly installed. (5) Fasten transformers, lights, fixtures, and other devices securely. (6) Glue or otherwise fasten all wires in place to prevent sagging and possible snagging and to reduce wire movement which can lead to broken wires and connections. (7) Test each bulb, lamp fixture, and circuit as it is installed, to assure that it lights and operates properly. If it does not operate properly, repair it immediately before proceeding to the next installation step. This is most important; if faults and troubles are

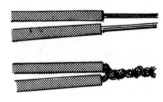

"PIGTAIL" SPLICE

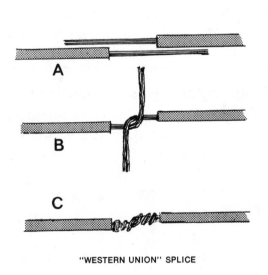

"WESTERN UNION" SPLICE

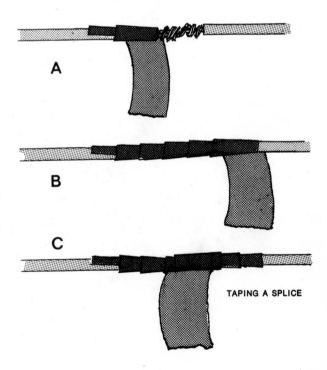

TAPING A SPLICE

allowed to accumulate, it may be impossible to analyze and locate them after the entire system is completed. Under no circumstances should the entire system be installed before power is applied.

Components

A miniature lighting system comprises three main parts. These are: (1) the power source, (2) the terminal devices (bulbs, lamps, wall sockets, etc.) and (3) the wiring. The power source is that source of electricity used to light the bulbs and lamps. The best power source for dollhouse lighting is a transformer which plugs into the wall outlet of your home and converts (transforms) the 115 volts obtained there to a lower, safer voltage. Batteries may also be used to obtain a low voltage.

For a small dollhouse, or one which will be equipped with only a few bulbs, a 10-volt doorbell/chime transformer which is obtainable at most hardware stores, may be used. Although rated at 10 volts, these transformers actually deliver between 12 and 14 volts and therefore are compatible with good system requirements for a 12 volt transformer and 16 volt bulbs.

The bulbs used in miniature lighting systems may be of the screw-base type which can be screwed into tiny sockets or of the grain-of-wheat type which are equipped with wire leads about 6

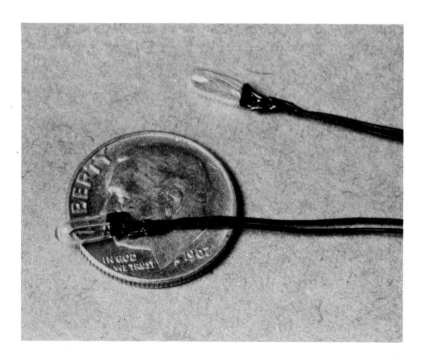

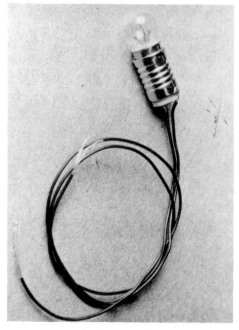

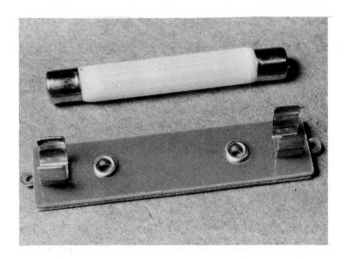

inches long used to connect the bulbs to the wiring. These, because of their very small size (1/8″ diameter, 3/16″ length) are the only type suitable for applications where authentically scaled lamps and fixtures are desired. Either of these two types of bulb is commonly available with 16-volt ratings.

Another type of bulb especially suitable for general room lighting in dollhouses is one that has a tubular shape and resembles a miniature fluorescent tube. These, called fluorettes, measure about 1/4″ in diameter and about 1 1/2″ in length and fit into a special socket which permits easy replacement. The long, slim shape of these bulbs makes them ideal for concealed applications where they are hidden behind ceiling beams or recessed into the ceiling of a room.

The wiring which is used to connect the bulbs, lamps and other terminal devices to the power source may be divided into two classes: feeder wiring and circuit wiring. Feeder wiring is that which suppies or "feeds" electricity from the power source to a number of circuits or to several floors of a dollhouse. Circuit wiring is the wiring which connects the bulbs, fixtures, wall sockets, etc., to the feeder wire.

Lighting Circuit Arrangements

The basic circuits for connecting one or more bulbs to a transformer are shown in the sketches of the basic circuits. For simplicity, a transformer having screw terminals for the secondary winding is shown. The method for connecting a single bulb is shown at "A." When a second bulb or light is required, it may also be connected to the transformer, as shown at "B," or may be

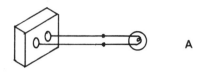

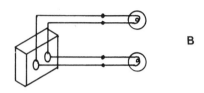 A

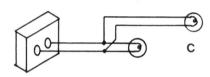 B

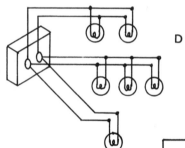 C

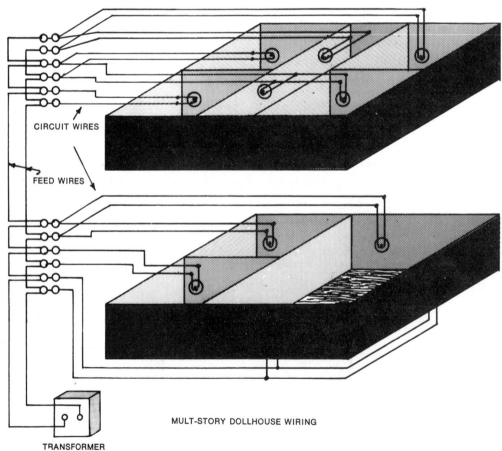

connected to the circuit wires at the first bulb, as shown at "C." When additional bulbs are required, they may be connected either directly to the transformer or to other circuit wires, as shown at "D." The method of wiring shown in these sketches is called "parallel wiring."

Some experimentation with the transformer and light fixtures or bulbs will help to develop familiarity with the methods for connecting lights and bulbs. It is recommended that the beginning mini-electrician splice a line cord to the transformer and connect different combinations of bulbs and circuits to the transformer secondary terminals or wires in order to gain firsthand experience and develop confidence. Be sure to properly insulate the splices between the line cord and the transformer even though this may be only a temporary splice.

Multi-story dollhouse lighting systems necessitate the connection of a great number of circuit wires to the transformer. A typical two-story dollhouse lighting system is illustrated in the sketch of the multi-story dollhouse wiring, where because of the great number of wires involved, the feed wires from the transformer

CIRCUIT WIRES

FEED WIRES

MULT-STORY DOLLHOUSE WIRING

TRANSFORMER

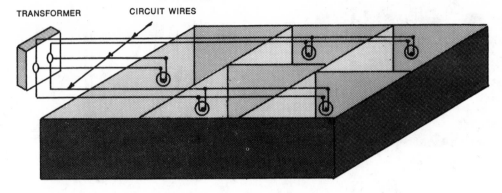

ONE-STORY DOLLHOUSE WIRING

have been extended to terminal strips which, in turn, provide many sets of screw terminals to which individual lamps or circuits may be connected. The terminal strips simply provide a convenient means for collecting together the many circuit wires and for connecting these to feed wires which come from the transformer. They have no electrical effect on the system.

Connecting the Transformer Line Cord

Transformers used for dollhouse lighting are generally of two types. One type has wires extending from the primary winding which must be spliced to the line cord and has screw terminals to which the feed wires or circuit wires are connected. The second type of transformer has wires extending from both the primary and secondary windings. In order to connect either type to the 115 volt wall socket, it is necessary to splice a line cord to the wires which extend from the primary winding. It is important that proper identification of the primary and secondary windings be established before the line cord is connected. On most transformers the primary winding is identified by the word "pri" or "primary" stamped on one side, close to the wires which connect to that winding. The secondary winding is identified by the word "sec" or "secondary" stamped near the wires leading to that winding. THE 115 VOLT LINE CORD MUST BE CONNECTED ONLY TO THE PRIMARY WINDING. If the line cord is inadvertently connected to the secondary winding, an extremely hazardous voltage may be produced on the primary leads when the cord is plugged into the wall. The line cord used should be of the three-conductor type which will permit "grounding" the case of the transformer to protect against the introduction of hazardous voltages in the circuit wiring or on

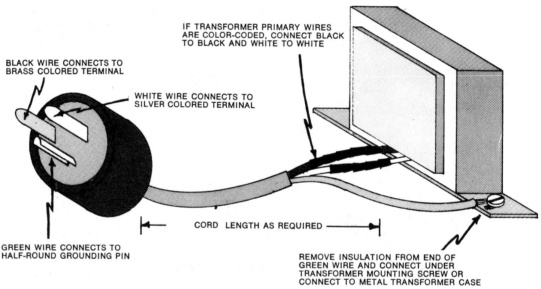

IF TRANSFORMER PRIMARY WIRES ARE COLOR-CODED, CONNECT BLACK TO BLACK AND WHITE TO WHITE

BLACK WIRE CONNECTS TO BRASS COLORED TERMINAL

WHITE WIRE CONNECTS TO SILVER COLORED TERMINAL

GREEN WIRE CONNECTS TO HALF-ROUND GROUNDING PIN

CORD LENGTH AS REQUIRED

REMOVE INSULATION FROM END OF GREEN WIRE AND CONNECT UNDER TRANSFORMER MOUNTING SCREW OR CONNECT TO METAL TRANSFORMER CASE

THREE-CONDUCTOR LINE CORD CONNECTIONS

the transformer case due to a fault inside the transformer. The method for connecting the three wires in this line cord is shown in the sketch above.

Wiring

If possible, plan the installation of the wiring before the doll-house is built. It may be possible at that time to shift the location of a wall or make other changes which will facilitate the wiring and lighting. During construction, provision may be made for hiding feeder wires or for routing circuit wires in a less obvious way. Special provision can also be made at this time for major components such as the transformer and terminal strips.

The small wires which serve individual lamps and fixtures can be installed after the dollhouse is completed. If the dollhouse has an attic, the wires which run to the ceiling fixtures of the top floor can be routed across the attic floor to holes drilled in the ceiling. If the attic floor must be kept clear, the wires can be routed around the edge of the floor and through a hole at the edge of the floor to reach the ceiling of the floor below. The wires may then be routed across the ceiling or along the wall to reach a ceiling fixture or a wall socket.

Horizontal runs of wire for fixtures, wall sockets, etc. located on the first floor of a multi-story dollhouse are best made beneath

WHEN NECESSARY, WIRE MAY BE CONCEALED BEHIND DOOR OR WINDOW FRAME, ON SIDE AWAY FROM VIEWER.

TO REACH WALL SOCKET, RUN WIRE ON TOP EDGE OF BASE MOLDING

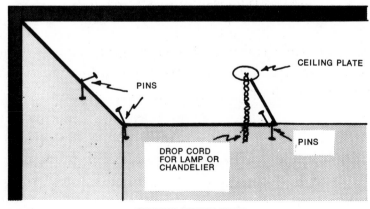

CEILING PLATE

PINS

PINS

DROP CORD FOR LAMP OR CHANDELIER

RUNNING CIRCUIT WIRES

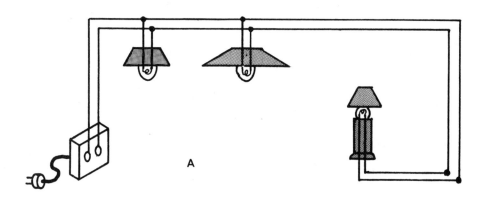

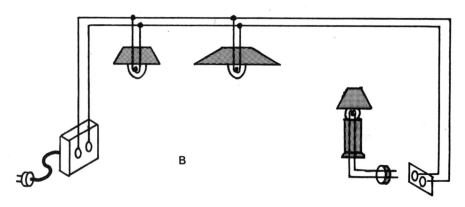

WALL SOCKET WIRING

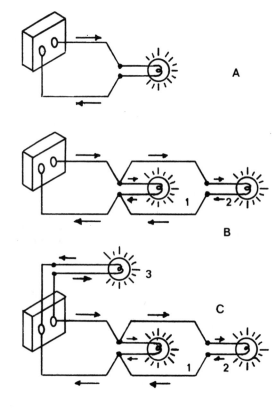

CIRCUIT OPERATION

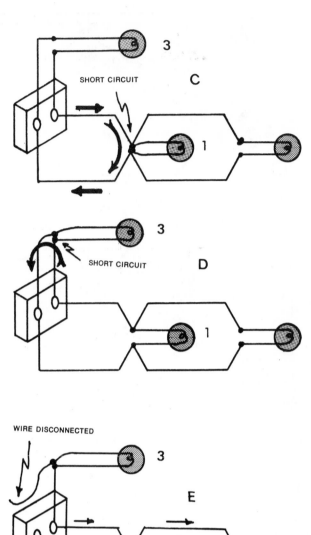

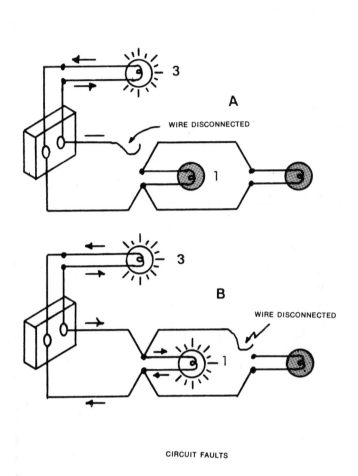

WIRE DISCONNECTED

A

WIRE DISCONNECTED

B

CIRCUIT FAULTS

SHORT CIRCUIT

C

SHORT CIRCUIT

D

WIRE DISCONNECTED

E

121

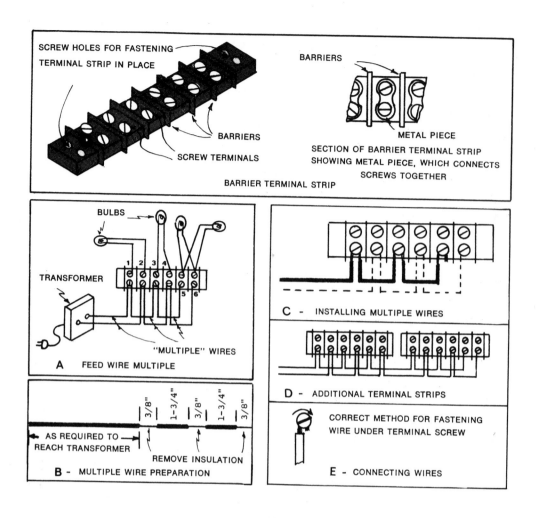

SCREW HOLES FOR FASTENING TERMINAL STRIP IN PLACE

BARRIERS

BARRIERS

SCREW TERMINALS

METAL PIECE

SECTION OF BARRIER TERMINAL STRIP SHOWING METAL PIECE, WHICH CONNECTS SCREWS TOGETHER

BARRIER TERMINAL STRIP

BULBS

TRANSFORMER

"MULTIPLE" WIRES

A   FEED WIRE MULTIPLE

C -   INSTALLING MULTIPLE WIRES

D -   ADDITIONAL TERMINAL STRIPS

3/8"   1-3/4"   3/8"   1-3/4"   3/8"

AS REQUIRED TO REACH TRANSFORMER

REMOVE INSULATION

B -   MULTIPLE WIRE PREPARATION

CORRECT METHOD FOR FASTENING WIRE UNDER TERMINAL SCREW

E -   CONNECTING WIRES

the first floor of the house. This requires that a clear space of at least ¾ inch be provided under the first floor. The space can be provided by installing a frame of 1" x 2" lumber under the house. 1" x 2" is a standard size lumber which may be obtained at any lumber yard.

In a finished dollhouse that has three floors, the middle floor is the most difficult to service because no direct access can be provided to individual fixtures from above or below. Wires which must reach the middle floor are best routed from a transformer or terminal strip located in the attic or the basement via a central stairway, a chimney or other device which reaches to all floors.

Installing Light Fixtures

Fixtures which are fastened to the ceiling are generally of two types. Some, such as bedroom and kitchen fixtures, are mounted flush to the ceiling and have no drop cord or suspension chain. Others, such as chandeliers, library lamps, etc. are hung from a chain or by a supporting cord. Commercially available fixtures of either type are supplied with only a few inches of wire extending from them. This means that the fixture wires must be connected (spliced) to the circuit wires which bring the electricity from the transformer or terminal strip. To avoid an unsightly appearance, these splices must be hidden. Most flush-mounted fixtures provide some space between the fixture and the ceiling where splices may be hidden. However, for chandeliers and other hanging fixtures, it is necessary to use a ceiling plate to hide the splices and support the fixture. A ceiling plate is a dish-shaped piece (usually metal) about ½ inch in diameter. The dish shape provides a hollow back in which to hide the splices. Ceiling plates are available from miniature lighting suppliers, or certain jewelry pieces may be used for this purpose.

When installing lighting fixtures which are fastened to the ceiling or wall, it might seem logical to bring the wires from the transformer or terminal strip to the fixture and then splice these wires to the fixture wires. This method can be used but it presents several problems. If the wire is run from the power source to the fixture, an excess of wire usually remains after the wires have been spliced to the fixture. This excess is often difficult to dispose of in a neat, workmanlike manner. Also, when the wire is run toward the fixture, gluing the wire in place is often complicated at the fixture location and the wire is sometimes pulled loose during the splicing operation. For these reasons it is recommended that the wire be run from the installed fixture to the source of power.

Handcrafted lamps and chandeliers can provide the special, unique touch often required for special or "period" dollhouses. This chandelier of turned wood was especially created by Jim Carlson, of West Chicago, Illinois, to grace one of the exquisite dollhouses for which the Carlson brothers are well known. The white, translucent chimneys are short pieces of plastic soda straw.

Before proceeding with the installation, the silicone insulation must be allowed to dry thoroughly. If the cement is air-dried, it will require at least three hours of drying before the cement is hard enough to proceed. The drying process may be speeded by application of heat from a lamp or hair dryer.

Primarily, when installing the circuit wires which run into and between rooms you want to achieve a realistic appearance by hiding the wires from view. Hiding them doesn't necessarily mean completely concealing them within walls and ceilings, however; when one looks into a dollhouse it is almost always from an angle above the ceilings of the rooms and if the wire is kept at ceiling height it will not be noticed by the casual viewer. The wire installed inside a room should be run in the corner or angle formed by the intersection of the wall and ceiling, or two walls. When the wire is run in this angle of intersection, the concealment is aided by the fact that the viewer's eye is somewhat confused by the changing angle of the two surfaces. Thus, wire which is run on the surface should always be run parallel with the edges of the walls or ceilings; when run at an angle to the edge it disturbs the viewer's eye and attracts attention to itself.

7 Wood Crafts

Wood crafts are the ones we encounter most frequently when we build our own dollhouse. From the time the frame for our house begins to take shape to the moment when we're ready to consider making a rose-carved Victorian settee, we are working with wood. And a satisfying thing it is, too, for in the world of woods and veneers we have a vast array of textures, colors, and rich grains.

Materials from India, Ceylon, Burma, Brazil, and Africa are now available to us, including avodire, kelobra, peroba, lacewood, and faux satine. My advice to you as you embark upon the adventure of woodworking is to order one of the groups of wood samples from one of the large suppliers, such as the already mentioned Constantine and Son, who offer fifty different samples for $5.95. I have had more pleasure from this treasure chest of woods than from anything I've ever purchased.

Garden Swing

We have to begin somewhere, and the most important step in any wood crafting is to select the proper wood for what we are making. Few of us can begin with the glamour products of the forest, such as rosewood, mahogany, and teak. So, for a first project, we offer the little garden swing that follows, and suggest using either balsa wood or basswood for the material.

I personally have always had good luck with balsa wood, but most professional miniature makers relegate it to the bottom of their list of favorites. It is very soft and light, as any maker of model airplanes knows, strong enough for most miniatures, and not nearly as "splitty" as some other woods. Also, it's easy to smooth with sandpaper, and in most instances you can push small tacks into it with your fingers.

Garden swing

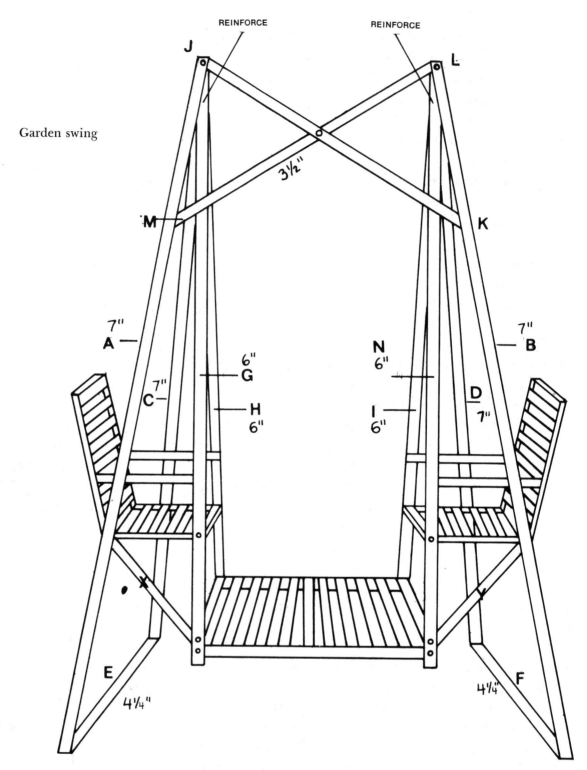

Basswood is probably the next most feasible wood for making miniatures other than furniture. It, too, is light and soft, but not as soft as balsa, and it has practically no grain, so it takes to paint and stains very nicely. Either is readily available, and a visit to your local hobby shop or a look through the catalogues of the wood-crafts firms will give you all the information necessary as to the sizes in which the wood may be ordered.

Materials Needed for the Garden Swing

 4 pieces balsa wood, 7" x ¼" x ⅛"
 4 pieces balsa wood, 6" x ¼" x ⅛"
 2 pieces balsa wood, 4¼" x ¼" x ⅛"
 4 pieces balsa wood, 3½" x ¼" x ⅛"
18 pieces balsa wood, 3" x ¼" x ⅛"
 2 pieces balsa wood, 3" x ¼"
 4 pieces balsa wood, 1½" x ⅛"
 4 pieces balsa wood, 1" x ⅛"
   Wire nails, ½"
 8 screw eyes, ¼"
   Glue
   Boston clips for gluing
   Enamel for painting

While the garden swing illustrated looks most complicated and professional when finished, it will probably be the easiest thing for you to make. It is made entirely of ⅛-inch wood, cut into ¼-inch strips, plus a few dowels and support pieces and some quarter-inch screw eyes. Cut four pieces (A, B, C, and D) 7 inches long to produce a swing on the 1/12 scale. Then cut four pieces (E, F, G, and H) 6 inches long. Cut two pieces 4¼ inches long for the bracing at the bottom. Cut four pieces 3½ inches long for bracing at the top. Cut two ⅛-inch dowels 3⅝ inches long, for bracing at the top.

On your work board, lay the four long pieces on the narrow side as shown in the reduced drawing below. Glue the wide side of braces E and F to the narrow, upturned sides of the long pieces. Allow to dry thoroughly. When these joints have set, glue one of the 3½-inch braces (J-K) from the very top of frame A-B, to a point 2 inches down from the top. Fasten with Boston clips until dry, then glue the other brace (L-M) in a like manner on frame C. Repeat with the other frame. Notice that in order for these braces to cross over, the first brace must be glued to the *inside* of supports A and C (and B and D) and the second, or crossing brace, to the *outside*. Hold with Boston clips (see p. 5) until completely dry, then tack a ½-inch wire nail through the point where they cross in the center. The nail will protrude a bit on the inside; snip off with a wire cutter. Repeat with frames C and D. Now, with your awl, make small openings at the top through frames and supports, and slip in a 3⅝-inch dowel from A to C, and from B to D. You now have a standing frame.

For the swing part, we will use the four 6-inch pieces as the frame. Sharpen the two remaining dowels to points, or until they are 3¼ inches long. Insert these into the ¼-inch supports G and H and N

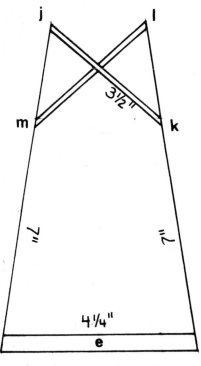

Diagram for garden swing

and *I*. The tops of these frame pieces must be strengthened a bit, so cut four $\frac{1}{4}$-inch squares of the $\frac{1}{8}$-inch wood and glue one reinforcement on each side, at the top of the frame, to furnish a grip for the dowels. Fasten with Boston clips until dry. Using $\frac{1}{4}$-inch screw eyes, screw these into the reinforced tops of the frame pieces. String onto the dowels supporting the frame pieces *A-C* and *B-D*. These are the supports for the seats; they will be hanging from the dowels.

To make the seats, you will use the eighteen pieces of $\frac{1}{4}$-inch strips of $\frac{1}{8}$-inch balsa wood, 3 inches long. The two pieces of $\frac{1}{4}$-inch balsa wood, $\frac{3}{8}$ inch wide and 3 inches long, will make the supports for the seats. For the back of the seats, lay two of the $1\frac{1}{2}$-inch pieces of balsa on your workboard about 2 inches apart and glue five pieces of the 3-inch strips, evenly spaced, to them. Weight with a book until entirely dry. Repeat for the other seat. Lay two of the 1-inch pieces on the workboard and glue four of the 3-inch strips to them, evenly spaced. These are the seats. Fasten the backs to the seat parts by fitting them against the 3-inch braces of $\frac{1}{4}$-inch wood, at right angles. Glue and allow to dry.

Arms and supports for the seats are cut from scrap pieces. Cut four 1-inch pieces to serve as arms; glue these about halfway up the end of the back, and against the swing frame, at the other end, one on each side of each seat. Cut four pieces $1\frac{1}{4}$ inches long and glue from the back of the seat portion against the swing frame about $\frac{1}{4}$ inch from the bottom of the frame. These are pieces *X* and *Y*. Repeat on the other side of the seat.

You are now ready for finishing the floor of the swing. From your scraps, cut two pieces ($\frac{1}{4}$-inch strips) of the $\frac{1}{8}$-inch balsa wood, $2\frac{3}{8}$ inches long. Reinforce these with $\frac{1}{4}$-inch squares at each end, as you did at the tops of frames *G*, *H*, *N*, and *I*. When dry, lay these on the workboard wide side up and glue to them five pieces, $2\frac{3}{4}$ inches long, of the $\frac{1}{4}$-inch strips. Let dry under a weight. Into each end of the supports, screw a $\frac{1}{4}$-inch screw eye. Gently remove the dowels supporting the seats, push through the screw eyes, and replace in the openings in the swing supports. If your corners have been properly squared and the top of the frame is absolutely square, the seats will swing free as they should. Paint as desired—most lawn swings, according to my recollection, were painted in yellow with red supports.

Privy

A privy adds a nice note of authenticity to houses up through the 1920s. It is one of the easiest pieces to make and will help you gain experience in woodworking at the same time. People-sized privies were never well-finished buildings, and in this miniature even though you make a mistake, it can always be covered up. Again, we will use ⅛-inch wood. This will seem a little flimsy for such a building, but you must remember that our ⅛-inch wood, on a ¹⁄₁₂ scale, would be 1½-inch wood in actual size; much too heavy for our purpose. Quarter-inch wood looks better, but this would be 3-inch wood in actual size, and is much too far from scale to be believable.

Materials Needed for the Privy

Cut all except the Miscellaneous strips mentioned at the end of the list, from ⅛-inch or no more than ³⁄₁₆-inch balsa or basswood.
1 piece, 4″ x 6″ (front)
2 pieces, 6″ x 5″ x 3″ (sides)
5 pieces, 5¼″ x 1″ (for roof)
1 piece, 3¾″ x 1⅝″ (for seat front)
1 piece, 2¼″ x 3¾″ (for seat)
Miscellaneous strips ¼″ x ¼″
Small piece leather for hinges
½-inch wire nails
Stain
Glue

The privy—the "necessary" of the nineteenth century

Cut the pieces shown on pp. 130–132 and stain on all sides, but don't attempt to finish smoothly; privies just weren't made that way. Cut the door from the front piece and then cut the moon in the door. For door braces, cut two pieces ¼ inch wide and 2¾ inches long, and one piece ¼ inch wide and 3 inches long. Glue one piece about ½ inch up from the bottom of the door as shown, trim the ends of the longer piece to fit against it, then glue the angled piece. Fit the second brace piece at the top of the angled brace. Allow to dry. Cut two leather hinges, as shown, from an old glove and glue to the door. Add a ½-inch wire nail to serve as a handle. You may prefer to use the ½-inch wire nails as added support for the hinges, also, as shown in the drawing. If this is done, however, they will protrude a bit from the back of the door, and must be snipped off with a wire cutter or pliers that will cut metal.

We found it a good idea to glue the two sides to the back in a butt joint inside the back piece. When these joints are dry, glue into the two back corners lengths of the ¼ x ¼-inch strips—5 inches long in the back, 6 inches long in the front, Allow to dry. Cut the seat piece 3¾ inches long (against the grain) and 2¼ inches wide (with the grain). Trim out the corners to fit around the braces in the back corners, then measure to be certain that the piece fits nicely between the two side walls. Glue in place. Cut the seat front 3¾ inches long

Diagram for privy construction.

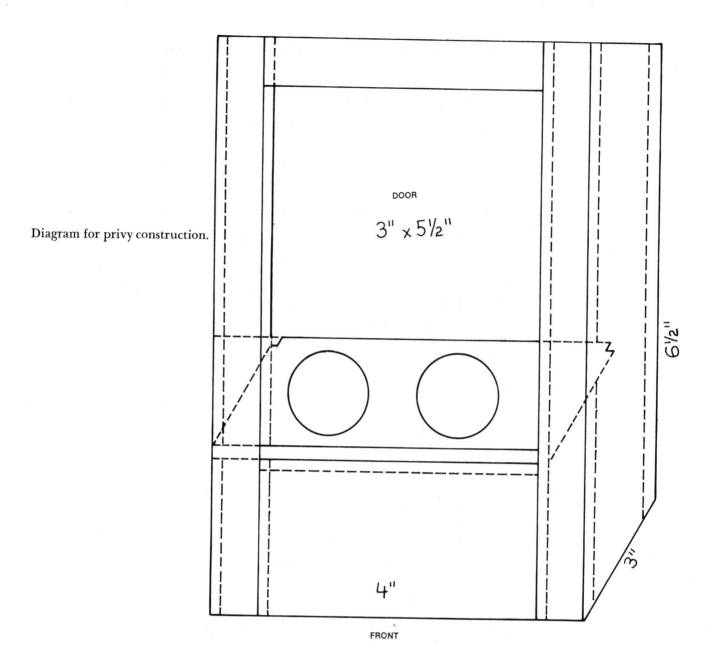

DOOR

3" x 5½"

6½"

3"

4"

FRONT

(with the grain) and 1⅝ inches wide (against the grain).* Slip this front up against the seat top about 2 inches from the front wall, or so the seat top protrudes about ¼ inch. Glue and, when dry, reinforce by gluing two pieces of the ¼ x¼-inch strips into the angle between the seat front and the side walls. These supports are shown in broken lines on the drawings, and go on the inside when attached.

Now you are ready for the front. First, attach the door by gluing (or tacking) the leather hinges as shown in the drawing, allowing ½ inch to go against the wall. Now slip the entire front into the ceiling,

* Author's Note: Where directions specify "against the grain" or "with the grain," this is very important to give added strength to the structure.

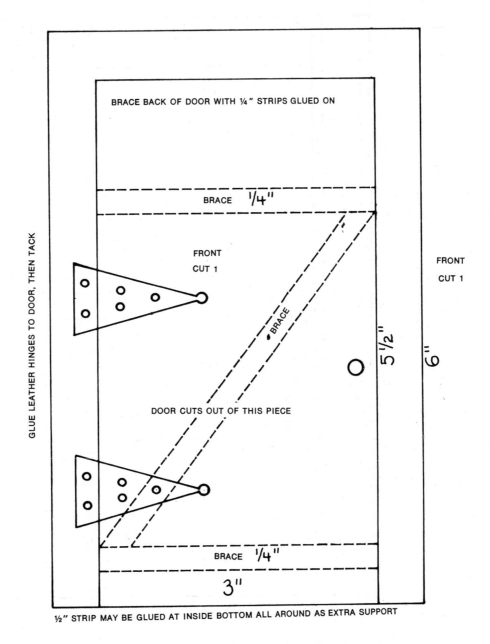

GLUE LEATHER HINGES TO DOOR, THEN TACK

BRACE BACK OF DOOR WITH ¼" STRIPS GLUED ON

BRACE ¼"

FRONT
CUT 1

FRONT
CUT 1

BRACE

5½"

6"

DOOR CUTS OUT OF THIS PIECE

BRACE ¼"

3"

½" STRIP MAY BE GLUED AT INSIDE BOTTOM ALL AROUND AS EXTRA SUPPORT

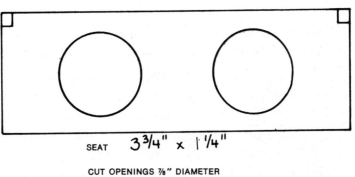

SEAT   3¾" x 1¼"

CUT OPENINGS ⅞" DIAMETER

Diagram for privy parts. (See also following page.)

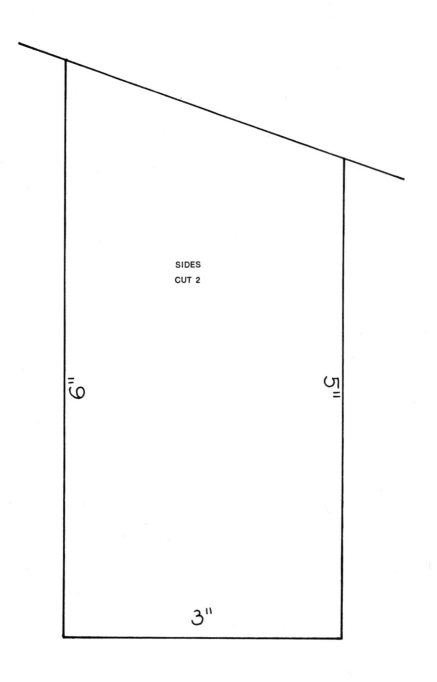

SIDES
CUT 2

6"

5"

3"

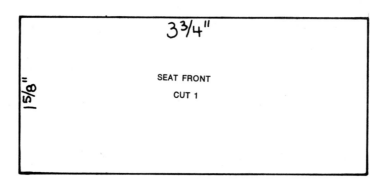

3¾"

SEAT FRONT
CUT 1

1⅝"

making a butt joint against the sides as you did in the back. Glue and let dry.

The five pieces of 1-inch wood are cut 5¼ inches long so as to provide an overhang for the roof. Stain on both sides, then, starting at the bottom of the roof slope (back of the building), glue against the top of the walls, allowing an equal overhang on both sides. Allow about a ¼-inch overhang at the back, too, which means that with the first plank laid, it must protrude over the back about ¼ inch. Always lay roofs beginning at the bottom. Glue each succeeding piece so it laps about ¼ inch over the one underneath. End up with a ½-inch overhang at the front.

One-half-inch strips may be glued on the inside of the building for added support, but we didn't find these absolutely necessary.

If you're a stickler for detail, make a little Sears, Roebuck catalogue 1 inch high by ¾ inch wide by cutting a piece of ¼-inch wood to this size. Cut a piece of paper, preferably yellow, and glue around the block to form a cover. Before the glue is dry, run a thread through against the spine, or back edge, of the book. Have some fun doing a little black lettering on the cover. Hang by the thread on a tack either on the door or at the side of the privy.

Butcher-Block Tables

There are few collectors who don't have a place somewhere in their mini-rooms, country stores, or dollhouses for a chopping block. This is, as a matter of fact, a most important piece, since it was the heart of the store, butcher shop, or kitchen. Crude versions were used in early periods in houses both here and abroad, and about 1915 a more sophisticated version made its appearance. The one pictured at the bottom of page 134, is part of the decorating plans for the most modern homes.

As a further example of the way in which the miniaturist sees possibilities in anything, model *A* was made from a slice of the trunk of a Christmas tree. Each year we try to make something of our tree when we've finished with it—a shillelagh from the trunk, that sort of thing. One year when we were short of ideas, my husband sliced a 1-inch piece from a smooth part of the trunk and a butcher-block table immediately suggested itself as a furnishing for our log cabin. It could be used in any early American home or country store.

The grain you get when you slice the trunk in this way doesn't run in circles; it is, rather, a series of delicately curved lines. This we used for the top, sanded well, then scrubbed to whiten. I would have

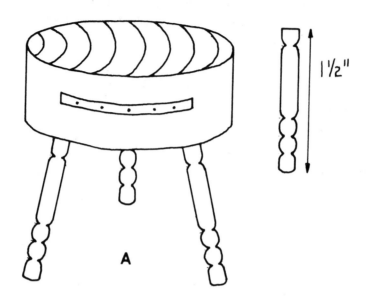

1½"

Butcher-block tables

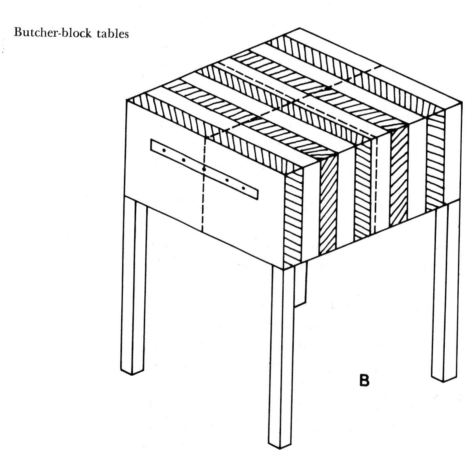

A

B

liked to use a dull varnish, but this was vetoed as not valid for such a piece. The bark (the side of the block) was carefully skinned off, and the sides were then stained brown and varnished. The strip you see in the drawing is a ⅛-inch strip of leather from an old glove, tacked onto the side of the block to hold the butcher's tools.

Materials Needed for the Butcher-Block Tables

Round slice of wood about 2″ in diameter, 1″ or 1½″ deep, *or*
16 pine planks ⅛″ thick by ¾″ or 1″ wide
Small bit of leather for utensil strap
¼″ dowels or square pieces for legs
Glue
X-Acto knife
Drill
File
Emery boards

The legs will give you a chance to make your first experiments in shaping; you will need three pieces ¼ inch square, 1½ inches long. Mark very carefully with a pencil, where you want the grooves to go. If you are lucky enough to have an electric drill in the house, put the drill in the chuck, tighten, turn on the drill, and file very carefully at the places you've marked. The Dremel Moto-Tool is perfect for this. You may spoil a few, but after all, you're not using much wood. Your small hand drill (p. 5) can be clamped in a vise and used in the same way. If you don't have these tools, just start filing on your marks, around and around. It's slower, but more easily handled.

Now, with your X-Acto knife, gently whittle off the corners of the wood, sloping the sides in a bit at the grooves. Try to keep everything uniform. When you're finished, stain, varnish, and slant the tops of the legs off a bit so the block is stable and the legs slant slightly outward. Glue.

Model *B* is made of a series of planks glued together to use the grain of the wood to make a design. Joen Ellen Kanze sells a package of pine planks ⅛ x ¾ inch, for about a dollar. Using enough planks to make a 2-inch block, laminate them using a good wood glue and let dry in a clamp. When dry, cut the block off so that it is 2 inches square. This will be only about ¾ inch deep, the width of the planks, rather than the 1 inch that we show on the drawing. You'll find, though, that the ¾-inch depth looks very nice. If you use this depth, be sure to make the legs longer so you have the tabletop about 2½ inches high. Sand carefully, bearing down on the edges and corners so they are a bit rounded. Varnish the sides and bottom.

Cut the legs from a ¼-inch square piece, making, as we mention above, pieces the tabletop needs to bring it about 2½ inches (the equivalent of 30 inches) from the ground. These may be left plain as we show in our drawing, rounded off a bit with decorative grooving as outlined above, or ¼-inch doweling may be used so you have round legs. Glue to the table and there you are.

You might try for an interesting finish on this little block, as we did. We cut the block into four equal pieces as shown by the dotted lines, then gave two opposite pieces a half turn and glued all together again. Let dry in a clamp. This gives a most interesting parquet pattern to the top and bottom of the block; simply sand smooth if it is a bit uneven after the gluing.

An interesting finish for this block is to rub salad oil into the wood; the old-time butcher's blocks, of course, were simply raw wood, and this gives an attractive approximation.

Gas Stove, ca. 1927

Jane Daniels, who perfected this design (it is an exact copy of a range in the 1927 Sears, Roebuck catalogue) tells me (and after making it I soundly agree) that it is probably one of the most satisfying pieces to be made, simply because so far as we know, no one has ever done it, despite its relatively simple requirements. We used ⅛-inch basswood for the botttom frame and ¹⁄₁₆-inch basswood for the remainder; light cardboard might be used for the top assembly, but it wouldn't be nearly so satisfactory.

Start with the legs, using ½-inch-square blocks of basswood or balsa, 2¼ inches long. Carve from the pattern; start by shaping one edge and rounding off by sanding or whittling. This gives the round edge of the leg which is at the corner. The other three edges are simply cut off flat. Take your time with these; doing them properly is very necessary to give the illusion of a real range. You may have to discard a few until your hand becomes more knowing, but it's fun even while learning.

Cut the piece for the bottom; glue the support pieces on all four sides on the edges, making butt joints. Cut a piece of ¹⁄₁₆-inch wood to go over this bottom, fitting exactly even at front and two sides but with ¹⁄₁₆-inch space left at the back. Glue. Cut the back and fit it against this piece, atop the back support, and glue. Cut the side *A* and glue to the burner side and back.

For the oven side, measure the two sides to make certain that when affixed they will exactly meet the back. This will leave about ½

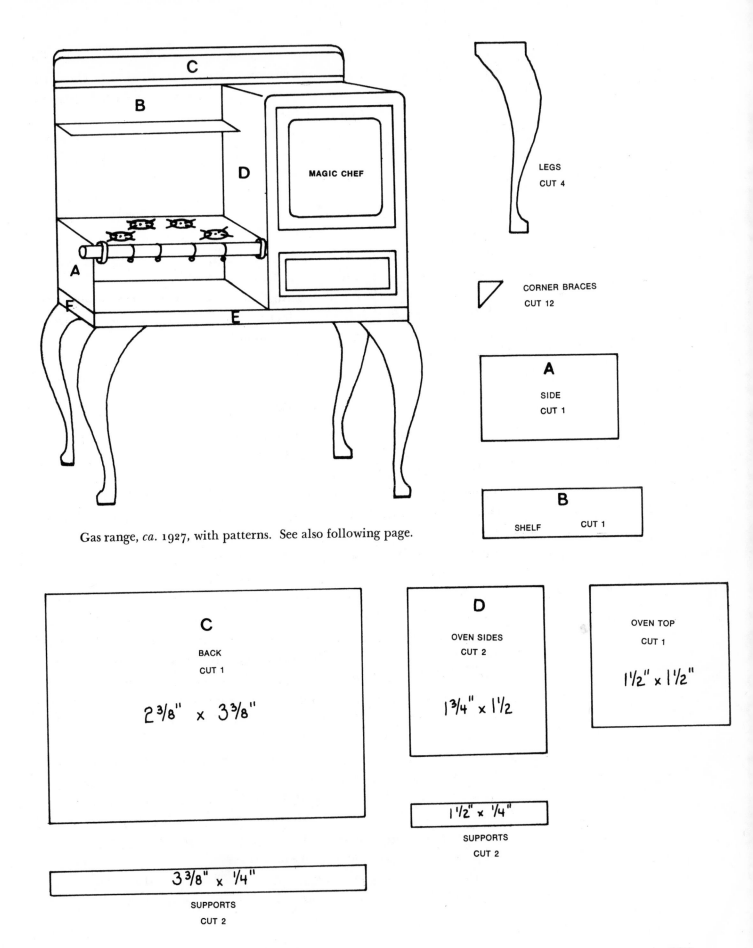

LEGS
CUT 4

CORNER BRACES
CUT 12

A

SIDE
CUT 1

B

SHELF   CUT 1

Gas range, *ca.* 1927, with patterns. See also following page.

C

BACK
CUT 1

2³⁄₈" x 3³⁄₈"

D

OVEN SIDES
CUT 2

1³⁄₄" x 1¹⁄₂

OVEN TOP
CUT 1

1¹⁄₂" x 1¹⁄₂"

1¹⁄₂" x ¹⁄₄"

SUPPORTS
CUT 2

3³⁄₈" x ¹⁄₄"

SUPPORTS
CUT 2

MAGIC CHEF

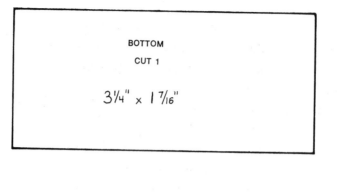

BOTTOM

CUT 1

3¼" x 1⁷⁄₁₆"

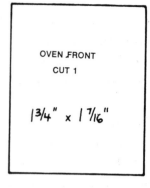

OVEN FRONT

CUT 1

1¾" x 1⁷⁄₁₆"

Gas range patterns

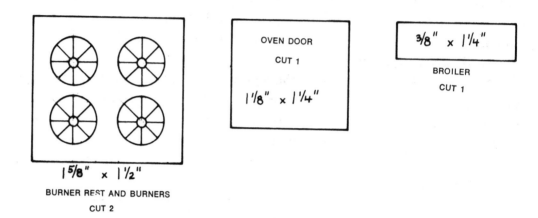

1⁵⁄₈" x 1½"

BURNER REST AND BURNERS

CUT 2

OVEN DOOR

CUT 1

1⅛" x 1¼"

⅜" x 1¼"

BROILER

CUT 1

inch above for a splash board. Glue the oven sides and top against the back. Allow to dry. Attach the shelf by gluing at the back and oven side, about ½ inch down from the top of the oven.

In a miniature piece which contains as many parts as this one, it is essential to measure the pieces against the parts to which they must join, for many things can make little differences that will ruin the fit. The width of your pencil point, whether you hold the pencil against the ruler exactly vertical or at an angle, will often make the difference between a well-fitting part and an awkward-looking finished piece. So make certain each part fits before you glue or paint.

The oven doors do not open. Glue four of the triangular corner supports ¹⁄₁₆ inch inside the oven at the corners. Make certain the oven front fits snugly into the oven. Cut the two doors from ⅛-inch wood and round off the front edges by carefully sanding the edges on the outside. Glue to the oven front, against the corner supports. For the handles, cut a strip of tin about ⅛ inch wide from a tin can, long enough to bend little handles and leave about ½ inch in the center. Bend just a little to arch the handle. Glue to the doors by the handle. Now paint the entire assembly with two coats of white model enamel.

Glue four more corner supports at each corner of the burner side (A and D), ¼ inch below the top of A. Paint the inside of this compartment, including the supports, with glossy black model enamel. Paint the burner rest and burner plate black also, after cutting the openings in the burner plate with a sharp-pointed knife, as shown. Slide the rest into the space, then the burner rest.

For the burners, cut a round toothpick to fit exactly the front of the burner rest. Cut two ⅛-inch strips of card about ¾ inch long and fold in half. Fold these around the toothpick about ¼ inch from each end. Glue the ends of the card between the burner rest and the burner plate, making sure they are equidistant from the ends of the toothpick. Cut ¼-inch bits from ends of the toothpicks and glue to the front of the burner rest, and resting upon this rod. Carefully paint the assembly with the black paint, let dry, then tip the ends of the toothpicks with silver or white paint.

Now all that remains is to set the legs on the inside of the bottom supports, glue, then glue the corner braces to hold them firm. Set your stove on the legs when dry and if not exactly even, sand off the legs as needed. Stencil or draw a design on the oven door, and there you are.

Materials Needed for Gas Stove, *ca.* 1927

- 1 square foot ⅛" basswood or balsa wood
- 1 foot ¼" strips ⅛-inch thick basswood or balsa wood
- X-Acto knife No. 1
- Sobo glue
- Black enamel model paint
- White enamel model paint
- 1 strip tin ⅛" x 1⅛"
- 3 toothpicks
- Small piece lightweight cardboard such as shirtboard

Be sure to study instructions. Trim all pieces before gluing.

In case you run into some difficulty in cutting out the burner openings on the burner plate, somewhat difficult to do with wood, try using Sculpey or some other sculpturing clay instead. Sculpey, made by Polyform Products, Inc., 9420 Byron St., Schiller Park, Illinois 60176, never shrinks, never hardens or dries out until it is baked. To make the burner plate, we simply rolled it out smoothly about 1/16 inch thick, then cut with a pointed knife to the same size as the burner rest. Cut out the round spaces which will be the burners, then bake at 325 degrees for 15 to 30 minutes. If it isn't baked long enough you can still bend it, and if it is baked too long it will take on a pinkish-brown color, but neither of these conditions prevents its being used after painting. Paint black with the model enamel.

Early Victorian Cook Stove, ca. 1840

About the end of the eighteenth century, when the first rumblings of the industrial revolution were beginning to be felt, ironmongers began to work on designs for stoves that would hold the fire better than the fireplaces still in vogue. The first stoves, naturally, were fitted into the fireplace space. By about 1840, these were in general use.

Vivien Greene, in her book *Family Dolls' Houses*, shows a number which were put into English dollhouses and shows a drawing from which our stove is adapted, which is in *Loudon's Encyclopedia of Cottage, Farm and Villa Architecture and Furniture* (printed in 1842). Jean Latham, in her book *Dolls' Houses: A Personal Choice*, shows us several beauties, including a tiled stove in a Dutch doll kitchen dating from the end of the seventeenth century, but we find few in American dollhouses or American people's houses either, for that matter, dating from this period. Perhaps progress was just slow in reaching America!

At any rate, such a stove is a fascinating thing to make because so many variations are possible. While there are dozens of fireplaces and hundreds of the iron stoves, which came in at the end of the nineteenth century, there are few of these little gems to be seen.

Materials Needed for the Victorian Cook Stove

1 piece balsa, 12" x 3" x 1/8"
1 piece balsa, 10" x 3" x 1/2"
  Small piece aluminum or foil for nameplate
  Red brick wallpaper or stones for back and sides
  Sobo glue
  Black model enamel
  Silver paint for bordering doors
  Small piece red cellophane
1 tube black acrylic paint
  Assorted small rings for handles

We will use 1/8-inch balsa except for the 1/2-inch pieces that form the two sides, since most of the wood will be covered anyway, and it is easier to work with. First, cut a piece to form the back, 5½ inches wide and as high as you wish it to go. If you wish the slanting chimney breast as shown, cut it according to our sketch.

Decide whether you want the inside of the stove brick-lined, tiled, or painted black. Brick is probably the most authentic. If you use this, use brick-type wallpaper and cover the inside of the back and the two side pieces marked *C*. Smudge the upper half of the back with charcoal or soot. Finish the hearth as you prefer, either with the brick

Early Victorian cook stove, *ca.* 1840

BROWN'S IMPROVED

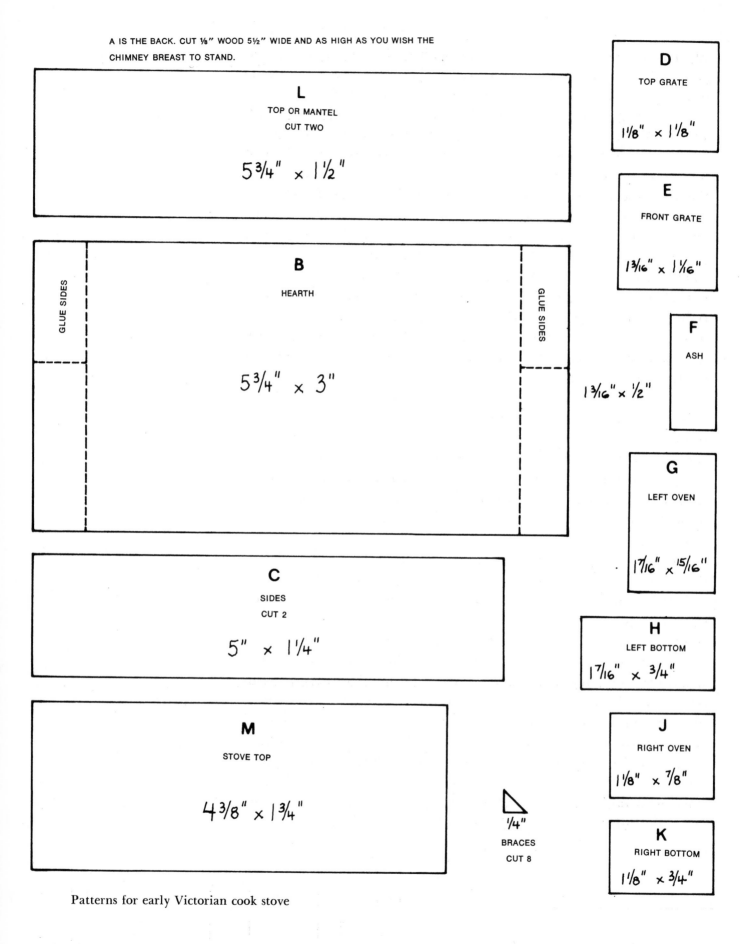

A IS THE BACK. CUT ⅛" WOOD 5½" WIDE AND AS HIGH AS YOU WISH THE CHIMNEY BREAST TO STAND.

L

TOP OR MANTEL

CUT TWO

5¾" × 1½"

D

TOP GRATE

1⅛" × 1⅛"

B

HEARTH

GLUE SIDES

GLUE SIDES

5¾" × 3"

E

FRONT GRATE

1³⁄₁₆" × 1¹⁄₁₆"

F

ASH

1³⁄₁₆" × ½"

G

LEFT OVEN

1⁷⁄₁₆" × 1⁵⁄₁₆"

C

SIDES

CUT 2

5" × 1¼"

H

LEFT BOTTOM

1⁷⁄₁₆" × ¾"

M

STOVE TOP

4⅜" × 1¾"

¼"

BRACES

CUT 8

J

RIGHT OVEN

1⅛" × ⅞"

K

RIGHT BOTTOM

1⅛" × ¾"

Patterns for early Victorian cook stove

142

paper, with your own "made" bricks, with stones, or simply painted gray or black. Glue the sides against the back, then glue the whole thing onto the hearth. Paint the outside of the back black.

To complete the stove assembly, cut two pieces 2¾ inches high and 1¼ inches deep, and one piece 4⅜ inches wide and the same height for the back. Glue these to the inside of the hearth, then glue four of the corner braces into the corners level with the top of the stove. Cut the stove top and check to make sure it makes a snug fit. Cut the stove front 4⅜ inches long and 2¾ inches high. Trace the pattern from our drawing onto this piece. For the front grill (E) and top grill (D) cut a piece of wood the size given in the pattern, then carefully round off the sides and corners with fine sandpaper. Glue a piece of red cellophane over each. Trace the iron work with black acrylic paint right from the tube onto each piece. Do the same with the ³⁄₁₆-inch space at the bottom of the center grill and add a few strokes of black to denote coal or wood burning. When dry, glue D to the center of the top and E and F to the front.

Cut the remaining doors and round off corners and sides as above. The doors will not open; glue them to the front and paint all with black model paint. The grill F is for ash removal; paint this a dull red, and glue to the front of the stove. If you have a hand that's steady enough, a border of silver paint around all doors is a great addition. Also, you might want to try cutting an oval of heavy aluminum foil to fit the center of the left-hand door, scribe a name on it, then glue to the door after it is painted.

Carefully fit this front up against the sides which are glued into the form. If it fits, glue against the hearth, sides, and back. Glue the grill (D) in the center of the stove top (M). Paint the top black, then slide in atop the stove, resting on the corner braces and the sides and front. Round the corners and paint black.

In the dollhouses, the chimney breast appears to be the same as it was before the dollhouse family decided to install a modern (1840) stove. Paint the top (A) whatever color you want to use in your kitchen, or finish with a wood finish. Set the two mantels cut from ⅛-inch wood atop the stove as shown in the drawing, one a bit shorter than the other, then a ½-inch piece similarly finished. Top with two more ⅛-inch pieces. Some dollhouses of the period show a shelf mounted over the stove, with various adornments on it. Others show the chimney breast left plain with kitchen utensils or cups hanging on hooks.

Victorian Wardrobe Trunk

In the days when the Grand Tour was a part of every well-bred young person's education, no one would have ventured forth without a wardrobe trunk, sometimes called a steamer trunk because the long trips for which it was intended were usually on steamers. The trunk held an entire wardrobe, and many of them were elaborate indeed. The one shown was made on the 1/12 scale to the exact measurements of the old trunk in a friend's attic, and it is one of the most entrancing miniatures I've ever produced. The trunk construction is of 1/8-inch balsa wood; the little drawers of thin cardboard such as shirt board; the hangers were bought from Pickwick Miniatures.

You will need:

2 pieces 2" x 3" x 1/8" balsa wood
4 pieces 3 1/4" x 7/8" x 1/8" balsa wood
4 pieces 2" x 7/8" x 1/8" balsa wood
1 piece covering material—leather, Con-Tact black patent paper, linen
1 piece lining paper, small pattern (about 1')
2 small hinges such as Miniature Mart's No. 261
    Light cardboard, such as shirtboard, for drawers
    Beads or pins for drawer handles
    Leather strip 1/8" wide for top handles
2 catches #3048 from Miniature Mart for front closing
    Tacky glue
    Pickwick Miniatures' clothes hangers

Victorian wardrobe trunk

144

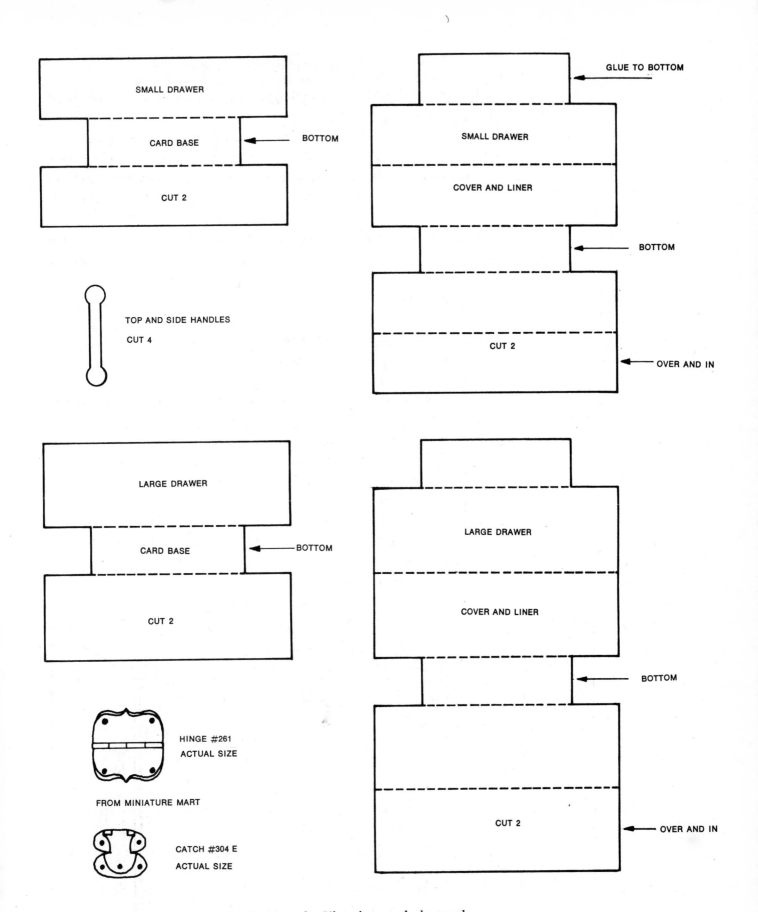

Patterns for Victorian wardrobe trunk

145

Be sure to cut the pieces with absolutely true corners, using the grain the length of the trunk. Glue the ends at the ends of the front and back as shown, the sides at the sides of the front and back. This will give you two small boxes 3¼ inches long and 1 inch deep (outside measurements). Use Tacky or Elmer's Glue-All; allow to dry completely before going on.

For the outside of this trunk we used black patent Con-Tact paper, because it is easy to handle and because the original was covered with patent leather—this was a very fancy trunk. For the lining, we used the Peddler's Shop wreath pattern, PA 102, but any very small-figured paper would be fine. You will need about a foot of each.

Cut a piece of the lining paper 3 inches long and ½ inch wide. Lay the two boxes on a table, two long sides about ⅛ inch apart. Glue the strip of lining over the top at the joining, to hold the two boxes together. Be sure to have a little space between the boxes, otherwise the trunk won't open.

Now cut a piece of the black Con-Tact paper 8½ inches long and 3⅞ inches wide. Fold it around your two little boxes, which have been folded together open side to open side, and crease where the paper goes around the corners. Very, very carefully cut a V at each corner the depth of the excess paper (this should be ¼ inch). Pull off the Con-Tact backing and press the patent in place, that is, around the sides, back and front, lapping over the ends and over the open edges at front. Press so that you have perfect adherence. Cut four pieces of the Con-Tact, ⅞ inch by 2 inches, and press onto the ends of the boxes. You may have to touch a bit of glue to these; Con-Tact doesn't stick very well to itself.

Now you're ready for the lining. The wreath paper mentioned previously is perfect for this. Cut two pieces 3½ inches wide (to fit exactly the inside of each box) and 3¾ inches high, to fit the up and down of the box, with a fraction over to glue to top and bottom. Glue each to the inside of the box, pressing the corners in well. You must measure carefully here; your measurements may vary a bit from ours. The lining should come exactly to the side-front edges to form a finish. Trim corners and·lap at top and bottom. Cut four pieces of the liner ⅝ inch by 1⅝ inches for top and bottom liners. Glue in. You should have a neat lining. Let dry thoroughly.

Now for the drawers. Although in the drawing we show the bottom drawer on the hanger side larger than the one on the other side (our original intention), we found that making them both the same depth made a better-looking trunk. Trace your patterns and cut, one from the thin cardboard and the larger from the lining paper. Lay the lining paper face downward and spread with wallpaper or decoupage paste.

Bend the cardboard on the dotted lines, then straighten out and lay on the lining paper so that the cuts fit. Press. Spread glue on the top (exposed) of the cardboard and fold the lining paper over. The cardboard should be completely covered with the liner. Fold at the dotted lines, fold in the flaps at the sides, and glue the flaps. Make sure the drawers fit into the trunk, then fasten the end flaps with paper clips and let stand until thoroughly dry. Snip off the ends of pins with round, colored heads and push the pins into the drawers to act as pulls. Either reach inside with needle-nosed pliers and bend the ends of the pins, or press a tiny square of $\frac{1}{16}$-inch balsa, spread with glue, over the ends and onto the drawer. It will hold when dry.

A word here. The original trunk had runners glued onto the inside sides, for the drawers to pull out on. We tried this with $\frac{1}{16}$-inch balsa, but found the effect wasn't worth the work. If the drawers fit snugly enough, they will stay in place without the runners.

The hangers hang from a metal gadget at the top of the trunk on the side opposite the drawers. In our hobby shop, we found a brass rod $\frac{3}{64}$ inch in diameter that was exactly to scale. Costs a dime for a foot and is easily bent with pliers. Cut a piece $1\frac{1}{2}$ inches long and fold to make a rectangle $\frac{5}{8}$ x $\frac{1}{4}$ inch. Fasten to the top with tiny doubled strips of the lining paper.

To finish the outside, we used two of the Miniature Mart hinges, No. 261, on the back (fasten first with glue, then with $\frac{1}{4}$-inch escutcheon pins, also from this shop—40 cents for more than you'll ever use) and two catches on the front, No. 3048, from the Miniature Mart. Cut handles using the pattern, from leather or imitation—ours came from an old eyeglass case. Fasten ends first with glue, then with the escutcheon pins. We even put legs on this trunk, using tiny gold beads about $\frac{1}{8}$ inch in diameter, fastened on with $\frac{1}{2}$-inch wire nails or escutcheon pins. Insert the drawers and—*voila!*—your doll lady is ready to travel!

Tongue-Depressor Whatnot

Tongue depressors are a staple in the kit of the miniaturist, serving for anything from roof shingles to floors to stair banisters, and they can be made into some charming pieces of furniture, too, as our whatnot proves.

These handy little sticks have been finished with some sort of filler, presumably to protect young tongues from splinters, so for furniture it might be well to sand them first with a fine paper, then cut them, and, after meticulous dusting, apply whatever stain and/or

The side pieces of the Tongue-Depressor Whatnot may be elaborately carved. Use your imagination (*Photograph by Sam Taylor*).

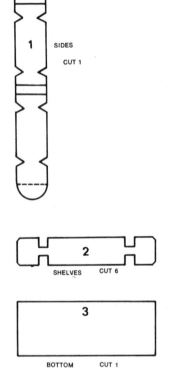

1 SIDES CUT 1

2 SHELVES CUT 6

3 BOTTOM CUT 1

Tongue-depressor whatnot patterns

varnish you prefer. Most tongue depressors are about $\frac{1}{16}$ inch thick, so you must be careful not to sand too deeply. We will need one stick for each side and three sticks for the shelves. Trace the pattern for the sides onto the full-length sticks, then cut the other three sticks in half. Trace the pattern for the shelves onto the sticks also, then cut. This is one place where the fine blade on the Dremel saw will prove its worth; the wood in the depressors is a bit too hard to cut with a knife, but careful sawing will handle the tiny measurements on the pattern easily. The back edge on the notches can then be knocked out with a tiny screwdriver or chisel, tapped with a hammer to drive it in. These cuts on the shelves must be exact, since they are to fit over the sides. The little triangular cuts on the side sticks are merely for decoration. An additional decoration, after the shelves are in, is to glue gold braid down the sides between the shelves. You might want to touch up these cuts a bit with a very tiny brush, in case the wood shows through whiter than the finish on the wood.

Materials Needed for the Tongue-Depressor Whatnot

5 tongue depressors
1 piece wood $1\frac{7}{8}$" x $\frac{3}{4}$" x $\frac{1}{16}$"
Varnish
Stain
Sandpaper
Sobo or Tacky glue

148

To make the shelves, at whatever height you prefer, we slip pattern 2 onto the side pieces, then slip another opposite so they meet snugly in the center. Repeat with the next two shelves, spacing the top shelf so the rounded end of the side stick protrudes about ¼ inch above the shelf. Saw the bottom ends of the sticks off on the dotted line. Glue the assembled pieces in the center of the base and allow to dry.

Steamer Chair, ca. 1900

One of the most charming miniatures I've ever made was copied from the November 1900 issue of a German magazine printed in St. Louis. It was suggested as a gift for a little girl's Christmas, and it was promised that this was an exact copy of a people-sized chair.

Construction is very simple. The side pieces are cut from ⅛-inch balsa or basswood, according to pattern. Crosspieces are ⅛-inch dowels, capped with wooden beads with a ⅛-inch opening. After cutting, the pieces are assembled according to the diagram on the next page.

Materials Needed for the Steamer Chair
1 piece balsa or basswood for uprights, 15″ x ⅛″
   Dowels for crosspieces, 12″ x ⅛″
10 small wooden beads such as for macramé
   Ribbon or linen material, 1½″ x 7″ (about)
   Baby ribbon, ¼″ x 15″ (about)
   6-ply embroidery thread for feather stitching
   Stuffing for pillows

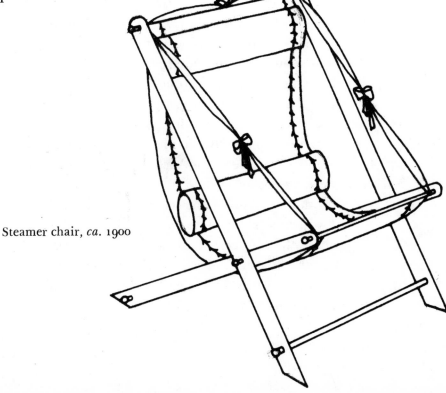

Steamer chair, *ca.* 1900

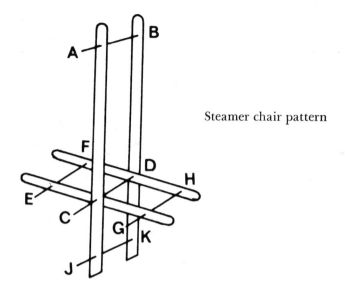

Steamer chair pattern

It is the wealth of ribbons, bows, feather stitching, and tassels that make the piece so endearing. A piece of 1½-inch ribbon is cut to a length that will allow the chair to lean back at just the right angle. After the wooden pieces are cut, punch openings with your awl at the points indicated on the diagram. Measure the dowels carefully to be certain they will be long enough to allow for the 1½-inch ribbon, plus enough on each end to go into the wooden beads. Attach a bead on one end of each dowel and fasten with glue. Slip the dowels through the uprights as indicated on the diagram, then fasten the bead on the other end.

Fasten the top of the ribbon onto dowel *AB* with glue. Bring down to dowel *GH*, allowing enough of a sag to make the chair comfortable for the doll people. Now, cut two pieces of the ¼-inch baby ribbon each about 10 inches long. Thread these on each side over dowel *AB*, down the back and through dowel *GH*. Tie a pretty bow that will hold the chair at just the right slant for relaxing. Repeat on the other side of the chair. The little tassels at the top are simply cord-stitched to the seat material and tied in the center, the edges then fringed— another example of the Victorian tendency to add decoration wherever there was a spot to hold it.

Make a bolster the length of which will fit the width of the seat; it will take about 1½ inches of material. The cushion at the point where the lounger's back will be supported is flat rather than round like the bolster, and will also take about 1 inch of the material. Now you're all ready to relax. Note: Feather stitching and edge stitching may be added to your taste.

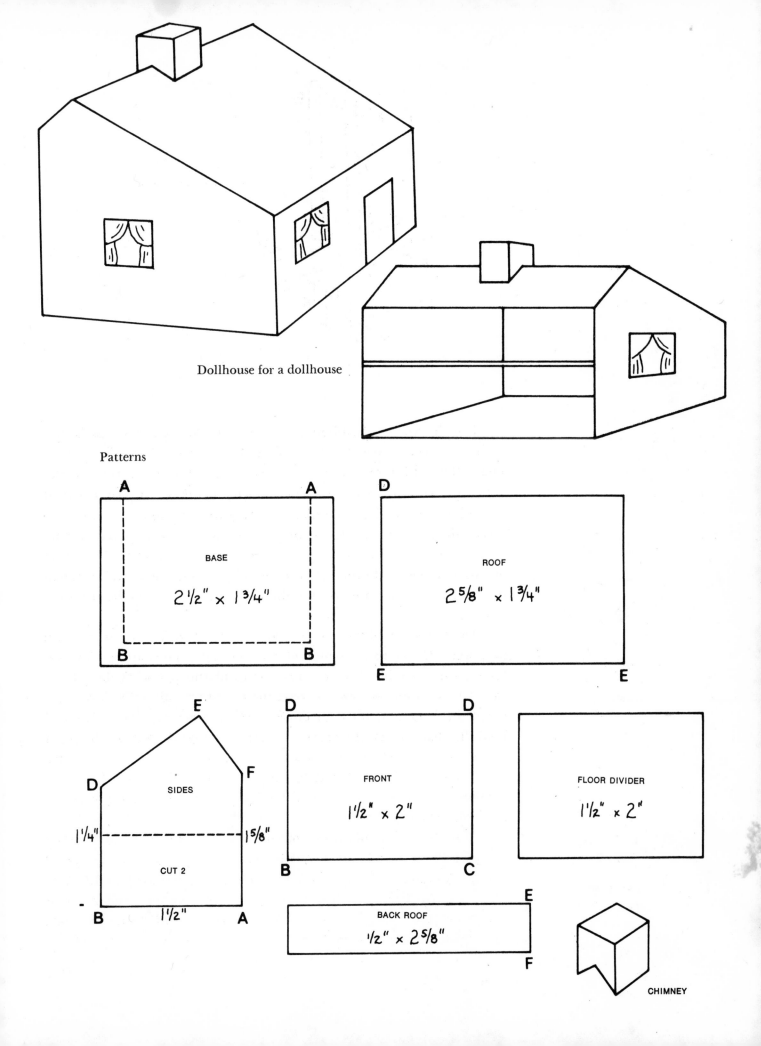

Dollhouse for a dollhouse

Patterns

BASE

A — A

2½" × 1¾"

B — B

ROOF

D

2⅝" × 1¾"

E — E

SIDES

E

D — F

1¼" — 1⅝"

CUT 2

B — A

1½"

FRONT

D — D

1½" × 2"

B — C

FLOOR DIVIDER

1½" × 2"

BACK ROOF

E

½" × 2⅝"

F

CHIMNEY

Dollhouse for a Dollhouse

Every self-respecting doll family does, of course, provide a dollhouse for the children of the group. This one was worked out by Annaleene Gard of Omaha, Nebraska, and is a delight to build because it takes so little time.

The pieces are cut from $\frac{3}{32}$-inch balsa wood, then edges are sanded with an emery board, to smooth them. Paint the front, sides, and partition on both sides, or paint on the outside and wallpaper within. J. Hermes offers a "Tiny Print" wallpaper especially designed for dollhouse dollhouses.

The chimney is simply a $\frac{1}{4}$-inch cube, two opposite sides cut in a peak at the bottom to fit over the roof. Cut the door from the piece marked "front," saving the piece you cut out to make the door. This can be paneled by cutting panels from $\frac{1}{16}$-inch wood and gluing them to the outside of the door.

Paint the door and chimney and stain the roof sections. Glue the front of the house to the base by placing the edge about $\frac{1}{4}$ inch in on the base and in the center. Glue the sides to the base and front, matching *B*, *C*, and *D*. Put the roof in place and glue. Add the back roof, the front door (fasten with a piece of masking tape), and the chimney. The windows are drawn on, or are cut from paper and stuck on. Add the partition last; it will be just a bit large, so that you can file it down slightly to make it fit snugly in the place indicated.

1

2

BOTTOM

Wastebasket and pyrography

Pyrographed Wastebasket

Pyrography, or wood burning, was the rage of the last quarter of the nineteenth century, as miniature crafts are today. Bookends, mirrors, boxes, wastepaper baskets, shelves, whatnots, any decoration the homemaker could dream up was burned into wood. Since the craze lasted well into this century, you may have a wood-burning set tucked away in a closet somewhere and if you have, get it out and put it to work. Many craft shops carry them.

The delicate little wastebasket shown here was made by Constance Simone of the Something Different firm. Make patterns for four of the No. 1 pieces and one of the bottom piece; then, using your emery board, file the two long edges of the panels to a 45-degree angle, being sure the smoothest side of the wood is on the outside. Now shape the curved tops with the emery board, or carve out and then finish with the emery board and sandpaper. Sand the five pieces lightly.

Apply three coats of varnish, sanding lightly between coats. Also apply varnish to a spare piece of basswood on which you can practice.

152

Using your No. 16 blade and your metal scriber, burn in the design on the outside surface of the four panels. (Practice this on the extra piece of wood you've varnished to achieve the finest line which cuts down through the varnish to the wood.) Apply a small amount of varnish stain to a soft cloth and rub it quickly into the scratched design. Immediately rub off the excess. If some part of the design doesn't show, it either needs more stain or to be recut.

Before gluing the four panels together around the square bottom, file the edges of the bottom piece slightly to fit into the slanted sides of the basket.

Materials Needed for the Pyrographed Wastebasket

1 piece basswood, 12″ x 1″ x ⁹⁄₆₄″
Varnish
Pyrography set
Mahogany varnish stain
Elmer's Glue-All or other wood glue
X-Acto knife with No. 16 blade
Emery board
Metal scriber
Extra-fine sandpaper

8 Furniture Crafts

I would hope that the miniaturist who reads this book will be of a purist turn of mind, that is, that he will want to make furniture such as he would like to have in his own house, rather than dollhouse furniture which is merely easy to make. I have made some of those pieces whose instructions begin, "Glue twelve pieces of cardboard together," or words to that effect, and have been enraged by them. If you are really an artist in the miniature world, you want to produce things that are esthetically appealing, that have a finished and professional look, not things which look as though they were turned out by a heavy-handed bungler working with a paring knife.

You can produce dollhouse furniture made from layers of cardboard, but it will not cut to make fine, sharp edges, it will not produce nice rounded corners when sanded, and it generally will not fool even the most casual of dollhouse residents into making them feel that they are keeping up with the Joneses—the dollhouse Joneses, that is.

Mattboard, we hasten to add, is a very different product. This is the very rigid board used in making mats for pictures, and because it is as sturdy as wood, it is often used by miniature makers instead of wood for furniture which is going to be painted. Elspeth of Bethesda, Maryland, whose patterns for furniture are so charming, suggests the use of mattboard in all of her room patterns. The material produces a fine effect, with sharp clear edges, and it even sands well.

For the moment, though, let's consider wood, which is usually used for making furniture. You may be able to produce a few simple pieces of furniture from balsa wood, but basswood, the next softer wood, is far more desirable, and almost without exception the true artists making miniatures say that working with the open-grained hard woods, such as cherry, walnut, and mahogany is no more difficult and produces much finer results. In the previous chapter on wood crafts. we discussed selecting the proper woods. As we begin to turn to furniture, we must think of the finishing of those woods.

154

Close-grained woods, such as maple, pine, fir, gum, and cedar, are easy to work with and do not need to be filled. But the previously mentioned open-grained hard woods should be filled in order to achieve a perfect finish. If the wood is to be stained, this should precede filling —or, there are a number of filler-stain preparations on the market now in a large assortment of colors that give the artist tremendous latitude. The best way to determine whether or not your wood requires filling is to look at it in a bright light, preferably with a pocket magnifier or reading glass, and if the pores look like small cracks, it needs filler. Select the color filler you wish to use and thin with turpentine to the consistency of thick cream or heavy paint. For very coarse-grained woods such as oak, the filler should be thicker and heavier than for less open-grained woods. Thin only as much as you expect to use, then apply the filler with an old but clean paintbrush. Brush it well into the pores of the wood, both with and across the grain. Watch until the surface gloss disappears, perhaps 10 to 20 minutes, then wipe off all surplus filler with a coarse rag, wiping *across the grain,* so as to press the filler into the pores. Use a clean rag to wipe perfectly clean. The next coat should be one of shellac, thinned about 25 percent.

Now the wood must be sanded smooth. Use a fine grade of garnet paper, then wipe clean with a soft cloth. I hope that you will have remembered to select woods with small grains which are in proportion to the scale in which you are working. Large grains never give much of an effect. Sand with progressively finer grades of the garnet paper tacked over a small block or merely folded so that it fits your fingers. For a very fine finish, instead of merely wiping the sanded wood, sponge off with a little water, let it dry, then remove the raised fibers with a light sanding with 7/0 garnet, used dry.

Dollhouse furniture made of twigs enjoyed a great vogue in the last half of the nineteenth century, but it was so fragile that little of it is found today. This photograph, reproduced from *Die Abendschule,* a German paper produced in St. Louis in 1883, shows an entire bedroom set. All you need are twigs in related sizes and plenty of sequin pins.

Wipe the stain on with a rag or sponge, and while still wet, wipe off the excess stain with the grain of the wood, using a dampened cloth or sponge. Wipe the grooves and crevices thoroughly. If the shade is not as dark as you wish, apply a second coat after the first coat has dried, and let it stand for about an hour. When the stain is dry apply a coat of interior clear finish liberally by brush, sponge, or spray (these finishes now come in an aerosol can), then two hours later apply another coat. Where the ends of your wood are going to show, you must take special care, for end grains tend to take up too much stain and become too dark. Moisten all of the end grain with water before applying the stain, or give the end grains a coat of shellac diluted with about 7 parts alcohol. This should prevent the ends from absorbing too much stain.

Cut all pieces, then apply a second wood-finish coat if you wish. Now you are ready to go ahead with the easiest of all furniture pieces, a chest.

Chest

The chest is one piece of furniture that has been prominent in all ages—blanket chests, silver chests, shoe chests, book chests—and every home housed a variety. The one pictured was made by Mr. C. E. Long of Branson, Missouri, a gentleman eighty-eight years young and full of ideas about making miniatures. It was originally intended as a wood chest, to be placed in the kitchen and filled with logs while it served as a seat. It is made of 1/4-inch plywood, but be certain that you use plywood finished on both sides, so that the inside of your trunk or chest will be nice, too. You will find plywood in this thickness available with almost any wood as the veneer—walnut, mahogany, birch, and so on, but you can also buy basswood plywood, which is a little less expensive. But remember that the basswood won't have a grain. It will, however, take enamel or paint perfectly.

Materials Needed for the Chest

1 piece plywood for front, 2 3/4″ x 1 1/8″ x 1/4″
1 piece plywood for back, 2 1/4″ x 1 1/8″ x 1/4″
2 pieces plywood for sides, 1 1/2″ x 1 1/8″ x 1/4″
1 piece plywood for lid, 2 3/4″ x 1 1/8″ x 1/4″
1 piece plywood for bottom, 2 1/4″ x 1 1/4″ x 1/4″
1 piece cardboard, 2 5/8″ x 2 3/8″
1 piece calico print material, 2″ x 3″
2 strips leather for hinges
1 strip leather for hasp, 3 1/4″ x 1 1/4″

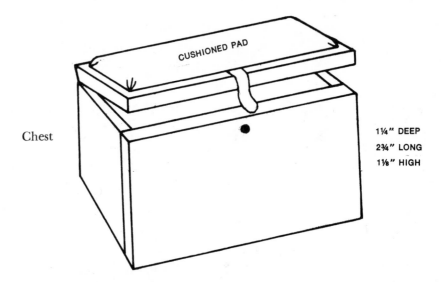

Chest

1¼" DEEP
2¾" LONG
1⅛" HIGH

Cut the bottom, four sides, and the top from the patterns given. Leave natural or stain and finish. Glue the front against the front side of the bottom, let dry; then glue the two sides on the outside edges of the bottom and allow to dry. The back will go on the outside edge of the bottom and against (or between) the two sides. Allow to dry. Finish the top by cutting two small hinges from an old glove or other piece of leather, and tack into place on the outside of the back, through the space between the lid and the back; then glue against the inside of the lid. Fasten a piece of leather to the top of the lid, center, to make a hasp. To pad the top, cut a piece of cardboard ⅛ inch smaller all around than the lid; glue a piece of small-print calico around the cardboard on three sides, then stuff a little cotton inside to pad the seat. Pull the open end around the cardboard and glue into place, then glue the whole thing over the top of the chest and put under a weight to dry. When making a chest with this thickness of wood, you'll find it a great help to tap ½-inch wire nails through the front, sides, and back to the bottom, and on all four corners.

Sofa Couch, ca. 1900

For about a hundred years, roughly from 1810 to 1910, every home had at least two couches or lounges in it; one in the library or den so that Father could lie down and take a nap after his arduous duties at the bank or mercantile store, and one upstairs so that if anyone on that floor felt tired or faint, he or she could lie down without mussing up the bed. The Sears, Roebuck catalogue for 1897 pictures a wide assortment of lounges in fanciful forms and also in strictly utilitarian design. Their best grade at that time cost a mind-boggling $8.00, which made it quite an important piece of furniture. Fine pieces such as this were invariably tufted, so our copy is tufted, too.

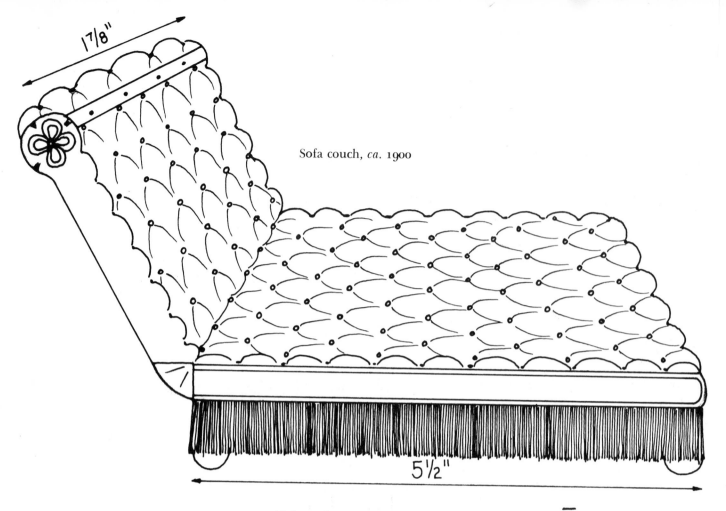

1⁷/₈"

5½"

Sofa couch, *ca.* 1900

Although some double couches were made, they apparently were not very popular; in fin-de-siècle days, two people didn't lie down together on a couch right out in the open for everyone to see. Widths ran from 27 to 38 inches, lengths from 74 to 78 inches, according to the catalogues, but these dimensions proved a bit overpowering in a ¹⁄₁₂-scale dollhouse. We reduced them to a width of 2½ inches (about 30 inches full size) and a length of 5½ inches (about 65 inches full size). This size will look much better in your bedroom. For this piece we worked with balsa wood, since we needed something soft enough for the pins that are used for the tufting to be pushed in.

Materials Needed for Sofa Couch

1 piece balsa wood, 12" x 3" x ½"
1 piece velveteen or soft glove leather, 20" x 4"
1 piece rayon lining material, 8" x 4"
1 piece polyurethane or foam rubber, 8" x 2¼" x ¼"
75 (about) ½-inch brass sequin or escutcheon pins
10 (about) ½-inch wire nails
2 ½-inch bell caps
Wooden beads or brass for legs
½ yard ½-inch gold fringe

158

Cut one piece of the ½-inch balsa 5½ inches long and 2 or 3 inches (whichever you are going to use) wide. Cut another piece the same width and 2½ inches long. Cut two pieces the same measurement as the width of the couch, and ½ inch square. One of these pieces is going to serve as the back round at the head of the couch; the other will be carved to form a wedge that supports the back. On the piece which will be the back round at the head, one side will go against the headrest, so sand off two sharp corners to produce a piece with one flat side and the remainder a nice round. Glue the flat side against the backrest, even with the edge of the backrest. Allow to dry thoroughly.

The second piece, which will be the wedge support, is now cut in half lengthwise on the diagonal, from corner to corner. Using an epoxy or other good quick-drying glue (a regular furniture glue is exactly right), glue one of the angled sides against the back edge of the couch proper. Allow to dry thoroughly. Fit the bottom side of the backrest against this wedge to make certain that the backrest leans backward at the angle you want. Some couches had backs in almost lying-down position; others were halfway between lying down and sitting up. Make sure the bottom of your backrest is going to rest against the top side of the wedge. If it doesn't, sand off each piece until it does, then glue and allow to dry.

Now we need a piece of polyurethane or foam rubber about ⅛- to ¼-inch thick, for the padding of the couch. Lots of this is used by dealers for packing minis, and you should save it so you always have a supply on hand. It may also be purchased in hobby shops. The piece we need is about 8 inches long and 2¼ inches wide. Spread a thin coating of glue over the whole surface of the couch and backrest and around the round at the back. Press the foam into place, then trim if the back piece is too long. Fit the covering material over this, starting at the foot with ½-inch overlap (tack into place with ½-inch wire nails), then fitting the corners closely. Tack into place on the underside along the length of the lounge. When you come to the angle created by the backrest, simply pull the cover material into the crevice quite closely and tack, then fit the cover up over the backrest and around the sides and tack. Where the cover material goes over the padded top of the backrest, simply let the edges stick out; we'll take care of that later. Bring the cover material up over the back of the headrest, folding in the sides so you have a neat fit. Tack quite closely with the escutcheon pins about ½ inch apart, right at the edge of the headrest padding. Then bring the remainder of the cover, edges folded in to fit exactly against the backrest, over the covering at the side and tack thoroughly—with escutcheon pins no more than ⅛ inch apart. Pull the rest of the cover material, sides folded in so it fits exactly over the base of the couch, down over the wedge and over the bottom of the couch base. Tack thoroughly.

Cut a piece of the lining material to fit the underside of the couch, allowing a 1/2-inch fold-in on all sides, and glue to the material on the underside with the edges folded in to fit.

For the tufting, tufts about 5/8 inch apart seemed most in keeping with the size of this couch. Start at the foot of the couch and lightly place pencil dots 5/8 inch apart. Measure the next row and mark off the dots 5/8 inches apart also, but staggered so that one escutcheon pin will be centered above the two escutcheon pins below. Repeat this up over the length and backrest of the couch, pushing the pins in firmly. You'll be amazed at the luxurious effect created by the gold-headed escutcheon pins. Don't go down over the back with the pins, just over the top of the backrest.

At the rounded top of the backrest, trim off the material at the sides so the material coming up the front and over the padded round just meets the material coming in from the back, then run a gathering thread through the cover material and draw tightly. Fasten and knot your thread. Flatten out the bell caps and make certain they fit against the round side of the backrest. Stitch into place with several stitches in each petal, covering the joining of the edges of the cover material.

For legs, you may find brass feet which are about 1 inch in height in shops where supplies for decoupage boxes, etc. are sold. The couch, of course, must be closer to the ground than a chair would be—probably about 1 1/2 inches from the floor. For our couch, we simply strung two 1/2-inch wooden beads on a 1 1/2-inch wire nail (this, with the 1/2-inch depth of the couch body, raises the top of the couch 1 1/2 inches from the floor) and pushed these beads into each of the four corners of the couch as legs. Drop a spot of glue at the bottom so the nails won't slip through the beads.

For the braid or fringe finish around the edge of the couch, fold in about 1/4 inch of the end of the braid or fringe and tack into place at the back edge of the couch, even with the top of the body. Tack along the sides and around the end with escutcheon pins at 1/2-inch intervals. At the end of the other side, fold under about 1/4 inch and fasten with an extra pin.

If you are using fine glove leather for this project (be sure to haunt all rummage sales or old attics for single long or elbow-length gloves made of French kid), you will have no trouble finding elaborate silk braid about 1/2 to 3/4 inch wide to finish the edges of the couch. I made one using brown leather for the covering material and an elaborate silk braid for the sides and end, and another covered with hot-pink velveteen studded with gold escutcheon pins and finished with gold braid and gold bell caps. Lovely!

Eighteenth-Century Wall Tables

Little wall tables with any number of legs were much in vogue during the eighteenth century. Those shown are adaptations of antique pieces in the Williamsburg collection, and make delightful additions to dollhouses. Also, the legs give the beginning miniaturist a chance to try out his carving techniques. The legs on all three tables shown here are carved on the shoulders and at the foot.

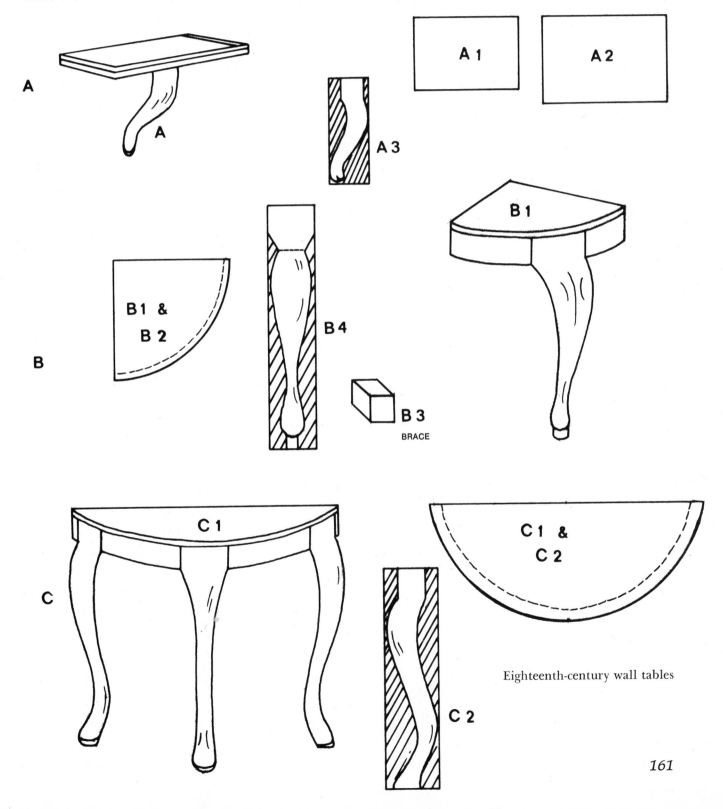

Eighteenth-century wall tables

The leg on the first table is simple enough. Cut a 1½-inch piece of quarter-inch wood, trace the pattern on it with one corner at the right edge. Trim off the opposite corner on a diagonal, then mark the ¼-inch top of the leg, round off the middle corner for the front of the leg, and sand carefully. Instead of trying to build up a gallery at the edge of the table, we simply cut two pieces, ⅛ inch thick and about ⅛ inch smaller on one piece than the other on the front and side edges. Back edge is even. Glue together, then sand as for finishing, and then stain and finish. Do the same with the leg, then glue it to the top at an angle that permits it to rest against the wall. Glue table and leg to the wall.

Table *B* is a corner table built on the same plan with only one leg. Cut a 2½-inch piece of ¼-inch wood the same shape as the top but ⅛ inch shorter on the round side. Cut the leg and carve as shown in *B-2*. When the leg is carved and perfectly finished, cut out an opening in the ¼-inch piece of the top into which the leg will fit. Glue. Glue the top (*B-1*) of the table to the bottom piece with the back sides even, which should put the bottom piece ⅛ inch recessed under the top piece. Note that the edges of the top piece (*B-1*) will be the edge of your table. These should be delicately sanded and rounded just as is done on furniture for adults. The ¼-inch piece to which the top is glued makes the skirt of the table, and should be just as carefully rounded and finished. This may take some care, since you must have the opening in the skirt piece of the exact size to accommodate the leg top.

Since table *C* is a bit larger, we cut from the pattern as given, then cut the underpiece from ½- or ⅜-inch wood to form a base and skirt. After the legs are carved, cut three openings in this piece (shown by the dotted lines on *C-1* and *2*) which will accommodate the legs. Again, the fit here must be precise. When the legs are cut and finished, fit into the openings, then finish the whole piece.

If the table has been stained, varnishing, waxing, or giving it several coats of decoupage glaze will ensure a nice finish. Candle wax is fun to work with too; drip a few drops of wax from an ordinary (uncolored) candle and rub it smoothly into the wood with OO steel wool. This gives a smooth satin finish.

Boston Rocker

A chair that will take you a bit further into the intricacies of furniture-making and finishing, is the Boston rocker pictured here. The Boston rocker, with its high back, painted finish, and gold-stenciled trim, probably came into being about the same time as

Hitchcock chairs, and in the same eastern vicinity. As may be seen, they are relatively easy to make; the only difficulty you will encounter will be placing the spindles in the back and under the arms.

Cut the pieces as shown in the pattern, cutting one of *1*, two of *2*, two of *3*, and one of *4*. Since these are to be painted rather than stained, we will skip the staining step, but the sanding and dusting must be very thorough if the painted finish is to be smooth.

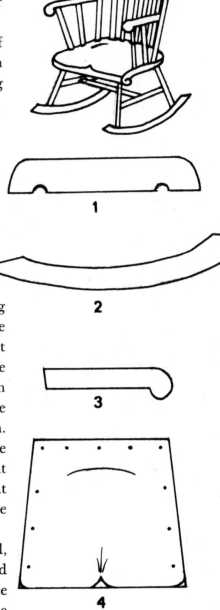

Boston rocker

Materials Needed for the Boston Rocker

2 dowels, 2¼″ x 1/16″
5 dowels, 2″ x 1/16″
4 dowels, 5/8″ x 1/16″
4 dowels, 1⅛″ x ⅛″
2 dowels 1¼″ x 1/16″
⅛″ pine or basswood for other pieces

Cut all pieces from the patterns, then sand carefully, softening the edges of arms, rockers, seat, and tops (particularly the seat, where front and front corners must be nicely rounded, the front in the sort of roll that is typical of the Boston rocker). Back and side edges are left sharp. To make the rolls at the ends of the arms, cut the arms from ⅛-inch wood. They will be ¼ inch thick. From the bottom of the arm and about ¼ inch from the front end, cut upward about ⅛ inch. With your fine knife, run this back to the back of the arm and remove the strip. It will take a little care. Then sand the knobs at the front and the edges of the arms, so they're nicely smooth and rounded. At the top of the back piece, sand well so the top edges are rounded; the wood should narrow quite a little here.

The spindles both in the back and under the arms may be glued, but it takes five hands to hold them until the glue sets. We preferred to use the awl and make 1/16-inch holes about ⅛ inch deep on the under edge of the top (*1*) and the same-sized holes in the seat. Set the two longest dowels at the outside edges of *1* and the five 2-inch dowels evenly across the back, in the holes you've made. Glue to *1* and to the seat.

Following the same procedure, set the dowels with a little glue into the arm pieces and the seat. Glue where the arms meet the back dowels.

Now we will make the rocker assembly. Drill similar holes in the bottom of the seat and at the front end of the rocker, ½ inch from the end at the back. Glue the last two dowels between the legs. Allow to set, then gently fit the ends of the legs into place with glue. I like to tack a ½-inch wire nail through the back spindles and the arms for support, but this isn't necessary and it is a delicate operation; tapping the nails may knock the whole thing apart.

After all is dry, the chair should be painted with a dull-finish black or dark red paint, then a small design painted on the top with gold paint. For a straight chair, omit the rockers and the arms. For a smaller kitchen rocker, make the back about 1/4 inch shorter.

Slipper Chair

Our slipper chair is the perfect project for a beginner, largely because you just can't go wrong on it—and no matter how beginning a beginner you are, it will have a professional look when finished. There is only one pitfall—the cutting of the curve at the back—and we hope to be able to guide you past that.

Materials Needed for the Slipper Chair
Heavy mailing tube of proper diameter
Sobo or Tacky glue
Square (about 8″) of upholstery material
Foam rubber or cotton for padding
Embroidery thread and needle for tufting
Silk fringe for finishing bottom
Silk cord for finishing seams
Cardboard for cushion form
X-Acto knife or jeweler's saw

Choose a very heavy mailing tube—we used one 2 1/2 inches in diameter, largely because that was what we had on hand, and it was in perfect scale. The height of the back will vary with the use to which the chair is to be put; the one shown in drawing B is a fairly formal chair and curves up to an almost-square back which measures 2 1/2 inches across the top—same as the diameter of the tube. In drawing A, however, notice that we have used much sharper curves at the sides; this gives a lighter effect, such as might be used in a boudoir. Drawings C and D show the curves at the sides, the solid line that of the B drawing, the dotted line that of the A drawing. Mark the curves very carefully on the outside of the tube, bringing the side curves down and tapering to a 1 1/2-inch front measurement.

This is a little difficult to cut. After trying all our tools, we found that a sharp paring knife, using a sawing motion, did the best job. The sides of the back should come down in a curve as shown in drawing C at the halfway point of the width of the tube.

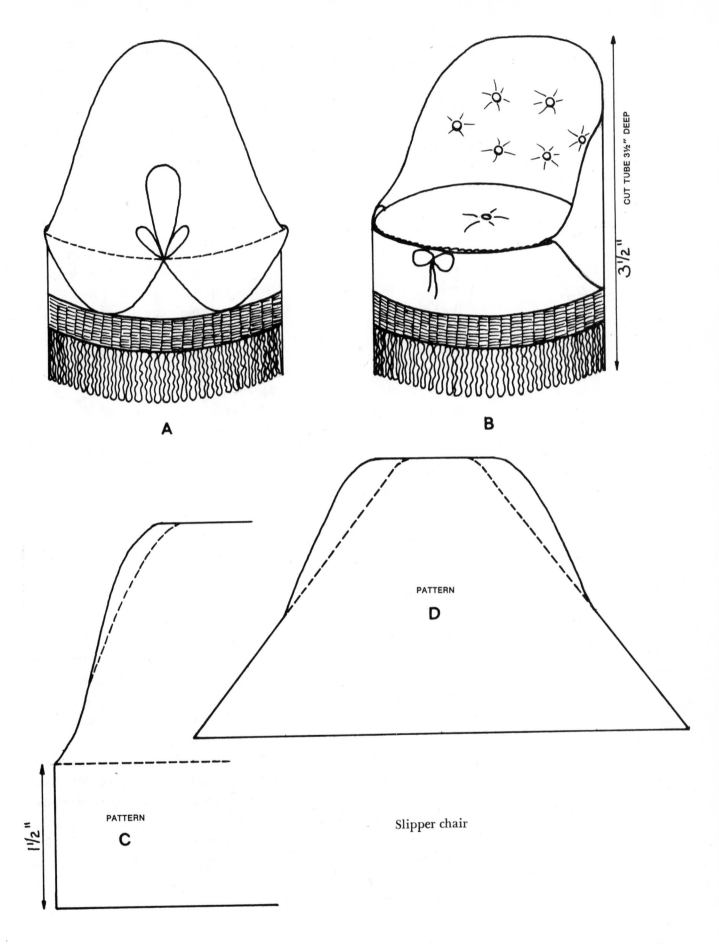

A

B

CUT TUBE 3½" DEEP

3½"

C

PATTERN

1½"

D

PATTERN

Slipper chair

You will need about ¼ inch of padding over the back of the chair; we used both polyurethane, which is the "foam-rubber" sort of material that comes wrapped around the minis you order, and plain sheet cotton such as you buy in a drugstore. Cut according to pattern *D*. Check to make sure it fits the back exactly, then glue. Now, with your awl, make evenly spaced holes in the back to take care of the tufting. Cut your upholstery material *with* the grain, from the same pattern as the padding, allowing ¼ inch all around to take care of the edging. Fold the ¼-inch allowance over to the back and secure with pins, then glue and allow to dry.

Nice ornaments for the tufting may be made with French knots. Use about four strands of a six-strand embroidery floss, bring the needle up from the back, and make three French knots at each hole you've punched. When you have three, bring your needle down to the outside, then over to the next hole and come up and repeat with the knots. You will not need to make a knot on the back until the last tuft; make it as flat as possible so it doesn't show.

Now to finish the back. The pattern (*D*) used for the back will be about ½ inch short on each side because of the curve of the back. Make a paper pattern to fit your tube and cut the upholstery material from the pattern, on the bias, allowing ¼ inch on the top and sides and using the same depth as pattern *D*. Pin this upholstery against the sides, and back over the glued inside of the back, making sure that it fits snugly. Then go over this seam with very tiny overcasting stitches. Glue at the bottom edge.

For the finishing touch, search your notions counters or sewing-supply shops for a tiny cord which harmonizes with your material. We're not going to use it as yet, but you want to have it ready. Choose one about ⅛ inch wide.

Cut a bias piece of the material 1¾ inches wide and 8 inches long. This is the covering for the bottom of the chair. Beginning at the middle of the front, glue it over top and bottom of the frame of the chair, coming around with it to your left. When you encounter the spot where the upholstering of the back joins the top of the front, you will have to make a small slit in the material so you can bring it around the back at the curve, then fold it under and continue on around the back, folding over and gluing as shown by the dotted line on drawing *A*. Where the curve of the back joins the bottom of the chair, make a slit in the material as above, and bring the material around to meet the other end in the front. Clip off, allowing about a ¼-inch fold-in, and glue. We will cover this joint with the cord.

Choose a pretty silk fringe about ¾ inch wide, to finish the bottom. Glue this over the covering, making the seam in the center of the back. Hold until the glue is set. Now glue or stitch the cord from the center of the front around up the sides and over the back, concealing the seams with it. At the front seam, make a pretty little bow from the cord or the thread in the fringe and glue this over the seam. Bring the cord down inside the chair at the point where the back joins the front (where you made the slit in the material) and bring the cord around in a graceful loop to the center of the back. Do the same at the other side, then form a decorative loop as shown in the drawing and glue or tack in place.

Now all that remains is to make the cushion. Cut a piece of cardboard 2⅜ inches in diameter (or a circle to fit your mailing tube). Cut a piece of the upholstery material about ½ inch wider all around than the cardboard. Bring this over the top and pleat so that it lies flat on the bottom of the cardboard; when you have it half folded under, stuff with a little cotton to make it soft and puffy. Finish gluing or tack with needle and thread to secure it. With your awl, punch a hole in the center and, bringing your needle up from the bottom, make a cluster of French knots to secure the tuft, then bring the needle back down under and secure the thread. Push the cushion into the chair. The bottom may be finished with a piece of construction paper glued on, or a piece of material fastened with whip stitches.

Variations on the slipper chair are endless, and as one explores them many other possibilities will suggest themselves. In these drawings, notice that a simple change in the shape of the back of the chair produces an entirely new effect, and attaching cabriole legs at the bottom emphasizes the change even more. In making this chair, we simply cut the bottom of the tube ½ inch deep instead of bringing it to the floor, and the legs were then attached on the inside.

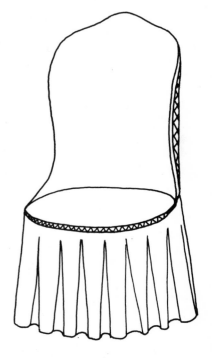

Colonial slipper chair

Queen Anne slipper chair

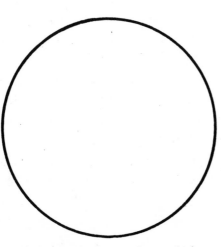

Cushion pattern for slipper chair

For the Colonial version, the top of the back was slanted down sharply but wide enough to give the effect of a wing chair. Here the tube was used full length as in the first slipper chair, but from the seat to the floor a dust ruffle was attached. Simply hem on both sides a piece of material which, when finished, will reach from the seat to the floor. Cut it double the measurement around the chair, then gather, leaving a ⅛-inch heading. This may be attached to the chair by gluing or tacking, and a tiny piece of tape or cord is then glued around to hide the stitches. The padded cushion goes over all.

Beds

The bed, one of the most important pieces in dollhouse furnishing, unfortunately is also the piece that so-called teachers of mini-crafts most often adjure their pupils to make out of a candy box stuffed with paper, or some such thing. That's too bad; a candy box stuffed with paper and using pencils for posts will, it is true, make something that may look like a four-poster bed, but the artist and owner will never take much pride in it.

If you will take time to master our four-poster basic design, however, you will be able to go on to other designs from other periods, to execute pieces which will be a joy to you and to your grandchildren for many years to come.

Materials Needed for a Basic Bed

4 pieces pine, cherry, or mahogany, ½" square, 1" long
2 pieces wood as above, ¼" square, 6½" long
4 pieces wood as above, ¼" square, 5¼" long
1 piece wood as above, 4" x 4" x ⅛"
2 dozen ½" brass nails
2 yards ⅛" sisal (brown) twine
1 piece wood as above for tester (⅛")
Glue
No. 1 X-Acto knife
Stain and varnish
Material for tester

Our bed is made approximately 4 inches wide and 6½ inches long; this is not exactly to scale of the original that was copied, but it is of a size which looks best in rooms on the 1⁄12 scale. Thus, we took the liberty of drawing posts only 5½ inches tall, rather than the 7-foot-tall posts which one generally finds on people-sized beds of this type.

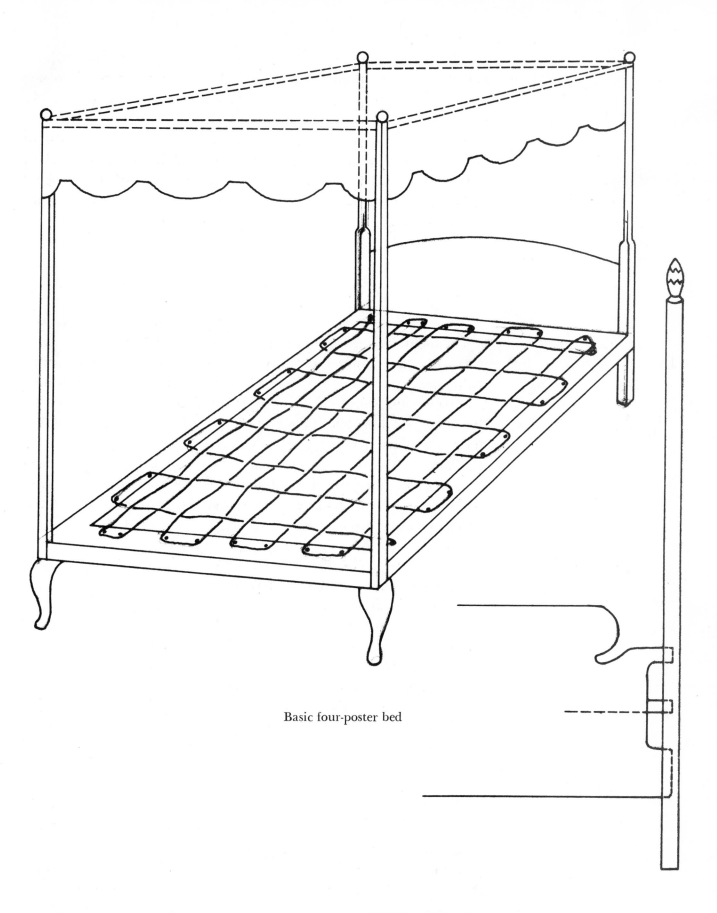

Basic four-poster bed

For the same reason, we have taken the liberty of picturing a bed 4 inches wide; in actuality, a double bed should be closer to 6 inches, a single bed 3½ inches, and the length over 7 inches. It might be wise to cut a cardboard pattern of these sizes and make certain that what you are making is going to be visually pleasing in your room. After all, no one is actually going to *sleep* in this bed, and if the dollhouse father and mother don't fit our measurements, we can just shorten or lengthen their legs. As an example of the variation in commercial dollhouse beds, we have one from Leo Fallert which measures 5 x 6 inches; John Blauer's Victorian bed measures 4¼ x 6¾ inches; and the usual commercial brass bed measures 4½ x 6 inches. Take your pick.

The legs on our bed are 1 inch long—not as much proportionally as real bed legs, but when you add this inch to 5½-inch bedposts, you have a pretty tall piece of furniture. We have made our drawings of the legs about 2½ inches tall, so that the design could be brought out. With a piece of graph paper, you can easily scale down the drawing to 1 inch.

For these, you will need four ½-inch blocks of wood 1 inch long. Our suggestion would be to use pine, cherry, or mahogany. This is your first excursion into carving, and we want it to be easy for you. Use your No. 1 X-Acto knife. Make your big cuts first, then whittle and sand to bring the curves to exactly the right effect. This curve— an undulating line based on the S, or cyma, curve (an unbroken line with a convex and a concave curve)—is typical of all Queen Anne furniture, so it would be well to master it now, since it is also the most simple of furniture designs. William Hogarth, the great eighteenth-century painter, called this curve the "line of beauty."

We'll assume that, while it may have taken a bit of time and you may have wasted a few pieces of wood, you're ready to go on to putting the bed together. You will need two pieces of wood ¼ inch square, cut the length of the bed, and two cut the width. These are left "as is." You will need four strips ¼ inch square and 5½ inches long for the posts. Notice that on this particular bed the back posts were tapered off 2 inches from the bottom, simply cutting in each corner at that point, whittling the wood away a bit above that point, then sanding the remainder of the post so that it slopes in to form a post that almost comes to a point. This shaping is not done on the front posts; in some cases these were elaborately carved, and in some left plain.

Cut the headboard according to one of the patterns given. Now you are ready to finish the pieces (see Chapter 2 for the process). When the finishing is complete and you are satisfied with it, drive in small brass nails (½-inch brass nails are best for this) so that they are protruding about ⅛ inch from the frame, about ½ inch apart. Then glue the frame together, so the four legs form the corners.

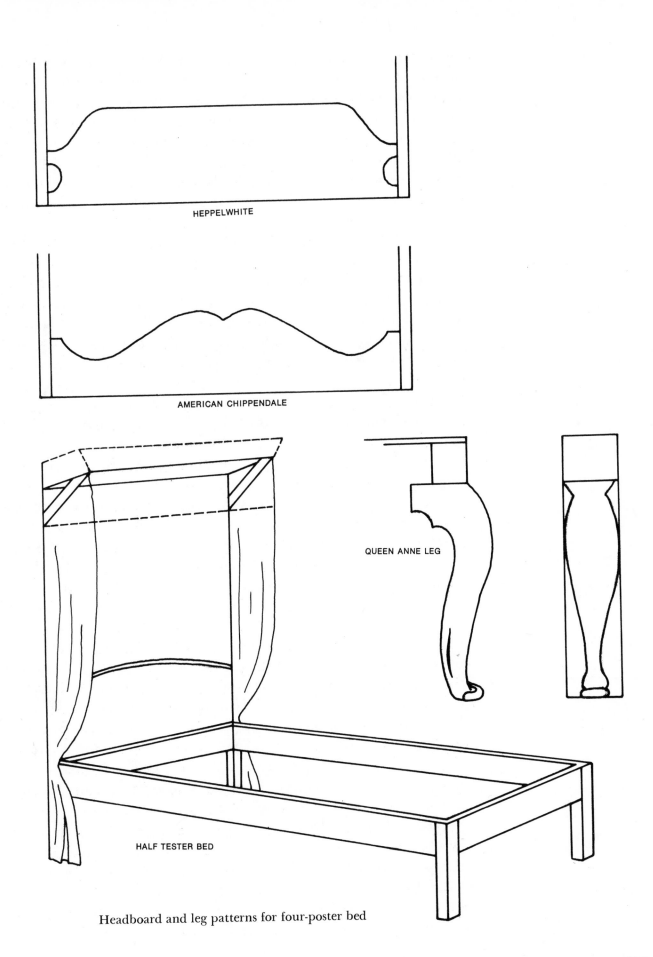

HEPPELWHITE

AMERICAN CHIPPENDALE

QUEEN ANNE LEG

HALF TESTER BED

Headboard and leg patterns for four-poster bed

The making of the rope spring is fascinating. Use ⅛-inch sisal (brown) twine. Tie a good knot in one end around the first nail head on the left side at bottom in the drawing. Bring this across and around the first two nails on the right side, then back to the left side. Notice in the drawing that when this is completed, we draw the twine diagonally to the first nail at the head (top-right corner in the drawing). This is now woven in and out of the crosswise twine until the bed is covered. Finish with a good tight knot at the upper-left corner. Then glue on the posts and the headboard.

The dotted lines around the top of the posts in the drawing indicate that you may go on from here to make a square canopy, or tester, for the bed. In the next drawing, we show a half tester, or half canopy, made by cutting a 1-inch-wide piece of wood, ⅛ inch thick, and gluing to the top of the rear posters. This is braced with two pieces of ⅛-inch-square wood, glued from the tester to the posts. In many old beds with testers or half testers, the headboard was omitted from the bed and a sheet of wood reached from the bed frame to the top of the posts. This was painted, carved, or covered with material to match the tester. Also, on some beds curtains hung from the sides of the tester shelf. There are endless posssibilities, all of them fascinating.

Or you might wish to make the posts from ¼-inch-square posts, sanded and rounded as shown in our inset sketch on p. 171, and carve the little pineapple finials at the top. An alternative to gluing is to cut the notches shown and fit the head- and foot-boards into these.

To make a full tester for a four-poster bed, as we show in the sketch, the frame must first be made as shown with the dotted lines. Then make a simple box of light cardboard, 1 inch deep, for the skeleton of the tester. Cover this by carefully gluing, inside and out, the material which will be used for the bed. Notice from the examples shown that the canopy needn't be simply straight-edged; a series of scallops or Greek rectangles or anything that occurs to you might be used to finish the edges—even tiny ball fringe, braid, or embroidered tape.

If you are planning on bed curtains, make these as long as the bed is high, and wide enough to reach from the back post to the front, doubled. Hem and line (we know a collector who lines every curtain with French voile), then gather up as close as possible and glue to the inside of the canopy. When all is finished, the box need only be settled over the bed, resting on the posts. Some beds of this period also boasted a dust ruffle to match the canopy, glued against the side boards or affixed to the mattress.

The half-canopy bed is even more simple. We have drawn a shelf arrangement which is explained above, but you could construct a little box exactly as described on p. 84 (section on curtains) and glue this at the back edge to the headboard or wall, after covering with the material to be used. The curtains will be made exactly as described for the full-tester bed, and they may be drawn back with a little cord and tassel, or with a tiny strip of the material.

We have drawn a "ghost" sketch of the draperies for this bed in order to show both the basic form of the bed and the form of the dressing. Notice that atop the tester we have a dotted line in the shape of a cornice; this was often used on beds of the era, and is easily made of ¼-inch molding or picture framing, mitered at the corners and glued on three sides (not on the back).

The French sleigh bed shown next is the most fun of all to make. It has never been very widely used either in people-sized houses or in dollhouses, but it does add a cachet of distinction to any arrangement you want to make. The end posts, which form the body of the bed, are seen in many shapes, but we liked the one shown here best; it doesn't have the heavy look that others do. Cut end and side boards according to the pattern shown; the head and foot boards are drawn to scale (3 inches long, or a single bed; we have never seen a sleigh bed in double size) but you may want to cut the side rails a bit longer than the pattern; actually, they should be at least 6 inches long.

If you plan to stain the wood, do this now. However, the period to which sleigh beds belong (last half of the nineteenth centry) boasted a great deal of painted furniture, and this is most appealing in a dollhouse. If you are going to paint, glue the bed together and, when completely dry, apply the paint. Notice that the head- and foot-boards are glued in at an angle.

When paint is the only finish, the artistic craftsman will make an effort to add a border, painted on with a fine brush and acrylic paint, as the French craftsmen did years ago. Another most effective finish is to glue paper to the wood pieces, both sides, just as was frequently done with the outside of the houses and with quite a few pieces of early German furniture. Because something light and delicate seemed indicated for a piece of this period, we used J. Hermes' Fern pattern, which is one of his Super Tiny line of papers and is beautiful in a silver-on-white print, or silver on tan. If you have used ⅛-inch wood for the frame of the bed, glue the paper to the bed pieces and dry under a weight, or use rubber cement, which does not cause wrinkles in the paper. Once dry, the edges of the pieces will have to be finished. If you decide to paint them, this should be done with a solid color before the paper is applied. Another possibility is the use of quilling paper, which now comes cut ⅛ inch wide and in many beautiful shades (see p. 215). This can be glued over the edges of the pieces after the paper has been applied, and it makes a charming finish.

Fern paper for side pieces of sleigh bed

French Sleigh Bed

2 pieces 3″ x 1″ x ⅛″ cherry or mahogany
2 pieces 3″ x 5⁄16″ x ⅛″ wood as above
2 pieces 6″ x 5⁄16″ x ⅛″ wood as above
4 pieces 2″ x 1¼″ x ¼″ wood as above
   Dowels or rounds for bolsters
   Glue
   Paper or paint for covering end pieces
   Materials for upholstering, tufting end pieces

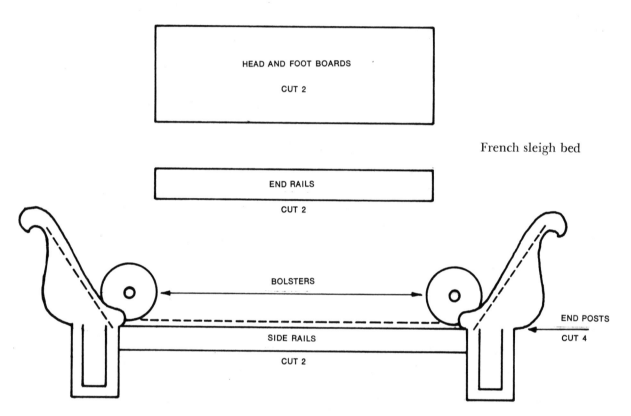

French sleigh bed

Once all this has been accomplished, a bit of decoration on the head- and foot-boards and even on the side rails is in order. If you have a bit of gold or silver cord, probably saved from a gift-wrap cache, this may be applied with glue.

Bolsters are an absolute necessity if one is to carry out the design of a sleigh bed. After much experimenting, we used those cardboard rolls which come on hangers from the cleaner. They slip off easily, but you'll find they are only about ½ inch in diameter—not enough for a bolster. Unless you can think of something else to use in place of these, cut them off in 3-inch pieces, then pad gently with a bit of sheet cotton to bring them to about ¾ inch in diameter. Glue the cotton in place. Now cut material for the bolsters wide enough to go around the bolsters with a 1-inch overlap and long enough to fit the length with a ½-inch hangover (about 4 inches). Tack the material around the bolsters with tiny stitches. Gather the ends and pull together, snipping off any excess length. Fasten with a tiny button or bead.

Springs and mattresses for dollhouse beds must necessarily follow a pattern dictated by the beds themselves. Some craftspeople like to use balsa wood, ½ inch thick, cut to fit the bed. Cover with material just as though you were wrapping a package, and glue or tack.

Others like to use ½-inch polyurethane, covered in the same way. Personally, I like wood used for the spring and a thin ¼-inch-thick piece of polyurethane used for the mattress, covered with ticking or harmonizing material. If you want to invest the time, it is very simple to carry realism a bit further and "button" the mattress by using three strands of embroidery cotton and making a French knot on one side, putting the needle through, then making a French knot on the other side. Slip the needle through the mattress material to the place for the next "button," and proceed as before.

Basic Wing Chair

Our Hepplewhite wing chair (English, *ca.* 1790) is a great piece for the mini-furniture-maker: first, because there is no wood on it to be finished other than the legs and, second, because it may be adapted to many designs. Make it twice as wide and use it as a sofa. Make it with or without the rolled arms shown, although the rolled arms are a Hepplewhite mark. Make it with straight tapered legs or with carved cabriole legs; these require little wood and will give you some fine experience in carving. They will also change your design to Queen Anne.

Materials Needed for Basic Wing Chair
1 piece 6" x 12" x ⅛" mattboard or balsa wood for frame
1 piece 10" x ¼" x ¼" cherry, birch, or mahogany for legs
   Cotton for upholstery
2 upholstery tacks with fancy heads
1 piece upholstery material, 9" x 15"
   Glue
   Stain
   Varnish
1 piece light cardboard, 6" x 15"

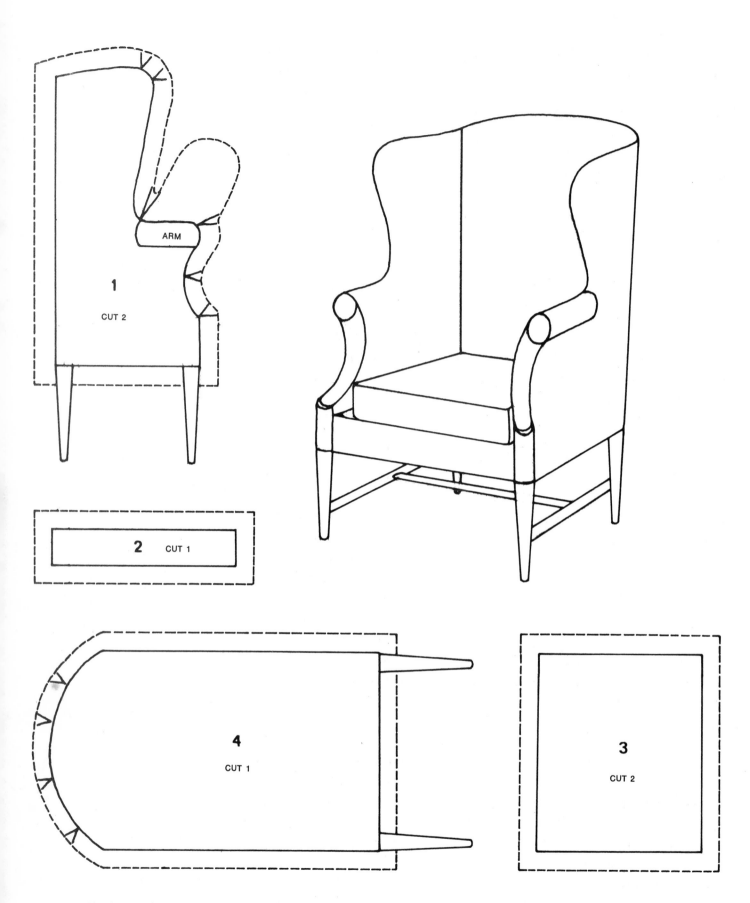

1

CUT 2

ARM

2 CUT 1

4

CUT 1

3

CUT 2

Basic wing chair

The frame of the chair may be a 1/8-inch thickness of mattboard, balsa or other woods, or cardboard, although we definitely prefer wood for all furniture bases. In the case of our chair, we used balsa wood because this is easy to work and has a feeling of great stability and it will, in any case, be covered.

Cut a pattern on the solid lines and cut the frame from 1/8-inch wood on this pattern. Cut a pattern for the legs from 1/4-inch wood and taper them nicely. Cut two pieces of pattern *1* and one of pattern *2*. Cut one of pattern *4*. None of these is cut with legs; the legs are added later. Cut, also, two of *1* and one of *4* from light cardboard such as shirt board or the back of a writing pad. Make two little rolls of cotton about the thickness of a pencil, rolling them very hard and firm. They should be as long as the arms, as shown on pattern *1*. Glue them to the outside of each No. *1* piece.

Now cut your upholstery material about 1/8 inch larger than the pattern, as shown on the dotted lines. Lightly pad the inside of the wood or mattboard pieces *1* and *4* with a thin layer of cotton, bringing the padding within about 1/4 inch of the edge of the pattern. Fit the upholstery material over this and bring the 1/8-inch margin over to the back and glue. Fit the upholstered pieces of *4* and *1* together and glue firmly on the inside where they meet. Secure the joint on the outside with strips of Mystik tape cut to fit.

Now we will cover the light cardboard, which is to be the outside of the chair. Fit the upholstery material over the No. *2* piece and glue. Place this against the No. *2* piece, which has been cut from wood or mattboard, and glue and let dry. Fit the No. *2* piece between the two sides of the chair in front. Check to make certain the seat is absolutely square. Glue the No. *2* piece in place, then cut a piece of light cardboard from pattern *3*, measuring first to be certain that this fits the seat of the chair from the back of the No. *2* piece to the joint at the No. *4* piece. This need not be upholstered. Glue into place.

The cushion of the chair is made by cutting two pieces of No. *2* from light cardboard and two pieces the same width (1/2 inch) the length of the chair from front to back. Cover the four pieces with material on one side only, lapping and gluing to the inside. Fit the pieces together to form the four sides of the cushion and fasten with tape on the inside—or stitch the pieces together with tiny stitches. Cut two pieces of pattern *3* from the material and fit over this frame, leaving one side of the bottom open. Stuff lightly with cotton, then stitch the open side with tiny stitches.

When you are upholstering the inside of No. *1* and No. *4*, notice that the pattern allows enough material to come down over the padding on the arm. Work this into place and glue, then work the material over the curved fronts of this piece and glue. Notches cut as shown on the pattern will facilitate working the material around the curved edges.

You will need another set of pieces to cover the light cardboard, which is going to form the back of the chair. Cut these and stretch over the cardboard; the cardboard should be cut out around the arm pieces, which have been covered from the inside. You are ready, then, to glue this covering on the back and sides of the chair for a nice finish.

Legs and stretchers may be cut from ¼-inch cherry or birch and tapered as shown in the drawing. The front legs were sometimes tapered a bit more than the back for a lighter appearance. The stretchers are also cut from ⅛-inch wood. After the legs have been stained and finished and glued to the bottom of the chair, measure exactly for the stretchers and cut these. Stain and finish them before gluing to the legs.

It is much easier than it sounds, and much easier than these detailed instructions would indicate. Finish off the arms with a fancy upholstery tack stuck in the front of each. Some miniaturists like to glue a very tiny braid down the front of the arms and around the bottom, just as we find on large chairs. Another possibility is the use of calico or small-patterned cottons for the upholstery, in which case you would omit the padding on the arms, and glue a ruffle or pleated piece around the bottom.

Chippendale Footstool, ca. 1760

The occasional seat, or bench, shown here is an exact copy of an English antique in the Williamsburg collection, made about 1760 and attributed to Chippendale. It makes a fine companion piece to the Hepplewhite wing chair shown as our "basic" design, and the legs may be tapered just a bit to match it more completely to the chair. It will be just the right height to push up against the chair to form a chaise, or can be used anywhere in the dollhouse.

Materials Needed for the Chippendale Footstool
1 piece mattboard 2″ x 1″ x ⅛″
1 piece ¼″ x ¼″ x 6″ cherry, birch, or mahogany
1 piece ¼″ x 6″ x ⅛″ wood as above
Light cardboard for cushion
Upholstery material for cushion
Glue
Stain and varnish for finishing

Cut two pieces of pattern *1* of ⅛-inch mattboard, balsa, or cardboard. Cut a piece of upholstery material following the dotted lines

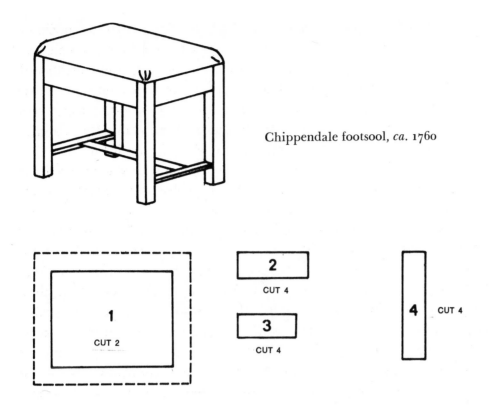

Chippendale footsool, *ca.* 1760

(petit point is used on the original) and fit this over one of the pieces, folding the excess material over and gluing on three sides. If you are making petit point to cover this little bench, be sure to allow about two rows of stitching outside the pattern to cover the puffing of the upholstery and about two meshes of canvas to allow for folding under. Fit it loosely. Stuff in on the fourth side a bit of cotton so the stool looks comfortable, then glue this end over too, and set to dry. When it is dry, glue to the second piece of base material. This is the top of your bench.

Finish all the remaining pieces carefully; the legs, as we said, may be tapered a bit to match the basic chair. When these are finished, glue pieces of pattern 2 to the side of a leg on each corner. Pieces 2 and 3 should be cut from $\frac{1}{8}$-inch wood; pattern 4, the legs, should be cut from $\frac{1}{4}$-inch wood and sanded down before finishing. When the legs are firmly dry on the No. 2 pieces, check the No. 3 pieces to make certain they fit exactly between the legs on front and back. When they do, glue these into place also. Measure the third of the No. 2 pieces and make certain it fits exactly between the two stretchers, which are side pieces. Glue into place. Glue the last No. 2 piece diagonally across the back of the seat, to furnish reinforcement. When dry, spread a thin line of glue along the top of the frame and fit the seat onto this.

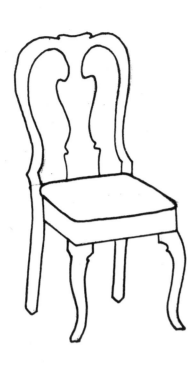

Queen Anne dining or straight chair, *ca.* 1735

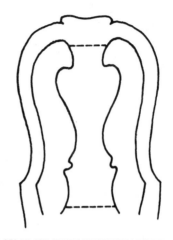

CUT SPLAT SEPARATELY BETWEEN DOTTED LINES

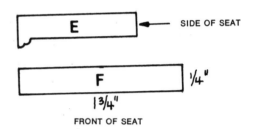

E ← SIDE OF SEAT

F 1/4"
1 3/4"

FRONT OF SEAT

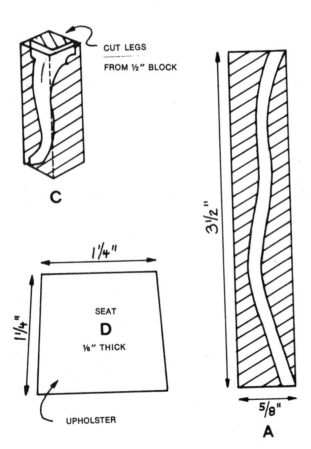

CUT LEGS
FROM 1/2" BLOCK

C

1 1/4"

SEAT
D
1/8" THICK

1 1/4"

UPHOLSTER

3 1/2"

5/8"

A

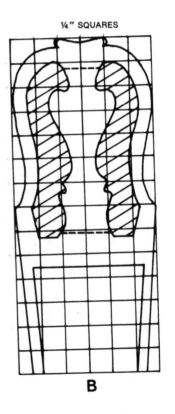

1/4" SQUARES

B

Queen Anne Dining or Straight Chair, ca. 1735

This basic straight chair in the Queen Anne style may be simplified by the use of a straight splat or made more elaborate by carving the crest rail deeper. Additional carving on the knee and leg looks nice, too.

Materials Needed for the Queen Anne Straight Chair
(One chair)

1 piece wood for back, 3½" x 1½" x ⅝"
2 blocks for front legs, 1¼" x ½"
1 piece wood for seat reinforcement, 4" x ¼" x 1/16"
1 piece cardboard or 1/16" wood for seat
Small piece velvet or damask for upholstery
Stain and varnish for finishing

Cut out the back from a strip of wood ⅝ inch thick by 1½ inches wide, using figure *A* for the curve and back legs and figure *B* for the back. The splat may be cut with the back if you have a saw that will handle this, or it may be cut separately along the dotted lines, then glued in.

Cut three strips of 1/16-inch wood as long as the sides and front of the seat and glue these on the wrong side at the bottom of the seat strips *E* and *F*. Cut the legs from a ½-inch block of wood as shown. Do any carving you wish to use. Now finish all pieces; while they are drying, cut out the seat pattern and then the seat from 1/16-inch wood or cardboard. Upholster with thin velvet or damask, being certain to make neat corners. Put the chair together with glue; the legs will be supported by gluing against the 1/16-inch strips at the bottom of the sides and front. The seat will rest on these. Stain and finish all pieces before gluing together.

Pedestal Dining Table, ca. 1820

This is truly a basic design from which all manner of tables might be made. Omit the pedestals, round the ends to an oval, add four tapered legs, and you will have a Hepplewhite design. Cut the table round instead of rectangular, use only one pedestal, and the whole thing has a very Victorian look. We cut our table to divide in the middle, although we have never been able to figure out why anyone needs an extension table in a dollhouse, where there is rarely room to spare.

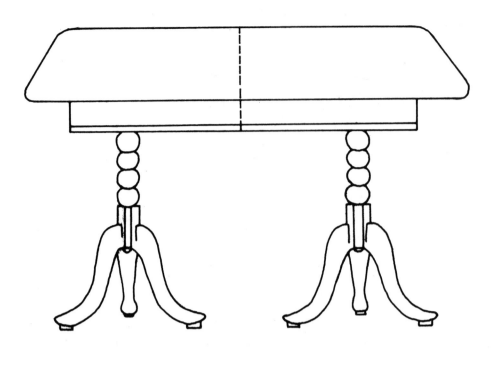

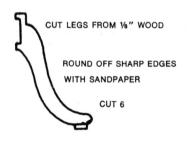

CUT LEGS FROM ⅛" WOOD

ROUND OFF SHARP EDGES
WITH SANDPAPER

CUT 6

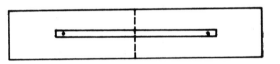

Pedestal dining table, *ca.* 1820, with wood channel for extension table

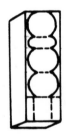

CUT FROM ⅜" SQUARE 1⅓" LONG

CUT 2

ROUND OFF BASE

Materials Needed for the Pedestal Dining Table
Any furniture wood—mahogany, walnut, oak, maple
1 piece for top, 7¾" x 3½" x ⅛"
1 piece for apron, 7½" x 3¼" x ¼"
2 pieces for pedestals, 1⅛" x ⅜" x ⅜"
6 pieces for legs, 1½" x 1" x ⅛"
6 tiny brass beads for leg tips
Stain and varnish for finish
Glue
Sandpaper
1 small piece wood for slide extension, 2¾" x ½" x ⅛"

If, however, you yearn for an extension table, cut the top of ⅛-inch wood 7¾ inches long and 3½ inches wide. Cut the facing from ¼-inch wood ⅛ inch smaller all the way around. Cut to the shape you prefer or round off corners, then cut each piece in half crossways. With your Dremel Moto-Tool or with an X-Acto knife cut a tiny beading around the edge. With the Moto-Tool, it is easier and more uniform. Glue the top to the facing, dry under pressure, then finish with a furniture finish.

Cut the pedestals from ⅜-inch-square wood cut 1⅛ inches long, mark off ¼ inch at the bottom of the piece and round off the remainder according to the pattern. If you have a jeweler's lathe, this is no problem. If you have a Dremel Moto-Tool, you can hold the square ¼ inch at the bottom with a needle-nosed pliers and shape the turnings with the smallest grinding tool. If you have neither, simply hold with the pliers and file the turnings with a fine hack-saw blade.

Fit the legs against the round quarter-inch at the bottom of the pedestals and glue. Be sure the legs are evenly spaced and level at the bottom so the table is solid. Finish the bottom of the pedestals with a dark bead glued in the center where the legs meet.

If you want an extension table, cut a piece of ⅛-inch wood 2¾ inches long and ½ inch wide. In the very center make a cut through this piece to within ½ inch of each end (see pattern). Fit the two halves of the table together and glue the end half of this piece of wood to one side of the table. Tap a brass tack ½ inch or ⅝ inch long through the cut in the wood, then allow to dry. Fit the other half of the table against the glued half, then tap a tack through the cut in the wood, but not through far enough to make it tight. Test the table to make certain that it will slide open on the tack; the tack must be at a point where it will hold firm but still slide. If you wish to make an extension board for the table, cut wood 1 inch wide, and face and bevel exactly as you did the table itself.

Cigar-Box Furniture, ¼-Inch to 1-Inch Scale

While there is some small-scale furniture coming into the market—some Limoges from France, pewter from Mexico, and polished wood from England in the ¼-inch scale—you'll find it an interesting test of your skill to make your own, as Charlotte Pack does. She writes that she uses ¼-inch-thick wood, but we think that's too heavy. In making the drawings below we used her dimensions but cut from ⅛-inch and sometimes ¹⁄₁₆-inch basswood.

Popsicle sticks work fine and the wider tongue depressors are very useful; these are made from orangewood and are quite hard. These

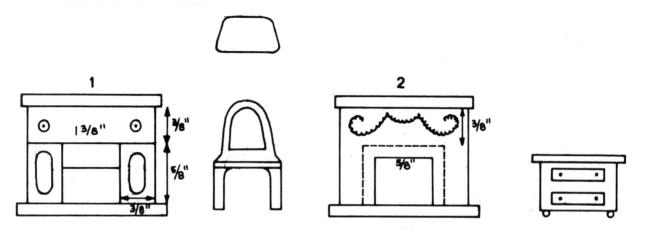

Cigar-box furniture, ¼″ x 1″ scale

are usually ⅜ inch wide and ¹⁄₁₆ inch thick; the rounded ends are fine for chair backs. A single bed is two sticks wide—a double bed, three.

Notice that fireplace No. *1* requires two pieces ⅝ inch long and one piece 1⅜ inches for the mantel, plus a tiny piece the same length to set atop the mantel for a shelf. No. *2* is reversed—two pieces 1⅜ inches long for the sides and one piece ⅝ inch wide for the middle. A tiny strip of wood should be glued under the shelf to give depth. A piece ½ inch wide cut a bit longer than the mantels and covered with brick or rock-effect paper makes the base. Do the two sides first, then the long front piece will hide the cut-off ends. The dotted lines on figure *2* indicate a facing for the fireplace, and the fireboxes may be lined with brick paper.

The two round pieces on No. *1* are two tiny metal buttons glued on; the oblong pieces are wood, cut and stained. The "carving" on the front of mantel No. *2* is a piece of heavy lace glued on, then painted over. Another idea is to paint the fireplace white and achieve a marbleized effect with black squiggles from a ball-point pen.

A good use for the sections between the two ends you have cut off is for chair backs. Cut the back long enough to reach the floor (1⅛ inches, as in our drawing) then cut out the center to make two back legs. Cut two front legs as shown and glue to the chair seat as shown. When dry, glue to the back and paint.

For a tiny dresser, Mrs. Pack cuts a piece of balsa ⅜ inch thick by ¾ inch wide, then cuts a piece ½ inch long (equivalent to 2 feet, the height of the dresser or washstand). The ¾-inch measurement is the length of the piece. With a ball-point pen, rule in the two drawers. Use ¼-inch copper nails for drawer pulls. (About the only way to manage this is to hold the nails with your long-nosed pliers.) We used tiny brown beads for feet. Mrs. Pack suggests that a piece of wood from front to back will do nicely if set just a bit from the edge. A ⅜-inch-wide piece, marbleized, makes the top. A back splashboard adds interest if the piece is to be a washstand. Increase the height for a chest of drawers—the length to make a kitchen range.

One piece of advice from Mrs. Pack is most important. She suggests that any little piece of wood you cut from other miniatures-in-the-making should go into a little box. You'll be surprised, she assures us, at how often you'll find just the right-sized piece in this miniature lumber pile for your next piece of furniture.

Victorian Screen

One of the handsomest dollhouse screens we've ever seen was the one pictured below, which won second prize for Mary Helen Beran in the 1974 contest for the Most Original Miniature which is staged annually by *The Dollhouse (and Miniature) News.* We liked it first of all because it could be made of almost any scraps in your workbox and, second, because it adapts itself to a wide variety of materials. Last, but most important to some of us, it looks exactly like a people-sized screen, rather than like a miniature. For a ½₂-inch-scale screen, measured to an actual antique in a Victorian home in St. Louis, cut three pieces of needlepoint canvas the desired width and height. Ours was

Victorian screen

cut in two panels 1⅞ inches wide, 4¾ inches long, and one panel 1¾ inches wide, 4¾ inches long.

Materials Needed for the Victorian Screen

5 strips basswood molding, 24″ long
4 hinges SR 39*
  Pins for the SR 39 hinges
  Needlepoint canvas
1 metal filigree piece J5914
2 metal filigree pieces H686
  Velvet, embroidered ribbon, or wallpaper for panels
  Embroidered or cut-out center design for panels
  Plain gold paint in spray can
  Gold fleck paint
  Wood filler
  Elmer's Glue-All or Quik Set epoxy
  X-Acto knife
  Scissors
  Needle
  Paint brushes for fine work

Using your X-Acto knife, cut tiny molding for the first side to fit the edges of each panel so that the ends are mitered. Before gluing the molding to the panel, set the hinges about 1 inch from the top and bottom on the center panel at the edge of the panel and push the pins in to hold them in place while gluing the hinge edges. Make sure not to let the glue set so the hinges won't move.*

Glue the molding down all around each panel, over the hinges so only the hinge mechanism shows. Hold until dry. When the entire screen has dried turn over and cut molding with mitered corners for the reverse side. Glue the molding on and hold until dry.

Now, using the filigree pieces (many such are available in hobby shops and art stores), set these on top of one side of the molding. Glue on and hold. Holding is important here, since weighting with a book or such procedure will not give an even pressure. Elmer's Glue-All works fine, but Quik Set epoxy would probably work faster. Fill in the spaces in the mitered corners and other gaps (these caused by your mitering not being perfect) with wood filler.

* Author's Note: These tiny hinges are very hard to find. The Miniature Mart in San Francisco is probably the best market. Tiny pieces of cloth or masking tape will serve as hinges and will be covered by the molding used as a finish.

Spray gold paint or other desired color over the whole screen including the filigree pieces (some sort of coating is necessary on the filigree to prevent later darkening which makes polishing necessary). If you wish the gold-fleck finish, apply it with a brush.

Cut pieces of velvet, heavy ribbon, wallpaper or, if you wish, needlepoint. Fit the pieces of material or paper over the canvas backing before attaching the molding. If you wish to needlepoint one or more panels, do this now. Don't attach the molding over the needlepoint canvas; simply cut the canvas to fit the space with an allowance for the molding to come right up to and meet the canvas.

Add any final touches like embroidery designs or edging on the first side before covering the panels on the second side.

We experimented with the possibility of tufting, and found this to make a delightful screen. In this case, fit the fabric over a piece of $\frac{1}{8}$-inch polyester foam with about $\frac{1}{8}$ inch of the fabric beyond the foam all around. Glue down on the canvas with the $\frac{1}{8}$-inch edge of fabric against the canvas where the molding will go, then glue the molding on, and finally, with embroidery thread, draw through one side, make a French knot, and end the knot on the opposite side. Then cover the opposite side.

9 Metal Crafts

New England Betty Lamp, ca. 1840

Our Betty lamp was designed and executed by William Burritt Wright, known as the Little Old Man. The Betty lamp consisted of a shallow dish that could be oval, round, or triangular. It was made of various types of metals, such as pewter, iron, brass, tin, or even silver. A "nose" protruded from one side of the dish, and the bowl was filled with tallow or grease. A wick was then made by using a twisted rag or a rush, placed in the grease and pulled through the "nose" until a short end was visible. The visible end was then lighted.

Betty lamps were often hung on a chair but the lamp presented on the next page was considered to be a great modern improvement. It had a wick tube within the reservoir, and was much cleaner and more desirable than the open-wick Betty lamp. From about 1800 to 1840, whale oil was probably burned in it.

Materials Needed for the Betty Lamp

1 soft-drink can or 36-gauge copper sheet, $2\frac{3}{4}''$ x $1\frac{9}{16}''$
1 piece sheet lead, $1\frac{3}{4}''$ x $1\frac{3}{4}''$ x $\frac{1}{16}''$
1 16-gauge copper sheet, $1\frac{3}{4}''$ x $\frac{3}{16}''$
1 $\frac{1}{16}$ o.d. round brass tube, $4\frac{1}{2}''$ long
1 piece 19-gauge copper wire, $1\frac{3}{4}''$ long
1 piece 26-gauge wire, $2\frac{1}{2}''$ long
1 straight pin, $1''$ long
1 piece heavy sewing cotton, $2''$ long
   Solder and soldering iron or Krazy Glue
   Drill and No. 20 bit
   Tinsnips or scissors
   Dividers and compass
   Small pliers
   Awl or round, pointed four-penny nail

Bill Wright advises that he finds such projects are much easier to bring to completion if the artist will read through the directions

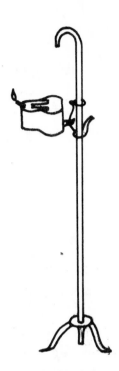

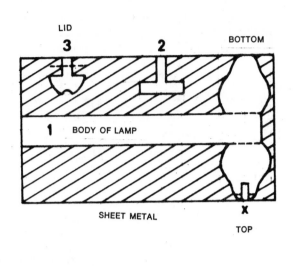

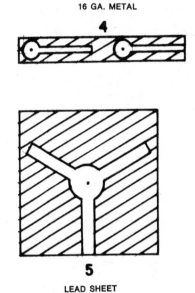

The New England Betty lamp, *ca.* 1840

completely, then cut out the pieces, then put them together in a sort of "dry run."

Here is more advice that will serve the miniaturist well in other projects too:

Aluminum cans for sheet metal should not be used if parts are to be soldered. And remember that sheet metal from cans is some times hard to cut without a good pair of tinsnips. If you have had trouble working with sheet metal, try 36-gauge copper tooling foil, which can be cut with ordinary scissors. The lead sheet used by Bill Wright was salvaged from the liner of an old shower. He preferred this to provide weight to the base of the mini-lampstand. This writer was given a nice piece of lead sheet which was intended for cutting into small pieces to be used in weighting fishing flies. If you cannot obtain lead sheeting, use any sheet metal but spread the lamp legs wider—a bit out of scale.

Any sheet metal may be substituted in place of copper if one is going to use glue instead of solder. This miniaturist finds heavy-gauge aluminum great to use, as it cuts much easier than copper.

The 1/16-round brass tube with .014-inch wall was purchased from the Brookstone Company, Peterborough, New Hampshire 03458; you should have their catalogue, since it lists many other hard-to-get tools for miniature crafts. Any friendly electrician will let you have short pieces of copper wire for the asking. When stripped of insulation, this copper wire in various gauges can be used in many ways. This project calls for a short piece that will fit in the brass tube. Any wire will do for the 26-gauge wire specified in the requirement list, just so it is fine enough to permit both ends to go into the brass tube at once. Try for a straight pin that will fit snugly into the brass tube; the closer the fit, the better.

Cotton thread is required for the wick. For our purpose, two strands in the brass tube works well. Other threads simply will not work.

Remember not to use Krazy Glue for the lamp if the lamp is to be filled and lighted. And *never* use Krazy Glue until you have read the directions. Do not allow children or pranksters to have it. It can be dangerous.

Putting It Together

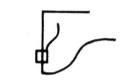

Form of holder for Betty lamp

Clean both sides of all metal and trace the patterns on p. oo on the appropriate pieces. Cut out all parts; you will have five parts. With the No. 20 drill bit in the Dremel Moto-Tool make two holes in part *4*, shown as dots on the pattern. Then shape part *4* to form the holder for the lamp. Try to match this form; the holes should be lined up in a straight line to admit the brass tube post. Part *3* should be placed on the inside back of the holder and the tabs folded around the holder. Shape this to act as a spring when in place on the post. Do not place this assembly on the post at this time.

Now, cut two pieces of the round brass tube, one piece ¾ inch long and the other 3¾ inches long. Drive a pin through part *5* at the center point. Put a drop of glue on the pinhead and allow to set. Then turn the part over so the pin is upright, and put a drop of glue on the point of the pin so it runs down the shaft. Slide the long piece of brass tube onto the pin and press it tightly on the base part (*5*). Shape the three legs as in the illustration of the completed lamp on p. 189.

Shape part *1* by bending the bottom on a fold line at right angles to the body. Curve and shape the body around the bottom until it meets the back of the lamp. Solder, if you intend to put oil in the lamp (or glue if you do not intend to light the lamp), around the edge where the body and the bottom meet. Fold the top down to meet the sides and after bending the tabs up at right angles on the fold lines, solder or glue around the top edge. After this is dry place a piece of 19-gauge wire about ½ inch long in the tab fold line and fold the tabs over the wire to leave a small space marked *X* on the pattern. Into this space slip the tab of the lid (part *3*) which has been bent on the fold line to a right angle. After the tab is through space *X*, fold it forward to make a hinge for the lid.

Solder or glue the body of the lamp to the holder and slip the entire unit on the post. It should be at right angles to the post and

190

level with the floor or base. A small piece of 19-gauge wire may now be pushed in the top of the tube post until about ¼ inch extends from the top. If all is straight and level, disassemble and spray-paint the stand and lamp.

While waiting for everything to dry, take a ¾-inch piece of brass tubing and pass two ends of a thin piece of wire through it so a loop is formed to pull the wick through the tube. There should be a double strand of wick in the tube with ³⁄₃₂ inch of the wick at one end of the tube and ¼ inch at the other. If your lamp and stand are now dry, place the lamp on the stand and turn the ¼ inch of wire at the top of the post to a crook shape.

Now, to use Bill Wright's words, prepare for the big moment. Open the lid of the lamp and place the wick tube in with about ¼ inch of the tube extending beyond the nose of the lamp. Fill the reservoir about three-quarters full of lamp oil—whale oil is very hard to find these days. Close the lid. Secure an ember from your fireplace and light the wick. Use a match if embers are not available. The flame should be about the size of this letter *O*. Absolutely no larger, or the flame will be out of scale. The flame may be made larger or smaller by lengthening the wick or shortening it. For the best adjustment, pull a bit more of the wick through the tube than is needed, then cut off the excess to the proper length. CAUTION: *Never* allow the lamp to burn dry.

Hammock

Materials Needed for the Hammock
1 piece netting from a frozen ham or turkey
   Heavy cord for tying
2 pieces 1½″ x ¼″ x ⅛″ balsa
6 inches materials to make 2 pillows the width of the hammock
1 1″ S-hook
1 ½″ S-hook
1 heavy coat hanger for frame
   Varnish for "spreaders"
   Pliers to form end supports

No matter what the period of your dollhouse, a hammock is almost a required accessory. Hammocks were especially popular in the Victorian days, although they originated in Roman days and have been in use ever since. Ours is one that you can have fun with. It is made from netting that once contained a frozen turkey. The red nets that enclose hams are narrower and of smaller mesh than those that encase turkeys, but either will do nicely.

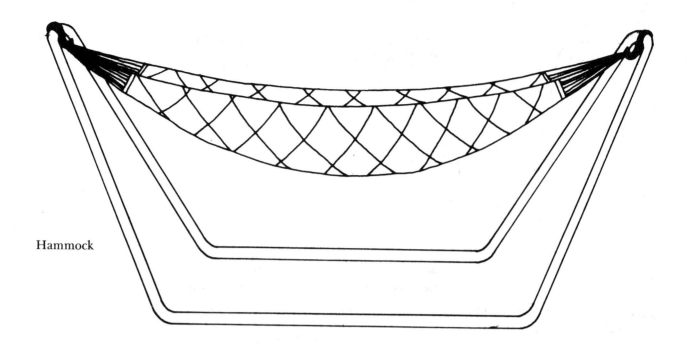

Hammock

Cut off a piece of netting about 10 inches long—about one-half of the netting. Pin on your ironing board in the width you desire (about 4 inches) and press with a damp cloth and a fairly hot iron. The netting will stiffen and hold its shape. One end will already be pulled together and fastened with a metal fastener; pleat the other end together tightly and press. Wind with embroidery floss or string very tightly, so it will be as firm as the metal end.

Using a heavy cord or string of single crochet, cut two pieces about 2 inches each. Fold these in half to form the loops for the ends of the hammock, and push into the roped ends with your awl. Dip each end in glue and let dry, pulling the loops so they dry in a proper shape. The "spreaders" at each end are 1½-inch pieces of ⅛-inch balsa wood cut ¼ inch wide and varnished. They may be glued to the netting (not very satisfactory, since they tend to become unglued), notched on the ends so they catch and hold the netting, or woven through the netting. We found the best-looking procedure was to stitch over and over the spreaders with needle and thread, catching the netting as we stitched. Make a little flat pillow about ½ inch by 1½ inches and tie to the spreader at one side. The hooks at the ends are S-hooks, which you will find at any hardware store. We used a ½-inch hook at one end to raise the head, and a 1-inch hook at the foot. Hook one end in the loop at each end of the netting and one end over the wire stand.

For the frame, use heavy coat hangers. With a wire cutter, cut out the bottom piece; it will be about 16 inches long. In the exact center, measure a piece 4 inches long. With a pair of pliers in each hand, bend the wire up at each end at about a 45-degree angle. We

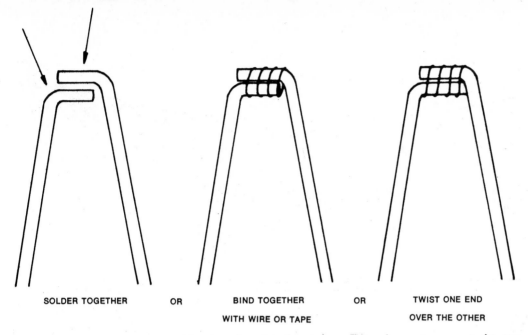

SOLDER TOGETHER   OR   BIND TOGETHER   OR   TWIST ONE END
WITH WIRE OR TAPE   OVER THE OTHER

Fastening hammock frame: solder together; bind together with wire or tape; or twist one wire end over the other.

want the uprights to be about 3 inches (feet) high, and to allow about ½ inch for fastening to the other side. Measure the 3 inches and at this point bend the wire at right angles to the upright. Cut off the ends about an inch from the bend. Do this with two pieces. The shaped bases and uprights are fastened together at the top bend in the upright either by lapping one piece over the other and soldering, or by placing one end over the other and wrapping with twine, or by twisting the wire ends together—this last looks best, but is quite a job. The tops of the S-hooks hang from these points.

Extension Rods

Extension rods are a prime requisite for a dollhouse if you plan to hang curtains. They may be made from ¼-inch or ⅛-inch wood dowels or from copper tubing such as we show here. These are much much more convincing. For the wooden dowels, simply rub with gold paint, then fit the ends with wooden beads of the proper size and paint them. For the brass rods, select a piece of ⅛-inch brass tubing from a model railroad counter of a hobby shop, and fit it with a ³⁄₃₂-inch solid rod, which will go in with exactly the right fit. These come in 1 foot lengths and can be cut with a hack saw to any length you desire. For example, for a 3-inch window, 2½-inch rod and tubing might be used. This will give you enough lap to make the rod solid. Fit the ends of the rod and tubing with little gold beads or with finials carved or whittled from ¼-inch wood, gilded. Make an opening in the bottom with your awl and fit the finial to the rod.

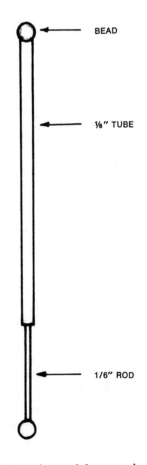

BEAD

⅛" TUBE

1/6" ROD

Extension rod for curtains

Eighteenth-Century Firebacks

We have always wondered why researchers involved with miniature reproductions have so far overlooked firebacks, those heavy metal backs made for fireplaces in the first half of the eighteenth century. They were originally used to reflect heat and protect the back wall of the fireplace. We could use them even today.

Firebacks were usually made of cast iron, and the three below, drawn in $\frac{1}{12}$ scale, were excavated while Colonial Williamsburg was being restored. The originals can be seen in restored Williamsburg houses and are most decorative. In our dollhouses, they do away with the awkward rubbing with charcoal or acrylic which the miniaturist resorts to, and in mini-rooms they show up beautifully because of the shallowness of the boxes. Firebacks must be a dull black to simulate cast iron. The one on the right bearing the Charles Rex monogram we made from tin, simply cutting a piece from the pattern on a piece of tin, and then placing another piece slightly smaller on top and punching the design in with our awl. A screwdriver serves very well for this work too. Don't worry if your design does not look perfect, for even the originals were a bit crude.

The fireback on the left we made of wood with a panel, properly beveled, glued over the back piece. The builder can be as artistic as he wishes with the paneling, and when completed the whole thing should be sprayed with dull black paint.

The center piece was made from sheet lead, a soft lead used by plumbers that is about $\frac{1}{8}$ inch thick. A tinsnips will cut it to any size you wish (these drawings are in actual scale) and the border may then be turned up using your needle-nosed pliers, or strips of the lead may be glued on. We then sprayed ours with the dull black paint and engraved the inscription with our Dremel Engraver, which was perfect for the job, but if you don't have the engraver the letters can be painted on with a fine brush and silver paint. I like the center (lead) one best.

Eighteenth-century firebacks

Punched-Tin Miniatures

We see few punched-tin miniatures these days. Few miniaturists are making them, possibly because they do take time and must be made by hand. However, these fixtures were an integral part of early homes, and when you make them yourself, they will be the heirlooms of tomorrow. Suzanne Ash of Mini-Things is one miniaturist who has researched punched-tin designs and now produces a pie safe (although not like our design shown below), a candle sconce shown at right, and a foot warmer which is similar to ours, shown at the bottom of the column. Early on, the perforations followed no pattern, but gradually the pieces became works of art, so that people-sized punched-tin pieces are today highly prized by antique collectors.

Tin of about the weight of beer-can metal is the best for our purposes. You might also use aluminum in the same weight, or the tin (which is not tin) in ordinary tin cans. Just remember not to attempt

Punched-tin miniatures

to cut it with an ordinary pair of scissors. Mark the guidelines on the metal. Then place the cutting edge of the upper blade of a tinsnips on the guideline with the metal extending far back into the space between the blades. The flat sides of the blades should be at right angles to the work. Keep as continuous a cutting action as possible, stopping just short of the tips of the blades. The tougher the metal is to cut, the larger the snips must be. I have one pair about the size of a small pair of scissors (9 inches) and another pair that measures 18 inches. Cut your metal a bit larger all the way around than the patterns, since the metal will shrink a bit from the piercing. To eliminate this, I like to scribe the pattern on the metal and do the piercing *before* cutting out. If your metal has a dull and a shiny side, choose whichever you prefer; I like the dull side better. You will need some sort of buffer under the tin; a square of acoustic tile is what I use, since the nail or awl will penetrate it easily and without noise. Place the tin on the tile with the right side up. Tape the pattern securely. Now, with a small hammer and whatever tool you plan to use—your awl, small nails—begin making the perforations at regular intervals. Be careful not to make the holes too close together, as this tears the tin and makes an ugly break in the design.

When you have finished (if you are using a nail, be sure that you tap it into the metal the same distance each time, otherwise some holes will be larger than others), antique the tin by spreading on and wiping off a thin mixture of black and raw umber oil paints. Let this dry overnight (thoroughly), then rub gently with linseed oil. Do not use varnish; this spoils the look of the tin.

For the first sconce, scribe the pattern at left onto a small piece of metal. Make the hole for hanging at the top with about a No. 8 nail. You are going to bend it at the dotted line; scribe your design above this and do the perforating. Now turn the metal over and drive a 5/8-inch tack or nail from the bottom through to the top where the bottom circle shows. Bend the edges of the bottom section up a bit with your needle-nosed pliers. This is easier if you make a small slit right at the dotted (bend) line first. This gives you a nice frame around the candle portion. Make a paper candle according to the directions in Chapter 11. Slip this down over the tack or nail.

The round sconces may be made any size you wish. We have seen them in Pennsylvania Dutch country over a foot in diameter. On p. 196, the hex signs form the pattern for the perforations. Cut the circle, cutting the tab on the bottom about 1/4 inch wide and 1/4 inch long. For the crimping around the circle, simply find a wood disk (slice off a dowel) or a button about 1/8 inch smaller than the metal. Center this over the metal; then, using a small screwdriver as a tool, press the

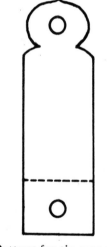

Pattern for tin sconce

outer edge of the metal up against the disk. Make the next crimp close against the first and continue around the circle. Be careful not to let the disk or button slide off-center as you do the crimping. Next, bend the tab up at right angles to the circle. Bend it in half, bending the bottom half up at right angles. This will give you a little shelf. Cut a tiny piece of tin about ¼ inch high and long enough to go around a pencil. Shape it into a circle around the pencil. Fasten to the shelf with Krazy Glue. Slip a paper candle into the opening. You may wish to make a hole at the top of the round sconce for hanging. We preferred to glue ours flat against the wall.

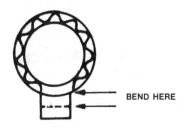

Punched-tin bent base

The foot warmer is enchanting. They were filled with coals or hot bricks and placed inside wagons or sleighs when travelers were forced to go out into the cold. Simply cut two ⅞-inch squares of ⅛-inch wood. Cut four pieces ⅝ inch long from a ⅛-inch dowel. In the pieces of wood that will be the top and bottom of the foot warmer, bore four ⅛-inch holes in each corner, then perforate the wood with a heavy needle in a nice pattern.

Cut a piece of tin about ½ inch wide and long enough to make four folds that will fit around the prepared piece of wood. Thus you will have a fold at each corner and the sides fastened with tape or glued at the other corner. As will be seen in our drawing, we sometimes carve a bit of a design in the dowels, then tip each with glue and fasten into the top piece of wood. Cut a 1-inch piece of wire, bend to make a handle, and force into the perforations at the top. Fasten underneath with a loop. Carefully fit the metal square of perforated tin between the dowels, pressing against each to make a tight corner. Glue all against the bottom piece of wood. Finish with stain or not, as you prefer.

10 Needle Crafts

Next to the glue pot and carving blade, there is hardly a tool in existence that is as important to the crafter of miniatures as the needle. The multitudinous stitches, fine thread, and variety of background materials available make almost any needle craft possible. Your only problem will be in deciding where to begin. You have available every size of English "sharp" needles, crewel needles, crochet needles (or hooks), upholstery needles, knitting needles, hooking needles, beading needles, yarn needles, tapestry needles, and basting needles. An imaginative needle worker with nimble fingers could almost furnish a dollhouse complete with the products of this art.

In the small amount of space which we can allot to needlework, we must necessarily omit some of the most detailed procedures. However, there are innumerable articles and books published these days with basic information, so we feel that even the beginner with meager instructions can turn out something of which his dollhouse family will be proud.

Needlepoint Rugs

Let's begin at the bottom, with the floors. Specifically, with needlework rugs and carpeting. This work is greatly enjoyed by dollhouse decorators; not only are the results esthetically pleasing, but also these projects are so easy to handle. The depth of the finished canvas is just about right for a 1/12-scale rug, and with it we need never worry about having to use something that in the dollhouse scale would be up to our knees in people-scale.

In the photograph, we show a variety of canvases in different sizes. All except the top right and bottom are double-thread, the so-called penelope canvas, as opposed to single-thread, or mono canvas. Since the double-thread canvas is easiest to use, we show this in several sizes from 5-mesh-to-the-inch (*top left*), to 40-mesh-to-the-inch at the

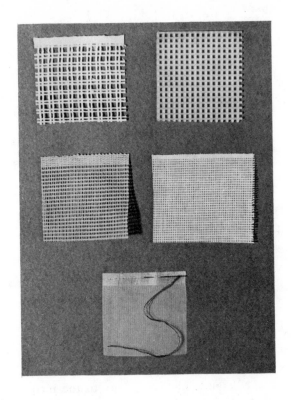

The various canvases available for needlework: (*top left*) a 5-mesh-to-the-inch piece; (*top right*) a plastic canvas; (*center left*) a 14-mesh-to-the-inch French canvas; (*center right*) an 18-mesh-to-the-inch French canvas; (*bottom*) a silk gauze, 40-mesh-to-the-inch, on which one strand of embroidery cotton is used (*Photograph by Elinor Coyle*).

bottom, with a 14-mesh-to-the-inch French canvas at right. The tiny mesh shown at bottom is actually a gauze and is now beginning to make its appearance here (it formerly had to be ordered from a Canadian supplier) and must be used with such threads as single-thread embroidery floss and the finest of needles. (See the bargello-work pillow and bell pull on p. 213, done on this gauze.) The canvas at top right is a new one, a plastic canvas that just became available in this country, which we find most satisfactory. The Oriental rug shown on the next page was made on this plastic canvas.

The threads used to work the various canvases must be suited to the size of the mesh, because if the thread is too small for the canvas or if it is pulled too tightly, you will end up with an incomplete cover. True needlepoint wool has a long smooth fiber that may be separated into three, four, or five strands, as opposed to knitting wool, which has a shorter fiber and tends to "ball up" when worked. Persian wool is finer, made of three strands and generally used on 10-mesh mono canvas. Tapestry wool must be used on a 10-mesh canvas, and crewel wool on an 18-mesh. Even the needlepoint wool will become thin to the breaking point, because of the continual drawing through the canvas, so it is better to use short strands—12 to 14 inches for petit point and 18 to 20 inches for needlepoint. If the wool becomes twisted while you're working, simply hold your work up with the needle hanging down, and the yarn will uncurl.

Needlepoint Oriental rug, 10 stitches to the inch, made by author (*Photograph by Elinor Coyle*).

English rose needlepoint rug, 12 stitches to the inch, made by author (*Photograph by Elinor Coyle*).

The two designs shown here, both executed by the author, were adapted from an Oriental rug found in an old dollhouse and an old English carpet. Both can be made with no trouble at all. The Oriental rug was made on the plastic 10-mesh-to-the-inch canvas illustrated, and the English rose carpet was made on the penelope canvas, 12-stitches-to-the-inch. We'll not attempt to chart colors, since you will want to choose your own. The English carpet has a cream-color background with natural-colored roses and violets and green leaves in the border, and the Oriental is in three shades of green with black, yellow, and orange touches, done in this combination so that it would match the wallpaper in a dollhouse dining room. I made a ½-inch fringe on the Oriental rug, a simple thing to do, since one has only to cut a quantity of wool and wrap it over and over a 1-inch-wide strip of cardboard. The wool is then cut at the top, resulting in 2-inch pieces of wool. Used double or triple, these are folded in half and a coarse (about a size 6) crochet hook is reached through the last row of mesh from the right to the wrong side and the loop is pulled through the mesh. The two ends are then pulled through the loop and are pulled tight. Repeat in each mesh.

It will be interesting to you to learn that the floral rug is almost an exact copy of one to be seen in an English dollhouse now in the Victoria and Albert Museum in London. I found the stamped canvas for it at a sale of needlepoint in a small shop where it was tagged as a footstool cover. A little judicious trimming here and there produced the exact size that I needed for a rug (9 x 12 inches plus ½ inch all around to fold under) so that all that was necessary was to fill in the background.

However, there will be times when you want to make your own design so that you have a completely original work, and this in itself is quite a craft. First, trace the design with black ink onto white paper or work out your own design on graph paper. If the design is too large or too small, you can enlarge or reduce it by redrawing it on graph paper on a larger or smaller scale.

Then be certain that you have the correct canvas mesh. A very small design to be worked with, say, embroidery floss, must be put on a small canvas, such as a No. 18 mesh, the canvas at right in the second row (p. 199). Tack the ink drawing over your canvas on a board and trace the design onto it very carefully. Use a light touch. If you can tape the canvas and pattern over a window and draw from an upright position, this is fine. Or, if you have a glass-topped table or one of the clear plastic TV tables, this works very well, too. Provide a source of light underneath, such as a flashlight, and you're ready to go. Use a completely indelible ink pen; be careful about this, otherwise your design may smear. If you have colored indelible pencils such as we mention in the section on wallpapers, you can do the design in the colors you prefer.

Remember that if canvas and thread are both of the right size, the thread must cover the canvas completely, Always work the background stitches in the same direction as those in the embroidered design, and be careful not to pull the yarn too tightly.

Before hemming, your carpet must be blocked. Lay a piece of brown paper on the ironing board or a cutting board, and mark in crayon the exact size you want the carpet to be, making certain that all corners are squared. Wet the canvas well from the back and gently pull it from all directions so that it approximates the size and shape you're after. Then spread it on the board over the outline you've traced, and start to tack it through the canvas, about ½ inch from the finished work. Tack first the top and bottom, then the two sides, first at the corners, then halfway down, then a quarter of the way, and so on. Let dry overnight on the board, and it will be ready to hem.

An easier way to block carpets and rugs if they're not too badly out of shape is to press on the wrong side with a hot iron so that they become a little damp, then pull into shape, tacking at each corner, then go over it again with a damp cloth and then iron.

I have had more inquiries from miniaturists as to how to bind miniature needlepoint rugs than on any other subject—and rightly, for this is a most important finishing touch. One method is to press down the edges of the rug right to the stitching, so that the edges lie flat on the wrong side. Trim off the corners so you have mitered corners that will lie flat, then baste into place. Fasten with a strip of masking tape all around. This is fairly good, but not perfect. Jennifer Bennett of Mt. Vernon, Illinois, who makes magnificent mini-rugs in any design you prefer at $1.50 per square inch, uses the binding stitch. For this the canvas edge must first be pressed flat so that only one mesh of the canvas is showing on the right side. Hold the canvas with the wrong side toward you and use wool of a suitable color and the same size as the needlework. Fasten the thread into the backs of nearby stitches. Working from left to right with the needle pointed toward you, go over the canvas and pull the needle through one stitch, then go over and through again in the next stitch. This will give you a diagonal. Be careful not to pull it too tightly. Simply go over and over, always coming up from the front in the *next* stitch, until you come to a corner. Then work four stitches in one mesh until you have come around the corner, and proceed as before. This will work satisfactorily on either mono or penelope canvas.

The miniature carpet with the English floral wreath and center was bound by folding over and fastening with tape; you will notice that the corners are not exactly true. The Oriental rug is made on the plastic canvas and so needs no binding; it doesn't stretch and will always have true corners.

Needlepoint Stitches

While there are a dozen different needlepoint stitches, only a small fraction of them are suitable for dollhouse rugs and carpets: the half-cross, the continental, the half-cross tramé, and the petit point. Remember, as we cautioned above, always to work background stitches in the same direction as those in the embroidered design, and remember, too, not to pull the yarn too tightly.

The half-cross stitch, shown here at left, is just that; half of a cross stitch, and most simple to do. It is worked diagonally from left to right. The continental stitch, shown here at right, is worked diagonally from right to left, and you will notice that the needle, in working the stitch, is brought up in place, then goes into the canvas

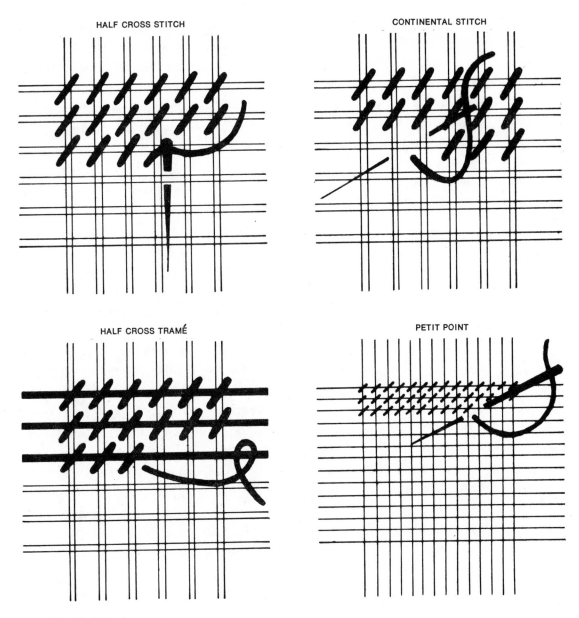

HALF CROSS STITCH   CONTINENTAL STITCH

HALF CROSS TRAMÉ   PETIT POINT

Needlepoint stitches

one mesh to the right and above, and is brought up two meshes over and one below. Thus, the work starts in the second mesh from the right side. The continental stitch is not often used for dollhouse rugs, since you will notice that this stitch gives a double thickness of wool on the wrong side, making the work almost too thick for our purpose.

The half-cross tramé is used on pieces having a background of tramé, or underlaid, work. One strand (the tramé thread) is laid along the canvas and the half-cross stitch is worked over it. This, too, produces a rather heavy rib, but it's fine for copies of Aubusson and similar-type carpets. You work diagonally over the tramé threads from left to right.

For true petit point, one must use penelope canvas but separate the horizontal and vertical threads of the canvas in order to get the smallest possible mesh. Split your yarn and work in the same manner as the continental stitch, from right to left. Petit point is counted 20 stitches to the inch or smaller; needlepoint is counted 14 to 18 stitches to the inch, although for some pieces, workers prefer 10 stitches to the inch. Mary Jane Hubers of Davenport, Iowa, who has some exquisite needlepoint rugs in her dollhouse, works with 14 stitches to the inch, using Persian wool which she splits into three parts, using only one strand.

Crocheted Rugs

There are dozens and dozens of possibilities for braided or crocheted rugs for the dollhouse, but we believe the finest one we've ever seen was one that was made on a backing of felt which kept it as flat as the most dedicated mini-housekeeper could desire. Entered by miniaturist Mary Ann McLafferty of Kirkwood, Missouri, in the annual contest for Original Ideas sponsored yearly by *The Dollhouse (and Miniature) News*, this one is almost too simple to believe. Mrs. McLafferty used a multicolored crochet thread in delicate tones of green, blue, pink, and yellow, and backed it against a pink felt base, producing a beautiful effect.

Use a No. 8 crochet hook and No. 30 multicolored Mercrochet; this rug, a fairly large oval measuring 10½ x 9 inches, required not quite two balls. To begin, start a slip knot and work a single chain stitch until you have 3 feet, working six strands of thread together. Spread a little Tacky glue on the center of a piece of felt cut the size of the rug you want to make and start an oval by pressing down 1 inch of the chain. Curve at top and bottom and make successive rows of the chain by gluing to the felt. The important thing here is that Mrs. McLafferty glues the chain down flat, so that the chain loops themselves show up and are flat on the felt; this is important to the design of the rug. Crochet a number of chains about 4 feet long and glue these to the felt, starting from the end of the center oval. Continue until the rug reaches the size you desire. Notice that no finishing of the edges is required here; simply glue the chain to the very edge of the felt. Use of the multicolored crochet thread gives a beautiful effect. Another rug with a more peasant effect is made of red, gray, black, and white embroidery thread using 6 strands and glued onto black felt for a base.

Material for Crocheted Rug

1 No. 8 crochet hook
2 (about) balls No. 30 multicolored Mercrochet
1 piece felt the shape and size you want

Crocheted Potholders

A very easy item to crochet is a little potholder. This one works up to a circle about ½ inch in diameter, depending upon the tightness of your stitch. Use a No. 30 crochet thread (notice, now; this is a crochet thread, whereas the thread in the previous project was an embroidery thread) and about a No. 14 crochet needle.

First round: With white thread, ch 2, then make 7 sc in the second chain from the hook, join with sl st to the first sc.

Second round: Ch 1, work 2 sc in each sc in the circle, ending with 14 sc. Join.

Third round: Ch 1, work 1 sc in joining, then work 2 sc in the next sc, * 1 sc in the next sc, 2 sc in the next sc, then repeat from * around and join. You should have 21 sc. Break off. Then, with some sort of contrasting thread, join to a sc, ch 1, sc in the same place and in each sc around. Join with a sl st to the first sc, ch 5 (to make a hanging loop) then sl st in the same place. Break off and pull the threads through stitches with a finer needle so as to hide them, or thread into a sewing needle and thread through.

Quilts

One can almost trace the course of history in a study of old quilts; some are pleasing in their very ugliness, and some are beautiful beyond compare. Some are patchwork, some are embroidered or appliquéd, and some use the quilting as the sole decoration. With quilts, you can give your imagination full rein. And, whereas a people-sized quilt represents an investment of untold hours, a 6 x 7-inch quilt for a miniature bed will require at most a few evenings of pleasurable handwork, will be just as impressive to show, and just as valuable to keep.

It is relatively simple to use a people-sized quilt design for a dollhouse quilt, since the majority of large quilts are made in squares, and one square is easily copied. Stitches, of course, must be minuscule, as must patches. In the quilt for a child's bed shown at the bottom of the

Quilts. Random Square quilt (*upper*) and Texas Star quilt (*lower*), both made by Selma Webber (*Photograph by Elinor Coyle*).

photograph on p. 207, **a** very tiny rosebud-print crepe was used, alternating with solid baby blue squares. To obtain ½-inch squares, they were cut ¾ inch in size and then hemmed, reducing the finished squares to ½ inch. After piecing, a thin layer of cotton was used as batting, delicate pink crepe de chine was used as lining, and these were quilted together. Then the whole was bound with ½-inch pink satin ribbon.

Selma Webber of Mexico, Missouri, generally considered the doyenne of miniature-quilt makers, follows a similar procedure. She suggests using only very fine, soft, pliable fabrics and says that fine cottons are the very best. Use small-patterned materials, or solids. She, too, uses a thin layer of cotton for filling, or perhaps a layer of Dacron and polyester. I personally have found that a good quality of flannel makes a very luxurious, soft quilt when used as lining. She reports that she does every bit of stitching and sewing by hand. Some quilts can be machine-stitched, she goes on, but the finished work will be stiffer. Also, although close lines of quilting are most effective, she tries to keep the lines at least ½ inch apart; if quilted too closely, the finished article has a tendency to be too stiff. She holds the tiny quilts in her hands as she quilts, working from the center out. I have found embroidery hoops to be a big help, if one is careful not to let the batting "bunch up" at the edges.

In making the Random Square quilt shown at top of the photograph opposite, Mrs. Webber uses squares of the size given above in a variety of tiny prints, trying for a balance between dark and light, complicated and plain. This quilt, she reminds us, would hardly be appropriate in an elaborate room or setting, but in an old-fashioned home or a log cabin it is most charming. A Texas Star quilt is shown beneath, also made by Selma Webber.

As for the velvet Crazy quilt shown below, this was one of the great favorites of Victorian days. We can't all be so lucky as Mrs. Webber, who has a great supply of old materials which she has been

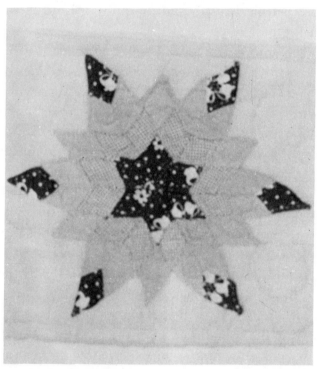

The finished Texas Star quilt, shown here, is approximately 6″ x 7″. Dark points are a navy print with white, light rows are pink and blue check. It is sewn onto a background of very delicate blue. Made by Selma Webber (*Photograph by Elinor Coyle*).

Three classic quilts. Yo-Yo or Flower Garden quilt (*top*), made by the author; Crazy quilt (*center*), made by Selma Webber; Checkerboard quilt of alternating squares of pale blue and a rosebud print (*bottom*), made by the author (*Photograph by Elinor Coyle*).

saving for years, but if we keep our eyes open, we will come across such treasures, and in this case a piece of thin silk or satin the size of our quilt is what we must look for. We will then need odd-sized pieces of various velvets, silks, or satins, and these are basted to the lining in a way to emphasize the odd shapes. The first piece is basted on with no hem turned, then the next pieces are basted over that with a ⅛-inch hem turned under. We go on in this fashion until the entire quilt is finished, then make the pieces permanent with various edging stitches—feather, crewel, and so on. In addition, the Victorian Crazy quilt also had a bit of embroidery on each patch—names, insignia, and designs. Victorian ladies vied with each other to produce the most intricate embroidery on their crazy quilts. Mrs. Webber reports that, actually, she doesn't use much real velvet; she prefers velveteen or chiffon velvet, and crepe de chine for the lining. When all pieces are stitched, the basting is pulled out. No batting is used, and no quilting is done, for it would interfere with the design.

Mrs. Webber has even gone so far as to design and execute a difficult Texas Star quilt, a real test of patience, since the bias sides of the tiny triangles have a tendency to stretch out of shape in the sewing. This one, shown in two different color combinations (see pages 206 and 207), is of extraordinary beauty (as are almost all patchwork quilts based on diamond shapes) because the star, after piecing, is appliquéd onto a very fine pale blue cotton. This, combined with the pinks, dark blues, and light blues used in the star itself, produces a most attractive effect. The diamonds are cut as shown on p. 209, on a base measurement of ⅞ inch, which will produce diamonds, after stitching, of about ⅝ inch on each side. The longer diamonds are necessary to piece out the finial (lengthwise) points and, on the right, what the quilter calls the east-west, or side, points. In our diagram, which gives one-half the quilt pattern, quilting lines are broken. It is interesting to notice how she has worked the quilting into the overall design of the finished piece.

There is one more quilt the beginning or experienced crafter can have a great deal of fun with, and that is the tied quilt which was so popular in past days. For the homemaker who was far from quilting centers or who simply couldn't take time to quilt, the "tied" comforter was both an outlet for her creativity and a boon when she needed more bedcovering. It consisted of two sides of material, put together with thin batting between the sides (in the case of miniatures, use a thin layer of cotton), and then tied every 6 inches or so with a bright knot of wool. Stitch the two sides of the quilt over the cotton with a basting stitch, and then go down from the top and up from the bottom with a length of contrasting thread or wool. Tie a double knot and a bow,

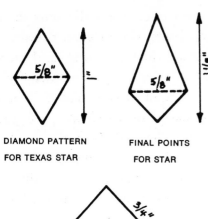

DIAMOND PATTERN
FOR TEXAS STAR

FINAL POINTS
FOR STAR

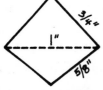

EAST-WEST POINTS
FOR STAR

Diamonds for Texas Star quilt pattern

One-half Texas Star quilt pattern

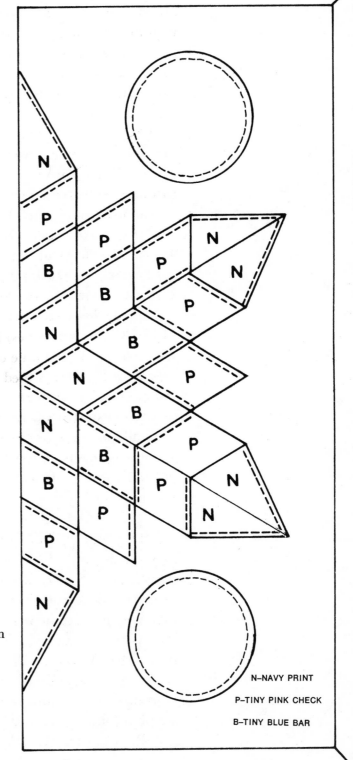

N—NAVY PRINT

P—TINY PINK CHECK

B—TINY BLUE BAR

then cut off the wool and proceed to the next tie. If you can find very small prints of similar design, say one with a red background and one with a navy background, this makes a very pretty coverlet, as does one with a print side and one with a solid side. When you are finished with the tying, simply baste the edges together, turning in a 1/4-inch hem on each side, and stitch together, preferably by hand with small quilting stitches or by machine.

You will find that quilts and spreads rarely lie properly on the miniature bed, with the edge dropping over the side; they have a tendency simply to lie flat, without dropping. To overcome this, mark the quilt or spread at the edge of the mattress, then run a seam the length of the quilt by hand or by machine. This will fold the quilt at the proper place, and you'll have no more trouble.

Sunbonnet baby patch for appliqué quilt

Appliqué quilts are not so simple for the needle craftswoman, since the pieces would be almost too small to stitch, if cut in scale. The sunbonnet baby design so popular at the turn of the century, however, is easy to make, looks utterly charming on a dollhouse bed, and takes but minutes to complete. In making ours, we used tiny figured calico for the bodies and solid matching colors for the bonnets. Cut according to the drawing. Don't attempt to turn in edges; simply pin the dress to a 1½-inch square of fine white percale and anchor with the tiniest of blanket stitches around sides and bottom. Glue the bonnet in place and decorate with a band of outline stitch. The feet are just three or four up-and-down stitches in the same color as the blanket stitches, with a holding stitch across the bottom. Turn the squares in 1/4 inch all around to stitch together. Use about five squares across and seven vertically, or whatever is needed to fit your bed. Line and quilt just inside the edges of the squares. Finish with a pretty binding, either one of the solid colors or the prints.

The Yo-Yo Quilt. Or Flower Garden Quilt. Or Pom-Pom Quilt.

This old favorite has a dozen names, and is as pretty today as it was when the pioneer women stitched it as they rode westward in the covered wagons. Also, it is a "natural" for the dollhouse seamstress, since the little puffs can be made almost any size. Cut in the size of the pattern given here, the puffs draw up to about the size of a nickel, and are perfectly to scale on a 1/12 bed. A quilt for a double bed should be eight rows in width in order to give a nice drop at the sides, while six puffs long is about right for most beds.

Remember, this quilt was not made for warmth; it was made, rather, for beauty and used as a spread. However, the one shown in our photograph on p. 207 was made for a small child's bed and after the pom-poms were completed and sewn together, the square was laid upon a square of fine French flannel, thus giving both extra body and warmth. For the child's bed in a dollhouse, it was made five pom-poms square.

Trace a template or pattern from the size given here (about 2 inches in diameter) and then cut your patches. Remember that in this, as in any quilt, it is best to use the same materials throughout, that is, all cotton, all polyester, all silk, and so on. Try to use five or six similar tiny designs, too, so there will be some continuity in the pattern. To sew the little pom-poms, use a double thread of about No. 50 or 60, since you will have to pull quite hard to bring the pom-poms together. Turn in the edge about ⅛ inch and, bringing your needle up from the bottom so that the knot will be on the wrong side, stitch around in tiny even stitches. When you have gone the whole way around, pull the circle up very tightly and fasten with two over-and-over stitches on the center opening. Then pull out the pom-pom so that the gathers are evenly spaced and the circle is evenly folded. The pom-poms are attached by placing two pom-poms together and making three tiny cross stitches to join them. Continue to do this to make one row; then with the second row, attach a pom-pom to the first row at top and at the side, to the next pom-pom. I lined mine by cutting the lining ½ inch larger than the spread, stitching a ⅛-inch double hem all around, then folding over so that the lining fits the spread. Stitch down at each pom-pom with three little cross stitches in the same way that you attached the circles.

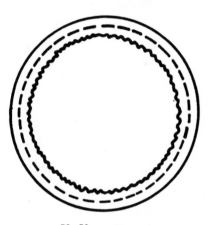

Yo-Yo quilt

Yo-Yo pattern

Quilting Stitches

Pictured on p. 212, enlarged, are three stitches generally used on people-sized quilts which are readily adaptable to miniature work. At top, the feather stitch. Notice that this is worked from right to left, using a size 5 to 8 needle (5s are so fine they are prone to break, but they give a prettier stitch). Bring the needle up at *1*, then down at *2*, and as the resulting loop is pulled down, place the thumb of your left hand over it to hold. Bring the needle up at *3*, inside the loop, then down at *4*, hold the loop again, and bring the needle up at *5*. An intricate double feather stitch is easily made by making one stitch up, as at *1* and *4*, and the next stitch down.

The tack stitch, shown next, is often used for so-called tailor tacks and some sorts of basting, but is dainty and effective on small quilts. Here we work from left to right, bring the needle up at *1*, down at *2*,

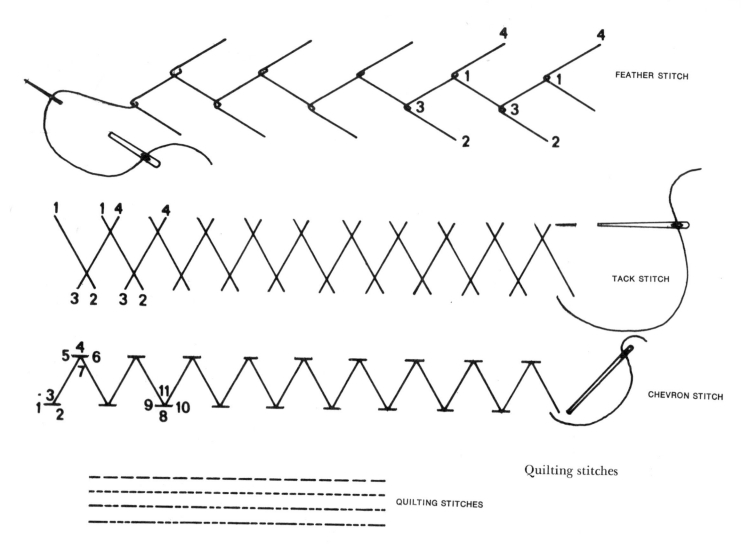

FEATHER STITCH

TACK STITCH

CHEVRON STITCH

Quilting stitches

QUILTING STITCHES

then up again at *3* and down at *4*. On a small quilt these stitches shouldn't be more than ¼ inch long.

The chevron stitch is perhaps the most difficult, but it was often used on old quilts. Working from left to right, put the needle down at the point labeled *1* and bring it up at *2*. Make a tiny stitch to *3*, down, then bring the needle up in the middle of this stitch. Take the needle up to point *4*, down, then up at *5* and over to *6*, down, to make the little stitch. Bring up at *4* again, then down to *7*, up at *8*, down at *9*, and up in the middle again. The whole procedure is much less complicated than it sounds, and after the first two or three stitches, you will have no difficulty with it. Any of these three stitches are effective with various patchwork quilts and especially around the edges of the patches in patchwork crazy quilts, and may be used equally well around the edges of the quilts.

The quilting stitches shown here are done with a fine needle, are merely variations of the single running stitch which was worked out to give variety to the background of the quilt. Many such varieties were used, and will be effective on your miniature beds.

212

Bargello

The bargello stitch, which is simply a variation of the Gobelin stitch in needlepoint, is usually seen in the well-known flame design, the simplest of all the bargello patterns. While the stitch is not difficult to do, learning it requires a very detailed explanation. There is, in fact, one whole book devoted to this stitch, but like swimming or bicycling, once it's learned, it is never forgotten. The bell pull and cushion shown here, worked by Carol Frumhof of the Threaded Needle Guild, is particularly worthy of note because it uses the bargello in a horizontal pattern, which is seldom seen, rather than the more usual vertical pattern.

Our diagram, the worker should note, is done on squares of 10-to-the-inch, while the work in the photograph was done on 40-to-the-inch gauze. However, the diagram will be easier to follow in this size, and you may make the adjustment when you decide which canvas or gauze you wish to use. Worked as shown, this is the medallion pattern of the bargello stitch. Starting two rows above *A*, make the single stitches which connect the medallions, using only one strand of three-ply Persian wool and a tapestry needle of an appropriate size. Your thread should be no longer than about 15 inches, as in work this fine the thread has a tendency to ravel if it is too long. Then work the three stitches we have marked *A* (this will be Row 1) and come down the sides of the medallion through Row 2, and so on. Some crafters prefer to work the medallion completely on the right side when working on a small piece such as this, and then come up along the left side.

The borders shown in the photograph are dark green on the outside and olive green on the inside; the center flower is then worked according to your own imagination with mercerized embroidery cotton

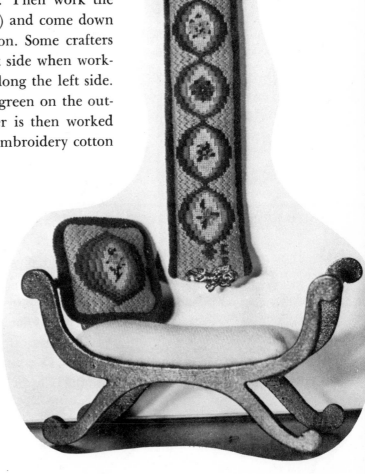

Bell pull and cushion, shown slightly larger than actual size, are done in two shades of green in the bargello stitch, a variation of usual needlepoint stitches (*Photograph by Elinor Coyle*).

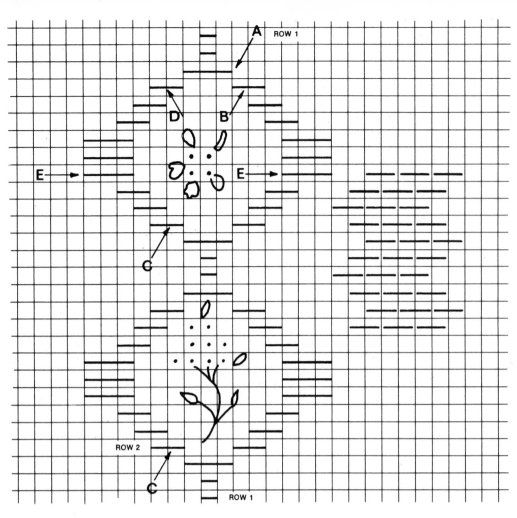

Pattern for bargello
pull and cushion

using only one or two strands, then the background within the medallion is worked with ivory-colored embroidery cotton. Fill in the background of both the pull and the cushion with a shade of green a bit lighter than that used on the inside border.

When needlepointing on miniatures, cotton embroidery thread is a fine thing to try. Use D.M.C. cotton embroidery floss; it has a sheen that resembles silk and it comes in a wide variety of colors. Avoid the Perle cotton, which has a twist and doesn't allow the stitch in miniatures to lie flat. A combination of cotton and wool is lovely, as in the bell pull and cushion described above, and if you go to 14- and 18-mesh mono-canvas, a 3-ply thread is fine. Use the same-sized needle you would if you were using wool, and cut the thread into 15- to 18-inch lengths; no longer, or the thread will fray and separate. Be very careful not to work with a twisted thread, as the stitches must lie even and flat.

If a stray thread separates from the ply and makes a loop on the canvas, just pull on it from underneath and it will easily work back into the body of the six-ply. Pull tight against the canvas, then unthread the needle and run the thread tightly between your thumb and index finger. If the problem continues, simply end off, cut the thread, and start with a fresh one.

214

11 Paper Crafts

The art of paper crafting has so many facets that one wonders where to begin. One facet involves folding and cutting and producing beautiful patterns from paper itself. Another ancient art, origami, produces whole forms which seem to convey a feeling of motion. Sometimes the beauty of the paper becomes an integral part of the design.

Quilled Picture Frame

One of the easiest paper crafts is quilling. The name derives, undoubtedly, from the fact that the paper strips were first wrapped around a quill. At that time, perhaps as early as the fifteenth century, quill work was known as paper filigree or rolled paper work. In the eighteenth century, the nuns of southern Europe used this simple method to produce scrolls, volutes, and rolls (still made by wrapping around the quills from birds), which were used to decorate religious plaques, paintings, and as backgrounds for statues.

By the time these decorations became known in France and England, the ladies of the nineteenth and twentieth centuries were ready for a new fad to replace the embroidery crafts. They took quilling to their hearts because, while it did require skill, it involved little expense. Probably for these same reasons the women in the American colonies taught quilling to their children, and so perpetuated the art. Today one may see examples of quilling in the Metropolitan Museum of Art in New York and in many old books of the period.

Basically, quilling consists of making many small rolls of various shapes and gluing them together in a design which has been worked out on a pattern sheet. Today quilling paper, precut in many different widths, may be found in craft and art shops, and is most inexpensive. A corsage pin or a round toothpick is used for the rolling. A bit of glue is the only other prerequisite. For the picture frame shown on

Basic quill patterns

p. 217, worked out by Annaleene Gard, neither pattern nor experience is necessary. First, practice making rolls. Moisten the end of a strip of quilling paper and bend a bit at the end so the pin or pick fits into the bend. Holding this between the thumb and first finger of the left hand, roll the paper around the pin or pick, keeping the paper evenly aligned as you roll. The length of your paper, of course, will determine the size of the roll. When you have the size you need (or have used the length of paper called for), simply cut off the paper and fasten the end with a tiny bit of glue—which you have added with the point of a toothpick.

Many books have been written about quilling, coiling, and curling paper, but the six shapes shown at left are the basic forms; from these nearly all other shapes are made. At top, we show, enlarged, a tight roll. Moisten the end of the paper with your tongue, bend the paper a bit at the end, then fold around your toothpick or long pin and begin to roll, holding the roll between left thumb and forefinger and the pin in your right hand. Fasten and pull out the pick or pin. To make the roll looser, shown next, simply let the roll unwind a bit in your fingers before gluing. The "leaf" shape, shown next, is made by making a loose roll, then pinching at one side with the thumb and forefinger of the right hand, and drawing this side to a point. The opposite side, of course, will remain round.

To make the S shape, shown next, roll one end of a strip under and the other end of the strip over and hold for a moment until the paper holds its shape. It will take about a 3-inch piece of paper to make the tiny S's used on the picture frame shown in Fig. 117 or, if you're making a very fine frame, a 1½-inch piece. The scroll shape, shown next, is made by turning the ends of the paper either up or down, and the heart shape calls for a fold in the center of the paper and the ends rolled in to form the heart. We have pictured quite a large frame here in order to show how the quilling shapes are affixed; it could be made still larger, and much smaller ones are very effective. A good size for frames which are to stand on tables or to be hung in groups is ⅞ inch by 1¼ inches. The drawings are just twice this size.

From lightweight cardboard such as that found on the back of writing tablets (a bit heavier than shirtboards), cut the rectangle in the size you wish to make. We would suggest starting with the size shown, until you have acquired a little experience in gluing the rolls. On any sizes up to the size shown, glue a border of quilling paper at the edges of the rectangle. For larger sizes, you will have to cut ½-inch strips of construction paper, or you may find ½-inch quilling paper in some shops. Glue the borders as shown, let dry under a weight.

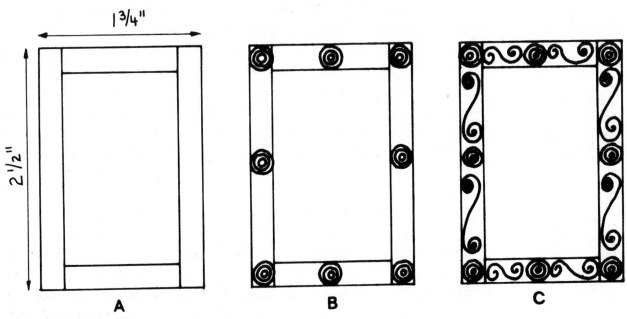

Quilling on picture frames

Now, make eight S shapes using 3-inch quilling strips for the size shown above, 1¼ inches for smaller frames. Make eight tight rolls using the same-sized strips. Glue the ends to keep the rolls tight. Position the eight tight rolls as shown in drawing *B* and glue in place, keeping them on the border. Use a white, clear-drying glue. Place four of the S shapes between the tight rolls on the sides of the frame. The remaining four S shapes may be a bit too large for the spaces between tight rolls at the ends of the frame. If they are, snip off a bit and curl them again. Glue these between the tight rolls at the ends of the frame. Now the frame should look like drawing *C*. Dry thoroughly, then spray with clear acrylic to seal and stiffen it. When dry, stick the corsage pin or a large straight pin into the back and, using the pin as a handle, dip the entire frame into a jar of aluminum or gold paint. Shake off the excess paint and stand up on waxed paper to dry.

To cut a stand for the back, for smaller frames cut a strip ⅞ inch long and 3⁄16 inch wide. For larger frames the strip should be about 2 inches long and ¼ inch wide. Dip the stand pieces in the paint also and when dry bend the tip a bit, dab with glue, and attach to the back of the frame to make a stand.

Any color paint may be used, of course, instead of the silver or gold, and you may prefer to use spray paint instead of dipping paint. Either way, beautiful effects can be achieved in any size you wish. If making very large frames, it is best to work out your design on a piece of graph paper, so you're sure to have rolls and shapes in the right proportion to the measurements of the frame.

Materials for Quilled Picture Frame
Lightweight cardboard such as tablet backs
Quilling paper
Corsage pin or toothpick
Corsage pin or round toothpick
Paper glue such as Sobo
Paint or spray paint
Spray acrylic for finished frame

Rubber Tree Plant

Few homes in the nineteeth and twentieth centuries have not boasted of a rubber plant tucked away somewhere in a bay window, the curve of a stairway, or beside the entrance in a foyer. Today rubber plants seem to be coming into their own again, especially in modern homes whose stark lines and unornamented walls seem to need such relief.

We searched for months before we found exactly the right paper for this project. Crepe paper won't do because its grain is too heavy. Even the thinnest of plastics won't do, because leaves cut from these won't hold the lovely curves which the leaves of *Ficus elastica doescheri* assume. But one lucky day we came across a roll of plastic-coated shelf paper, the exact color of olive green which nature chose for the rubber plant, and from then on out, everything was easy.

A very fine commercial rubber plant, 4½ inches high and with eighteen leaves, is in great demand at $25.00, thus making it one of the miniatures that is well worth spending a little time over. You'll find it simple to duplicate, once you've practiced a little. Once your paper is located, search for a pot. Perfume and cosmetic bottle tops seem to offer the most decorative possibilities. They should have a flat base on which to stand, and should be large enough to be logical for a plant of such size—at least an inch high, it seems to us, and perhaps another inch in diameter.

You will need, in addition, a good glue such as Sobo, a spool or card of fine beading wire, and a roll of Scotch plastic tape, ¾ inch wide. Plastic tape comes in many colors; we chose this brand, because it is available in a brownish terra cotta, which is the exact color of the bark of the rubber plant.

Most mini rubber plants are a bit stiff looking, made entirely on one stalk. Thus we chose to make two stalks, one 4½ inches long to carry twelve leaves, one 2½ inches long to carry six leaves. Cut twelve leaves from the large pattern. Six from the middle-sized pattern shown,

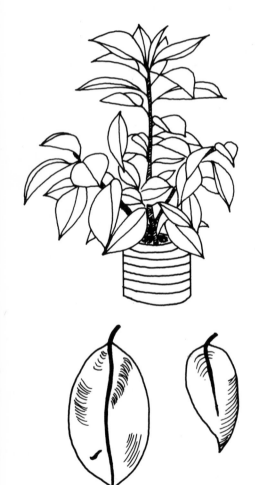

Rubber tree plant

218

and six for smaller leaves, about half the size of the middle-sized pattern. Cut one strand of the wire 9 inches long and four strands 8 inches long, four strands 6 inches, and three strands 4 inches. These will make the main stem. Fold the 9-inch strand of wire in half, pressing the bend hard so it will be sharp. Spread glue on one of the smaller leaves, lay the wire on the glued side about halfway up the leaf, and press another leaf on top. Press to make the glue hold. As you press, the impression of the wire will come up on the paper exactly like the vein in the leaves of this plant.

If you will look closely at a rubber plant, real or artificial, you will notice that the new growth comes out in the fold of an old leaf, a dull green sheathed in a pinkish red. This spot of color, repeated down the stem, makes the plant tremendously interesting. There are two ways to make it: One, find a paper the right color (we found a very light-weight notepaper and a light-weight construction paper) and cut a strip ½ inch wide and about 2 inches long. Roll into a tight roll and glue. Using three strands of embroidery cotton of approximately the same color, tie a knot in one end and with a needle, bring the thread through the roll of paper and out the top. Holding the roll between the thumb and index finger of the left hand, pull slightly; the thread will bring the rolled paper up into a point. Cut off the thread and drop a bit of glue into the roll.

Another way to make this pinkish-red point is to use a 6-strand embroidery cotton. Cut off a piece about 3 inches long and lay on a piece of waxed paper. Spread with a clear glue. When it is almost dry but still tacky, roll this between your fingers until it is like a cord. Allow to dry, then cut off ½-inch pieces and roll between the fingers at one end, to make the bud.

About every fourth leaf, bend the leaf in half lengthwise. Spread the bud with a little glue and lay it on the leaf where the wire makes the center vein. Add a bit of glue and fold the leaf up, to encircle the bud. Hold for a minute or so until the glue sets.

Cut a piece of the plastic tape about 5 inches long and ¼ inch wide. Starting at the base of the leaf on the 4½-inch wire, wrap around and around, pressing well and stretching the tape so that it fits tightly. About ¼ inch down, add a leaf on a 4-inch wire, and continue to wrap, remembering to pull the tape tight. About another ¼ inch down, add another leaf opposite the first, and so on.

For the smaller stalk, start with a wire 5 inches long and bend in half, then glue on the middle-sized leaf with a bud, to form the end of the stalk. Repeat as with the larger stalk. When finished, the two stalks are forced into whatever jardinière you have decided upon. Modeling clay makes a fine earth to use in packing the jardinière. It is available in either terra cotta or brown to simulate earth, and if your pot is deep enough, will hold the rubber plant nicely. Bend the smaller stalk so that it curves gracefully away from the larger, and bend a few of the leaves a bit over the curve of your finger, so they will seem to be drooping.

Materials for the Rubber Tree Plant

1 jardinière at least 1 inch deep
1 card beading wire
1 small piece olive-colored plastic-coated paper
1 roll Scotch plastic tape, brownish color
1 small piece thread or paper for bud
   Any clear-drying glue
   Decoupage scissors

Just one amusing thought on this project: As we were searching for the perfect material for making the buds, our eyes happened on a tiny bunch of plastic red peppers about ½ inch long. Their shape was perfect for the buds, their color not right for red peppers but perfect for rubber plant growth. We used them on one plant and they were pronounced perfect.

Nile Grass Plant (Umbrella Plant)

The Nile grass plant shown here, a creation by Charles Claudon, is related to the Egyptian papyrus and was found in every Victorian home. It is perfect for dollhouse corners because the real plant often grows to four feet or more. Despite its professional look, it is simple to create. Simply cut out and glue a circle to fit the bottom of the spool which will be the holder, and fill the center hole with clay—this helps to hold the branches upright. Paint the entire spool with a base coat of off-white. When dry, pencil in your own design lightly and then paint the design with blue acrylic, varying the intensity of the paint by thinning with water, to suggest Delft. Cut a ¼-inch strip of gold paper long enough to make a ⅞-inch-diameter ring. Tape it together, then glue the ring onto the top of the spool to simulate an inset pot.

Now you're ready to begin making the plant. Following the pattern in our drawing, cut four leaf rosettes. Vary the length and shapes slightly to make the plant more realistic. Cut three lengths of 18-gauge wire for the stalks—more if you want a larger plant. Insert the stalks as shown. Make a hole in the center of each rosette and glue it onto a stem, leaving about 1/16 inch of stalk above the leaves.

Using scissors, crease the center of the leaves, then bend them into shapes similar to those shown. Then cut seven stamens per plant or stalk, about ½ inch long. Using Krazy Glue or any very quick glue, glue the stamens in a cluster onto the 1/16-inch top of the stalk. When set, put a drop of white glue on each stamen and dip the end into the sawdust. When dry, paint the stamens and stalks green and the sawdust flowers white.

To finish, spray the entire project with decoupage spray. Fill the gold ring with white glue, then drop in Kitty Litter to suggest pebbles. And don't forget to sign your name and date on the bottom.

Nile grass plant

Materials Needed for the Nile Grass Plant

Empty spool about the size of the drawing
Forest green or medium green drawing paper
A small piece of clay
Decoupage scissors
Acrylic paints—Prussian blue and green-gold
Pencil
Thin paint brush
Strip of gold paper or gold foil
White glue
Transparent tape
Wire—both 18 and 22 gauge
Sawdust
Decoupage spray
Krazy Glue
A pinch of Kitty Litter

Charles Claudon's idea for using a spool as a jardinière, described here, is a valuable one; you'll be able to use it in many ways.

Of Making Many Books

Probably one of the greatest pleasures you will have from your crafting of miniatures will come from the making of books—and it comes not only from the fact that making the tiny volumes is relatively simple, so that anyone can do it, but from the fact that books are universally loved, and it is such a pleasure to stock the homes of our doll families with good reading.

Norman Forgue of Chicago, a great artist in the making of people-sized books and the designing of type, also produces small books of exquisite workmanship and beauty of design. These are a bit too large

A variety of books from the author's collection (*Photograph by Elinor Coyle*).

for collectors of miniature books, being close to two inches in height, but by working at this size, Forgue can use paper and design bindings which are a joy to behold.

There are two makers of books in this country, however, who do very creditable jobs with books about an inch or so tall, which is a bit closer to the dollhouse scale. Judy Jacobs of Merry Miniature Books makes hers from photographic reproductions which are then reduced to fit the size of the book she is making. She has, in fact, produced a copy of this writer's *The Bible Cookbook* less than one inch high, which actually has a jacket carrying the author's photo, and includes a title page and one full recipe.

Carol Wenk's books are a bit more professional looking, but neither of these is printed from movable type, as are Forgue's, and neither is of a quality to match his. However, Forgue's books are priced at from $15.00 to $25.00, and we have been told of many of these being snapped up at three times these prices.

As with most things *in parvo*, one must begin searching for the necessary materials before the work begins. Very fine French kid gloves make nice book bindings. Bookbinder's papers may sometimes be had for the asking, and at the end of this section is a suggestion for making your own papers. Small-scale wallpapers are always good, and these may be combined with small-grained leathers for half-and-half bindings. As for papers, a fine grade of rice paper is available at art or hobby shops, light-weight all-purpose white sketch paper is quite good, but for very fine paper which doesn't make too bulky a book, I have always preferred tracing paper, even that tracing paper which is used by dress designers to trace patterns and is very inexpensive.

Cut the two pieces for the cover from lightweight cardboard such as you find on the back of writing tablets. Cut the paper the size of the pattern, half as many as you want pages in the book. Cut the cover material along dotted lines of the bottom drawing. Cut off corners as shown. Something to be remembered here: if you are making a very thin book, say sixteen to twenty pages, you won't want a spine as wide as that shown in our drawing. The space we show will accommodate about forty pages (twenty of the size shown in the pattern, folded) but if you want to make a smaller book, simply make the spine a little narrower. Cut out the little rectangles at the top and bottom of the spine. Lay

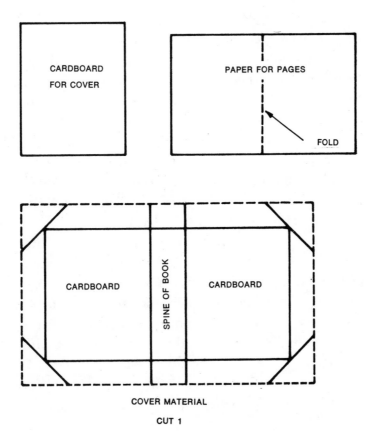

CARDBOARD
FOR COVER

PAPER FOR PAGES

FOLD

Patterns for covers
and pages of book

CARDBOARD

SPINE OF BOOK

CARDBOARD

COVER MATERIAL

CUT 1

the cover material right side down, then position the cardboards over it. Moisten the edges of the cover material with glue and fold over carefully. Dry under a weight.

If you are making the wider book with more pages, we would suggest that you now cut a bit of reinforcement for the spine from cardboard, to fit the spine minus the two end cutouts. Glue this to the cover material between the two cover boards. As before, dry under a weight.

If you are going to write or print a story in your book, it is best to do this before the pages are sewn together, but if you do this, it is important to remember to do the writing, printing, or pasting on consecutive pages. The first page, folded, will be one and two on the left half. Three and four will be on the left half of the next paper. Five and six on the left half of the next paper, and so on. The last half of the pages are numbered consecutively on the right-hand halves of the sheets.

Fold your sheets and fit them together. Thread your needle and carefully sew the pages together, taking care to keep the end of the thread long enough to tie after the sewing is completed. You will find that you can sew about six pages together comfortably. Repeat with the next six pages, so that when all your pages are fastened together, you have a series of little books.

Take your first stitch about 1/4 inch above the bottom edge of the fold in the pages, come up with your needle about 1/4 inch up, then down through the pages another 1/4 inch ahead until you come to the top of the page, then come down with another series of stitches through the holes you have made, to complete a solid line of stitches. End your stitching at the outside bottom and tie the ends securely. Clip the ends, then drop a dot of clear glue right on the knot, to hold it securely.

Now you are ready for your end papers. You can make your own (see the following pages), use regular book papers, or use any small-patterned paper that will glue well. Cut a piece the size of the pattern for pages, then another (two pieces).

First, glue your pages to the spine by spreading a bit of glue onto the spine, fixing the folded and sewn pages in the center of the spine, and fastening closed with a rubber band (but not too tightly!). When this has completely dried, affix the end papers by gluing over the back of the cover and then up onto the first page. Press to fasten securely, rub out any bubbles, and allow to dry. Repeat with the back cover by gluing from the last page down over the cover. Fasten again with a rubber band until completely dry. You are now ready to insert photographs or do other lettering.

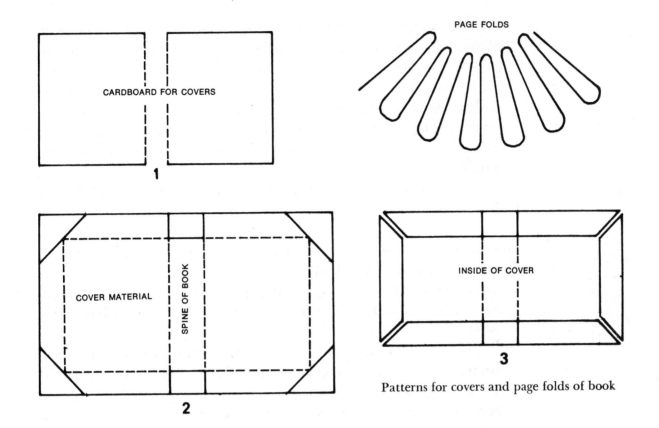

CARDBOARD FOR COVERS

COVER MATERIAL

SPINE OF BOOK

INSIDE OF COVER

1

2

3

Patterns for covers and page folds of book

Another method of bookmaking is followed by Mary P. Ross-Ross of Lancaster, Ontario, who has constructed a library of volumes that trace her family's history. Each volume covers one year and includes tiny reduced photographs of family members. Covers are of suede, although Mrs. Ross-Ross also uses purse and wallet linings because they are of fine texture and very soft. The volumes on her library shelves are a sight to behold. Mrs. Ross-Ross first conceived the idea for her "record books" from a souvenir booklet from Woburn Abbey, England.

As with the book described on previous pages, make the cover first. Cut the cardboard covers as illustrated in *1*, cut the cover material as shown in *2*, then lay the cover material right side down and arrange the cardboard over it. Carefully fold the cover material in over the cardboad and glue. Cut a small piece of heavy paper the size of the spine and glue this. Let dry under a weight.

Our pages are going to be 1 inch in width, $1\frac{5}{16}$ inches high. Choose the paper for your pages and cut a strip $1\frac{5}{16}$ inches wide and as long as you wish to have pages. The $1\frac{5}{16}$-inch width of the strip is the height of your pages. Now fold the strip accordion-fashion as shown in the drawing marked "page folds," so you have the number of pages you wish. Press together tightly to fit the spine of the book and glue heavily. Fasten with a rubber band while the glue dries. Now cut end papers 1/16 inch smaller than the boards in *1*, but twice as wide. You will need two. Glue these to the inside of the cover and up onto the first page of the book. Carefully press out any air bubbles. Repeat for the back of the book. Close the book again and fasten with a rubber band while the glue dries, then you are ready to go. Mrs. Ross-Ross uses tiny squares of black leather purse or wallet linings to glue on the spine of the books so they will look interesting as they stand in the shelves. One might even letter these strips with gold ink, as real books are lettered.

Norman Forgue, one of the greatest designers of miniature books, says that he doesn't see the need for making pages in books that are never going to be taken off the shelves. He uses tiny wood blocks or lead "quads" such as printers use to make spaces between lines for the book itself, and concentrates on the covers.

If you want to go a step further, you can have great fun making the handsome decorated papers for your end papers. One idea, based on the fact that oil and water don't mix, is to use those Easter-egg dyes which come with separate oil colors to be dropped onto a bowl or pan of water; the patterns that result are fascinating. Use a pan or bowl that will accommodate the pieces of paper which you will use for the end papers (the shallow foil roasting pans available in supermarkets are fine) and one deep enough to hold two or three inches of warm water. Start by using only one or two colors for the best effects, and a good grade of rice paper or medium-weight white sketching paper. Even high quality typewriter paper will do.

Drop a few drops of the oil dye into the water and then lightly swirl the surface with a spoon, or even blow upon the water. When nicely swirled, drop the paper onto the surface, making sure the center touches the water first to prevent air pockets which would leave white spaces on the paper. After a few seconds the paper will have absorbed the oil; carefully lift it out and set to dry, color side up, on newspapers.

On occasion, you'll see a beautiful new design as you lift out the paper. Have paper handy so that you can take advantage of this by dyeing another sheet. For a little variety, sprinkle about a half teaspoon of pale gold bronzing powder onto the paint; it has a beautiful effect. You may have to stir or twirl the water after each paper or each two or three; experimenting with it is half the fun. After the paper is completely dry, spray with acrylic or with artist's fixative—this is particularly necessary when you have used bronzing powder, or it will rub off on the rest of your book.

You will use these pretty papers in many ways—making fans, covering boxes, making fire screens, etc.—so do start to look for the Easter-egg dyes without delay.

Materials for Bookmaking Projects

Lightweight cardboard (such as is found on the back of writing
   tablets)
Materials for book bindings·
Thin paper for pages (rice paper, tracing paper, pattern paper)
Needle and thread for sewing pages
Glue for fastening pages to spine
Decorations for outside of book covers

A great idea for dollhouse hostesses, in our opinion, is to have on
hand a supply of blank books (Carol Wenk of the Miniature Book
Studio sells these in groups of one hundred at a very reasonable price)
into which each visitor is asked to pen a tiny greeting or story, as was
done with the volumes in the Queen's Dollhouse. This will soon build
up a most fascinating library!

Fire Fans and Screens

Since a cold, black fireplace opening was never a very pretty thing
to contemplate in an elegant room, homemakers, both people-sized and
dollhouse-sized, hundreds of years ago began to design screens or stands
that would be decorative and keep the ashes from blowing into the
room.

The fireplace fan was probably the first of these inventions, since
it required little more than paper or parchment folded and placed in
a stand. For your dollhouse so little of the paper is required that you
can be lavish with this ornamental detail.

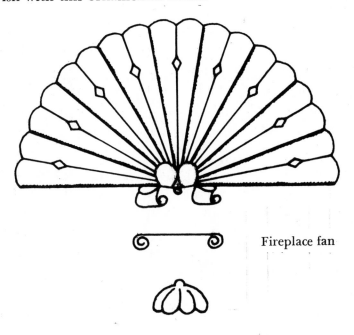

Fireplace fan

Our's is one copied from an 1850 fan in an English dollhouse, and it is so easy to make that one feels almost guilty that something so charming can be turned out in so little time. There's a catch to this, however; in order to make it really impressive it must be made from beautiful paper or foil, so start looking for the principal ingredient before you plan your fan. Ours is made from a heavy golden wrapping paper (gift paper) which was printed in a lovely Persian design of pinks and blues and then sprinkled with glitter. Gold or silver foil gives a lovely effect, too, as does any heavy lace which can be starched stiff enough to hold its shape.

The size of your fan will be determined by the width of the fireplace it is to stand against. This, divided in half, is the width of the paper to be used. In our collections the fireplaces averaged about $3\frac{1}{2}$ inches wide, so this is the dimension we used. Cut your paper $1\frac{3}{4}$ inches wide and $9\frac{3}{4}$ inches long—it takes about this length to make a perfect half-circle of pleats. Pleat the paper in $\frac{1}{4}$-inch pleats, turn the end pleats under, then with a stout needle and heavy thread run a thread about $\frac{1}{4}$ inch from the base of the pleats—you can get the needle through about four pleats at a time. When the thread is through, pull the pleats up very tight and knot and cut off the thread. Secure both the beginning and the ending knot with a dot of glue. Cut a pattern on the folds as shown.

Now open up a $\frac{1}{2}$-inch bell cap by spreading it flat. You will have two prongs on top, two on the bottom, and one on each side. Bend the top and bottom prongs up; there will be about $\frac{1}{4}$ inch space between them, the little loop which had been at the top of the cap will be below. Work the fan between the two pairs of prongs; the ends of the fan will come down and lie against the prongs which are sticking out at the sides.

You will notice from this that your folding must be precise; if any pleats are over $\frac{1}{4}$ inch, the fan will not fit into the prongs of the bell cap.

Now you are ready for the feet. Cut two pieces of $\frac{1}{4}$-inch brass banding, each 2 inches long. With a good needle-nosed pliers you will be able to catch the very end of the banding and bend, rounded, underneath. Repeat with the other end. If you have made the curves at the end nice and tight, the straight top of the band will be $1\frac{5}{8}$ inches long. Drop a droplet of Krazy Glue in the center of each brass band, on top, and set the screen on it. Be sure to remember the instructions for using Krazy Glue (p. 20); you will have a perfect bond. The only thing you have to watch is to be sure you have the legs parallel to each other, so they don't appear crooked from the front. Spray all with acrylic to keep the brass bright and stiffen the paper.

Materials Needed for the Fire Fan

1 strip material for the fan, 1¾" x 9¾"
1 ½" bell cap
2 strips ¼" brass banding, 1½" long
   Decoupage scissors for cutting patterns
   Tinsnips for cutting brass
   Needle-nosed pliers
   Krazy Glue

Paper Accessories

You can make some very nice candles by cutting a piece of paper about as wide as you wish the candle to stand tall, and 2 inches long, Moisten the ends of thumb and forefinger and roll the paper from one end, rolling in a bit of a slant. You will finish with a tapered roll that can be tipped with red, then yellow paint to make a perfect candle. Cut off at the bottom to stand straight. Make a larger candle simply by rolling more paper.

12 Bead Crafts

Crystal Chandeliers

We have an almost unlimited choice of designs of lighting fixtures to follow, from sixteenth- and seventeenth-century candlesticks and candlestands to today's model table lamps and other modern lighting fixtures. Some of the earliest light fixtures, such as the Betty lamp on p. 189 and the candle sconces on p. 195, almost demand metalwork, and these are relatively simple to make. Then we come to the early 1800s, however, and the oil lamps, and these are not so simple for us. Glass for the shades is hard to come by, and the bases are beyond the skills of the average homecrafter, even when made from metal.

But the next phase, the crystal chandeliers of the Federal, Victorian, and Regency periods, are perfect for the do-it-yourselfer, since our hobby shops and art shops today are filled with metal, crystal, glass, and wooden beads that can be manipulated into very impressive copies of the real thing. Our first one, and one of the handsomest we've come across, was created by Sue Thomas of Oak Ridge, Tennessee, and is made of crystal beads. These today are available in plastic (which certainly isn't very satisfactory so far as beauty is concerned), in plain glass, in crystal, and in what is called Aurora Borealis crystal, which reflects light in a whole rainbow of lovely colors. The latter costs a bit more, but the whole project is so very inexpensive when compared to the prices of crystal chandeliers available from shops that one can afford to work with the very best.

We illustrate here the shapes and sizes of the most commonly used crystal and Aurora Borealis crystal beads; glass and plastic beads are very similar. Those not found in the illustration, such as the flat-backed rhinestones called for in this chandelier, will be found packaged in ten-cent stores or hobby or art shops. Notice that some others, such as bugle beads, do not appear in this drawing. They too are available in packages in most ten-cent stores or art or hobby shops. The small bell caps, of course, are available in all shops; they are used for necklaces, but we use them in many ways. Your major search will be for the 2¾-

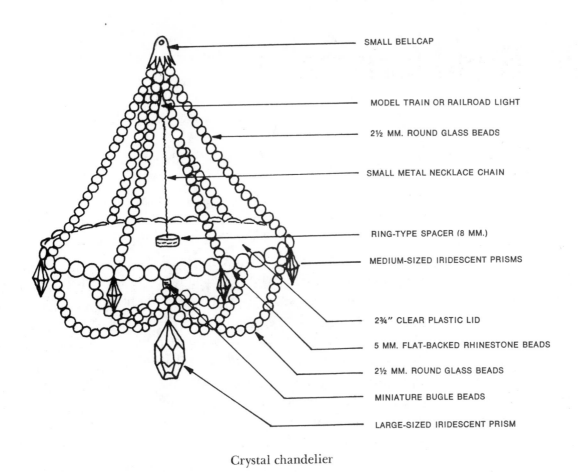

SMALL BELLCAP

MODEL TRAIN OR RAILROAD LIGHT

2½ MM. ROUND GLASS BEADS

SMALL METAL NECKLACE CHAIN

RING-TYPE SPACER (8 MM.)

MEDIUM-SIZED IRIDESCENT PRISMS

2¾" CLEAR PLASTIC LID

5 MM. FLAT-BACKED RHINESTONE BEADS

2½ MM. ROUND GLASS BEADS

MINIATURE BUGLE BEADS

LARGE-SIZED IRIDESCENT PRISM

Crystal chandelier

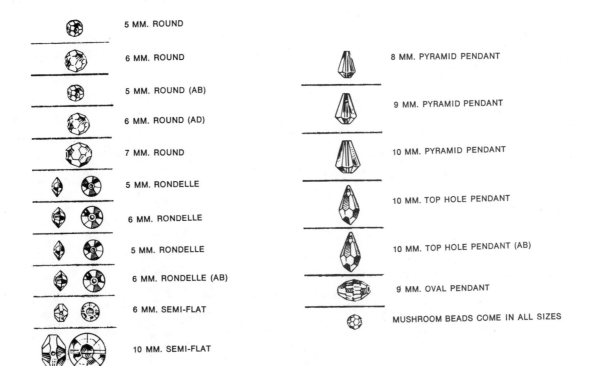

5 MM. ROUND

6 MM. ROUND

5 MM. ROUND (AB)

6 MM. ROUND (AD)

7 MM. ROUND

5 MM. RONDELLE

6 MM. RONDELLE

5 MM. RONDELLE

6 MM. RONDELLE (AB)

6 MM. SEMI-FLAT

10 MM. SEMI-FLAT

8 MM. PYRAMID PENDANT

9 MM. PYRAMID PENDANT

10 MM. PYRAMID PENDANT

10 MM. TOP HOLE PENDANT

10 MM. TOP HOLE PENDANT (AB)

9 MM. OVAL PENDANT

MUSHROOM BEADS COME IN ALL SIZES

Bead sizes

231

inch clear plastic lids; these are found in "smoked" or "clouded" plastic on containers of food, but usually with printed messages embossed on them; you will have to be on the lookout for clear ones suitable for this chandelier. We have made some from this pattern from the cloudy plastic lids and they serve very well, but are not quite so sparkly as the clear.

To make the top half of the chandelier, make six strings of seventeen beads each in the smallest size obtainable—not shown here on our drawings; $2\frac{1}{2}$ mm in diameter, using nylon thread and a beading needle if it makes it easier. Knot each thread at one end to prevent the beads sliding off and leave an extra four or five inches at the other end for attaching.

Choose a bell cap with seven holes; one in each prong, or a six-prong cap if you want a slightly smaller chandelier. We are going to use six prongs. Thread the unknotted end of each string of beads through one of these holes, threading from the top to the inside of the bell cap. Knot each thread several times and clip thread close to the knots. Using a toothpick or a pin, add a small dot of glue to these combined knots inside the bell cap. Allow to dry.

Now hold your plastic lid with the rimmed edge down; divide into six equal portions around the circumference. Using a large sewing needle held over a candle flame to heat, punch six small holes on top at the edge of the rim. Thread the other end of each of the six strings of beads through one of these holes; tie and glue as above, except allow about $\frac{1}{4}$ inch of slack in the thread between the last bead and the plastic cap. Otherwise, the beads will not hang straight. Be careful not to cross the threads in doing this.

Another hole should now be made in the middle of the plastic lid. Run the small metal chain through this; knot and glue on the bottom of the lid. Glue the 8-mm ring-type spacer (or a ring-type jewelry mounting set with Aurora Borealis stones) over the lead to further "fix" the chain, and then run the chain through the bell cap. A small piece of wire slipped through any link of the chain, and the top of the bell cap can be adjusted as to length. This will determine the drape wanted in the suspended beads. You can now use the wire to hang this from the arm of your desk lamp or a coat hanger suspended from a cabinet knob or handle so that it is upright as you work.

Make three strings of forty beads each ($2\frac{1}{2}$ mm) using the finest wire. Knot the wire at one end and allow a bit of wire for attaching at the opposite end. Attach one end of each wire in three consecutive holes in the plastic lid. Pull each wire string across the bottom of the lid and attach in a hole directly opposite on the plastic lid.

Curve the suspended wires into rounded shape underneath the plastic lid. Using about 6 inches of wire, attach the large prism in the center of the wire (by threading the wire through the hole in the top of the bead and then twisting both strands two or three times); lay aside temporarily. Arrange beads on each of the draped wires so there are ten on either side of the intersection. Use the wire with the large prism attached to "catch up" each of the three suspended drapes. Twist the wire around the middle of the three drapes (but not too tightly) and then continue threading these two loose pieces of wire through the small bugle beads (using as many as desired to get the draped effect you want), gluing and threading as you go. Continue threading the wire through the middle of the plastic lid and through the ring-type spacer on the top side. Clip the wire closely and bend to the opposite side and glue with a dot of glue.

Use about 3 inches of wire to thread through the hole in the top of each of the medium-sized prisms. Slide the prism to the center of the wire and twist tightly over the top of the prism for about $\frac{1}{4}$ inch; attach each of the prisms through one of the holes in the plastic lid, allowing enough slack in attaching so that it dangles.

Glue the flat-backed rhinestones around the rim of the plastic lid, covering as much as possible the wires which have been flattened and glued to the rim.

If you wish to electrify the chandelier, attach a small pea-light bulb, such as is used in model-railroad and car making, to the very top of the chandelier just under the bell cap. Since the $2\frac{1}{2}$-mm beads are of the Aurora Borealis variety and the others mostly rhinestones or iridescent, there is a surprising amount of light reflected down through the beads.

The light fixtures in the Spinka house (p. 31) are extraordinarily handsome and are made of brass tubing (available in many sizes at stores which carry model-railroad supplies), formed and soldered using jewelry findings and crystal beads and drops. They are intended to resemble gaslight fixtures and are wired with electric bulbs through six switches to six 14-volt transformers. The three-globe chandelier in the entrance hall is made from cup-shaped plastic beads and bell caps with bread-dough roses and leaves on a wire vine, all painted brass.

The drops of the crystal chandelier in the dining room are made from crystal bugle beads hung on hoop earrings, which are attached to each globe. The crystal bead chandelier in the library is an exact copy of an antique original, and the bead chandelier in the tower is made of beads and bread-dough flowers similar to the parlor one.

Materials Needed for the Crystal Chandelier

1   2¾″ clear plastic lid
222   2½-mm round glass beads
42   5-mm flat-backed rhinestones
6   medium iridescent prisms
1   large iridescent prism
1   6-prong bell cap
1   fine metal chain, 3 to 5 inches
6 or 8   crystal bugle beads
1   ring-type 8-mm spacer bead
    Nylon thread
    Spool of fine bead wire
    Glue or jewelry cement

Jeweled Ming Trees

It is strange that we never find miniature jeweled Ming trees, since slightly larger ones were brought here in such quantity when the China trade opened—and still, perhaps it is not so strange. For one thing, the Chinese considered <u>them</u> an art form, and perhaps didn't make them in miniature, and for another, even if there were miniatures (not one has even shown up in inventories of dollhouse furnishings), they were probably too delicate to survive.

Many modern-day miniaturists have not made them because they are, really, a job for a jeweler. Putting them together is such a delicate procedure that the miniaturist who is trying to sell them at a profit could never come out even. However, if you are not trying to sell them, you can have fun and be creative.

The first thing to do is search for a suitable container. For something so delicate as these trees, the cap from a large toothpaste tube is the right size, but not nearly nice enough for such a treasure. After a lengthy search of all our available pieces, we found the little handled pot shown at left in the drawing and in full size, in a batch of very pretty cobalt-blue pottery pieces from Mexico. The one upper right, also shown full size, is simply a small brass goblet. You probably have at least a dozen in your stock box.

The trees are built on brass wire. Your jeweler may be willing to sell you a foot or so of regular jeweler's wire, which is what we used in making the tree on the right. For the one at left we used a brass wire used for beading and purchased at the hobby shop for 29 cents for 24 feet on a spool. This is just a little lighter than the jeweler's

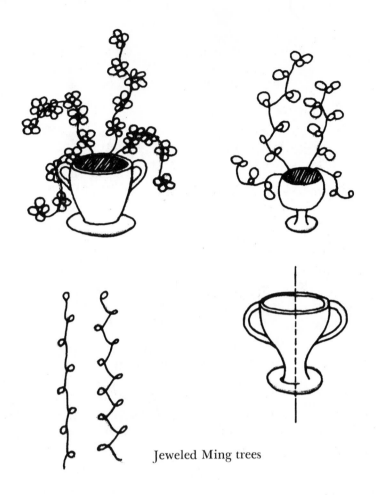

Jeweled Ming trees

wire, so we used it double. We liked it the better of the two. (A 32-gauge wire is just about right.)

You will also need a good pair of tweezers; the one made by Revlon is equivalent to a jeweler's tool at about a third the price. For trees the size of ours (about 1½ inches tall), which is about the scale of the people-sized jeweled trees, cut two pieces of wire 6 inches long and two pieces 4 inches long. Fold them in half. Now, using your tweezers in your right hand and holding the doubled wire in your left, bend the wire as shown in the small drawings; it should look almost exactly like a feather stitch. We used the loop at the end where the wire was doubled, for the first loop. Then, ¼ inch down, loop the wire over itself and down and around. Another ¼ inch down, repeat, remembering that in making the little loops the wire must always be bent *over* itself. When you have a stem about the height of the tree you have in mind, lay it flat on a table and bend it a bit in a graceful curve, the way you want your tree branch to bend. Repeat for the other branches, varying the length so the arrangement is graceful.

You will need about six beads or pearls for flowers, about twenty-four for leaves. We particularly liked a tree made with 5-mm semiflat (flat on one side) iridescent beads for flowers; the play of color on these is beautiful. Tiny pearls are pretty too, however, and we dug out several tiny faceted stones from an old earring that made lovely blooms. Choose glass beads for the leaves.

On a piece of waxed paper, lay out a stem. Using just a tiny droplet of glue, drop it into the loop at the top. Place a flower there. Squeeze a drop of glue onto the waxed paper. With your tweezers, dip a flower or leaf bead into the glue and then affix to the stem. Or, you might group two or three leaf beads around the terminal flower. Then come down to the next loop, dip a leaf bead into the glue and set into the loop. Set two more leaf beads around the central bead and drop one on top of the grouping to give depth. Try not to let any glue drop onto the paper, although nothing will be ruined if you do. Complete all the stems and let dry completely.

When all are ready to use, press a bit of modeling clay into your holder over half of it, vertically, as shown in the drawing. We do this because the stem wires aren't strong enough to force them into the clay. (Try to use terra cotta-colored clay so it will look like earth.) Arrange the stems against the clay in the pot, cutting off if they are too long for your taste. When the arrangement is exactly right, use your tweezers to press in clay to fill the other half of the pot, thus holding the stems firm. When the beads are completely dry, they can be rearranged a bit with the tweezers if they don't exactly suit you.

The tree on the right was not made from beads; the flowers are tiny pearls, but the leaves are jade chips obtained from a local jeweler. They are irregular in length and width, usually no more than 1/8 inch each way, and one is affixed to each loop in the wire.

Materials Needed for Jeweled Ming Trees
Tiny container for your jeweled tree
Jeweler's wire or brass beading wire
Terra cotta modeling clay
Iridescent beads or pearls for flowers
Green glass beads for leaves (or jade chips)
Sobo glue or Elmer's Glue-All
Tweezers
Wire cutters

Victorian Whatnots

The darling of the Victorian (and Edwardian) age was the "what-not"—that little shelf or group of shelves so necessary for the display of a nineteenth-century homemaker's bibelots. It is particularly appro-

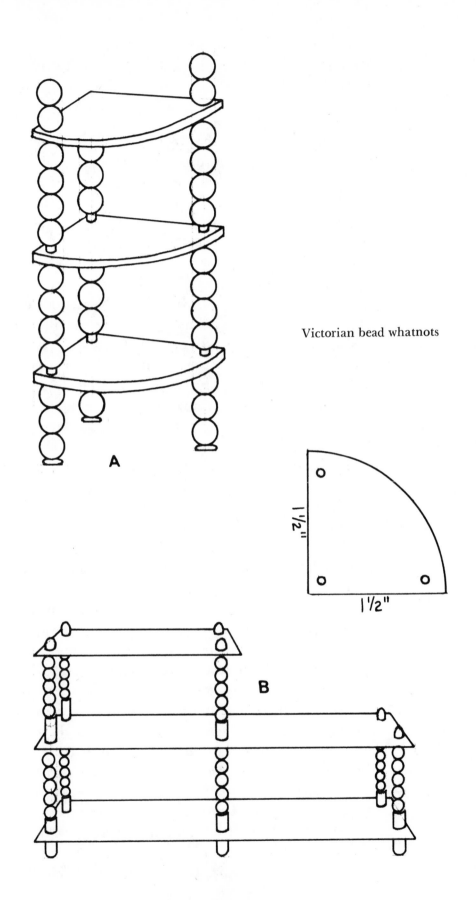

Victorian bead whatnots

A

1½"

1½"

B

priate for our dollhouses, too, since it can be made so easily and in so many different scales.

The one on page 237 was made using ⅛-inch cherry for shelves; the one at the bottom of the page, 1⁄16-inch wood, in order to keep the wood in scale with the beads. A fantastic array of beads is available for use in making furniture—glass, ceramic, and papier-mâché—but it is the wood (macramé) beads that are so perfect for furniture.

In the corner shelf at top we used a rather large bead in order to illustrate it clearly, and this one (found in most craft or art shops now) is made of olive wood from Jerusalem with little indentations on the sides—alway a nice conversation piece when Mrs. Doll has guests.

The ones drawn are ¼ inch, or 6 mm. You might check on sizes down to 3 mm, to see which you prefer. Never use heavy wire for these furniture pieces, as some craftsmen suggest; it will eventually bend out of shape and your work will be wasted. Ask for brass rods in the miniature-train department of your craft store. They come in all diameters to fit any bead, but 1⁄16 inch is about right for most. For the corner shelf cut a triangle no less than 1½ inches on the two sides—it can be as large as you wish. Drill three holes, as shown, to accommodate the rod on which you will string the beads. Use round, square, or "oat" (oval) beads to get the effect you want.

Fasten the bottom bead by filling the hole with a good glue (Sobo or Tacky), then insert the rod, making certain the bead is even with the bottom of the rod, and lay flat until dry. While these are drying, finish the shelves in any finish your prefer; we sprayed the corner shelf with gold paint and got an exact reproduction of a shelf from a book on Victoriana. Another authentic finish is one of flat black or maroon paint, with the edges of the shelf and, say, every other bead painted in gold. A bit gaudy, but most effective. Use as many beads as you wish to space the shelves; when you come to the top, finish off with an oat bead or a gold bead from an old necklace, attached with glue. Then snip off the brass rod exactly even with the top of the bead.

Shelves for the bottom piece, one still seen today in many shops and homes, are about 4 inches in length for the two at bottom, and one about 2⅛ inches (never use exactly half the measurement) for the top. Width should be about ½ or ¾ inch.

Materials Needed for the Victorian Whatnot
Wooden beads of size and number as you wish
Small scraps cherry or mahogany, ⅛" and 1⁄16" thick
Brass rods in the diameter to fit the bead holes
Stain or gold leaf to finish the piece
Good white glue, such as Sobo or Tacky

Wire snips
Sandpaper to prepare shelves for finishing
Small brush for paint

Children's Building Blocks

Eleanor Dunston of Pickwick Miniatures, Glenview, Illinois, makes beautiful little blocks for the doll children from square beads. Choose beads about $1/4$ inch square. Fill up the holes in the beads with plaster or plastic wood—just mix up a little in a teaspoon. If you are using natural wood beads, paint with bright primary colors, but if you search, you'll be able to find macramé beads already painted.

Now search through magazines for letter patterns $1/8$ to $3/16$ inch square—you'll find more than you can ever use. Cut these out carefully with a pointed knife, square and slightly smaller so that the colors of the block show uniformly around the edges. Glue the letters carefully onto the blocks, using Elmer's Glue-All and a small brush. The letters need not cover all six block faces, but should be so dispersed as to permit the spelling of words or names. Let dry, then apply three or four coats of decoupage coating to properly imbed the letters.

Materials Needed for Children's Building Blocks
$1/4''$ macramé square beads in various colors
Decoupage coating and a small brush
$1/8''$ to $3/16''$ block letters cut from magazines
Plaster or plastic wood
Elmer's Glue-All or similar glue

13 Accessory Crafts

Wall Pincushion

In the days when the seamstress came once a year and stayed for a week in order to complete wardrobes for all the ladies and children of the family, an entire room was set aside as the "sewing room," and here the lady with the needle reigned supreme.

Louise Allen Metzger of Prairie Village, Kansas, found one of the old wall pincushions, which were an important furnishing of the sewing room, at a country sale, and won second prize in the annual contest conducted by *The Dollhouse (and Miniature) News* with her 1/12-scale reproduction, the exact size of the drawing shown. You can cut from the drawing.

She writes:

The original, obviously made by loving hands, has lovely stamped brass corner plates, but my snippets from a gold border paper pretty well approximate the design. There was a hook in the bottom corner to hang the scissors on, so I made a hook with a bent pin and hung a miniature pair of scissors on it.

To reproduce the pincushion, first locate a tiny bit of old silk; the original seemed to be an old ribbed faille in a faded green. Cut a piece of light cardboard the exact size of the drawing and cover it with the faille, folding over and gluing in the back. Use 1/4-inch basswood or balsa strips for the border. Paint these black or dye with India ink, then cut to fit the covered square. No need to bother with mitering the corners here; they'll be covered, so simply make butt joints.

Now cut a square of the light cardboard the size of the center square and cut a piece of the faille or other material 3/8 inch larger all around. Glue one side of this, then two other sides, lapping over as with the larger square. Stuff a bit of cotton into the square, then lap the material over and glue this, too. Glue this square in the center of the larger square as shown. For the brass corners, we used pieces cut from decoupage gold banding; it worked perfectly. Or, you may

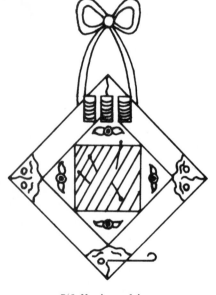

Wall pincushion

have a piece of brass banding from which you can cut the corners. The tiny roses we cut from an old valentine, but we now think it is much more effective to make roses and tiny green leaves from French knots. To cap it all off, you will need a piece of ribbon no more than ¼ inch wide; paste the two ends onto the back of the pincushion, bring up and tie in a bow.

Cut a square of harmonizing construction paper and glue over the back.

The little spools at the top of the pincushion are fascinating. Louise reports that she made hers using ⅛-inch dowels cut ¼ inch long. Pound a brad or wire nail into one end to use as a handle while winding on the thread. Fasten the thread ends with Elmer's Glue-All. When the brad or wire nail is removed and another pounded into the bottom, the tiny holes look like the spool holes. Glue three of these to the top of the pincushion. Be sure to wind threads that are bright and contrasting. The hook for the scissors is made by bending a small pin and forcing it in. Stick a few small pins into the pincushion.

Materials Needed for the Wall Pincushion

1 piece balsa or basswood, 8″ x ¼″ x ⅛″
Small piece of old silk
Light cardboard, such as used for tablet backs
India ink or paint for the wood
1 inch of ⅛-inch dowel for the spools
Tiny pins for the cushion
Piece of ¼-inch ribbon for the hanger
Hook at the bottom for scissors
Construction paper for backing
Elmer's Glue-All.

Tomato Pincushion with Strawberry Emery Bag

Several miniaturists make tomato pincushions to sell, but making them is such a pleasant job that if you have a good pattern such as this one supplied by Louise Allen Metzger, you'll enjoy making one yourself.

Using the end of a thimble as a guide, draw a circle on red percale. Cut out ⅛ inch from the edge of the circle. With tiny stitches, gather around the solid line. Stuff with a small wad of cotton, then draw the thread tight and sew down any loose edges.

Using two strands of green embroidery floss, bring your needle up from the bottom through the center, then down again and up again,

Tomato pincushion

pulling the thread tight to make the dimple in the top of the tomato.

To make the strawberry emery bag, cut a piece of the percale 1 x ½ inch. Fold into thirds, then turn in the corners diagonally as shown in the sketch and fold over to make a tiny cornucopia. Using four strands of the green floss, overcast the top to hold it in place and to simulate the cap of the strawberry. Bring the thread through the top of the tomato, allowing about ⅝ inch for the cord, then back again to the top of the strawberry. Fasten. Stick sequin pins in the top of the pincushion. If you wish to go a little further with the illusion, a few black dots for seeds of the strawberry may be dropped on.

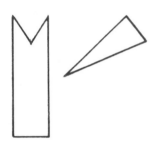

Vermont bootjack

Vermont Bootjack

A bootjack is a fine project for a beginning woodworker, and a necessary adjunct to any dollhouse. Use basswood, poplar, or any wood you have on hand. Stain, then cut according to the pattern. Glue the base to the top. That's all there is to it. We used walnut for the base and basswood for the top, to make a nice color contrast.

Love Letters

Jean Townsend of Albuquerque, New Mexico, sends along this romantic idea to make a stack of love letters to store in a desk or tie with a tiny blue ribbon, and store in the attic. Color the stamps, then cut out the patterns and fold into envelope shape on the dotted lines. Add a smidgin of glue to the inner edge of the bottom flap. Glue over the side flaps and fold the top down. (She even suggests adding a whiff of perfume!)

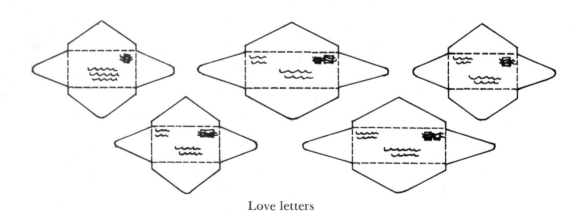

Love letters

Flower Arrangements

Gardens made in buttons are perfect for dollhouse flower arrangements. The button in the center of the photograph below is slightly enlarged. It is actually 1 inch in diameter. The shaft and metal lining was pulled out and the button turned over. The garden at left is Chinese. Note the pagoda at top, grasses and trees, aluminum-foil stairs ascending. The woodland garden at right has a tiny glass lake, many greens, tiny fawn drinking. All are planted in modeling clay. The shell pictured at top is planted with velvet mini-flowers. The tiny arrangement at bottom in the concave button has been given a wire handle.

Flower and garden arrangements in buttons. Made by the author (*Photograph by Elinor Coyle*).

Tin Hip Bath, ca. 1840

There is a dearth of tin bathtubs on the mini-market, a very odd thing since they were so universally used from about 1820 through the Victorian era. They were even carried westward in the covered wagons; hence, the ring at the head to hang them on the side of the wagon. The only other one we know of is that made by Al Atkins of the Village Smithy; his is of real tin and costs around $18.00, but according to the old photographs we were able to resurrect, his is much too low at the foot. You can cut the foot lower than our illustration if you wish, but these are the measurements as we found them.

Find an empty plastic bottle of detergent for dishwashing, and look for one which has an extrusion on the bottom which gives the effect of a little stand, as we picture. Wash out the bottle thoroughly (some hand lotions come in a similarly shaped plastic bottle), then draw the shape from our pattern onto the plastic with carbon paper or a soft pencil. The plastic will cut very easily with a razor blade; if it doesn't come out perfect the first time, just trim it down a little until it does.

We used Stain 'N Buff on ours; it takes to the plastic perfectly. Rub the inside with the silver to simulate tin, then rub outside with brass or copper Stain 'N Buff—both products are a paste and are rubbed in smoothly with the fingers. Then go through your catalogues to find small metal decorations which are affixed to the sides with Krazy Glue. (Try the Miniature Mart catalogue first.)

For the hanging ring at the head of the bath, you might use a simple ½-inch ring (get this at your hobby shop) and affix it with Krazy Glue, or cut a ⅛-inch strip 1¼ inches long, glue the ends together to make a circle, then affix the circle to the head of the bath.

A nice touch for this and any other appurtenance that should look as though it contains water is to fill with casting resin, allow to harden, then top with whipped candle wax for soap bubbles.

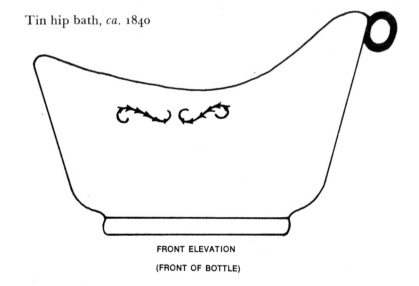

Tin hip bath, *ca.* 1840

FRONT ELEVATION

(FRONT OF BOTTLE)

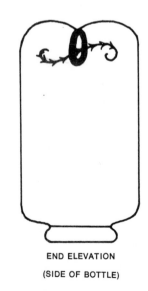

END ELEVATION

(SIDE OF BOTTLE)

14 Christmas in the Dollhouse

Christmas is a beautiful and happy time anywhere, but in the mini-world it is more beautiful than anywhere else, for we can indulge ourselves in making all of the lovely accessories that we'd like for our people-sized house, but sometimes can't quite afford.

Gingerbread Cookies

One can make, for example, huge (1-inch-high) gingerbread cookies to accompany our gingerbread house in either of two ways; the one on the left below is cut from cardboard, then coated thickly with Liquitex modeling paste, then when dry painted with acrylic paint (see the color combination suggested for the gingerbread house), and when dry, is dotted with Sobo glue and a few nonpareils sprinkled on. Finish with a coat of Deep Flex Decoupage Glaze.

The gingerbread boy's little friend, and the other tiny decorations here, were made from Polyform, a sort of modeling clay, rolled to a flat sheet a bit less than 1/8 inch thick, then the shapes were cut out, placed on a sheet of waxed paper, and baked in the oven for thirty minutes at 250 degrees. They were then painted with tube acrylic paints and decorated as described above.

Gingerbread cookies

This festive dollhouse setting displays, about ½ size, an array of Christmas decorations. In the center of the chimney breast, top to bottom, is a wreath, a swag, and another less sumptuous wreath flanked by two drapery rings each framing a petit-point figure. Food is on the table; the paper Christmas tree is ready for Santa (*Photograph by Elinor Coyle*).

Swag and Wreaths

Regular pipe cleaners, green if you can find them but white will do because you're going to coat them thickly with paint, are used for the two wreaths and the swag shown hanging on the chimney breast in the photograph. Twist three of these together to get a nice thick look, and fasten at the top after cutting off the excess. Dab on the modeling paste very thickly, trying for a rounded effect, then paint with dark green acrylic paint right from the tube—the rougher the paint, the better the effect.

In a saucer, mix a bit of yellow acrylic with the dark green and stir in a spoonful of fine breadcrumbs, the kind that comes in cans, but don't use the seasoned crumbs which are apt to contain cheese that will soften in the paint. Dab this mixture over the top of the forms so you have some variation in color—the paint with yellow in it gives a more realistic look. As the paint begins to set and acquires a tacky feel, use a wooden toothpick and pick and pull at the paint for a lovely feathery effect. Allow to dry overnight, then add a few dabs of glue and some nonpareils, then glue cookies and canes to the green.

The swag is made in exactly the same way. Most important to remember is to keep the acrylic paint watered down, which makes it

An elegant wreath in shades of brown, shown here twice the actual size, is made by gluing tiny pine cones, bits of dried leaves and stems, and minuscule dried flowers on a circle of thin cardboard. A red velvet bow is centered at the bottom.

easier to handle for these forms. Then, when you add the paint-and-crumb mixture, make sure the surface is tacky, but it must not be allowed to dry until you have drawn it out with the toothpick. The more ragged it is, the better the effect.

Petit Point Figures in Brass Rings

The petit point pieces in the brass curtain rings are really charming, and are an ever popular sale item for Christmas bazaars as well as for dollhouses.

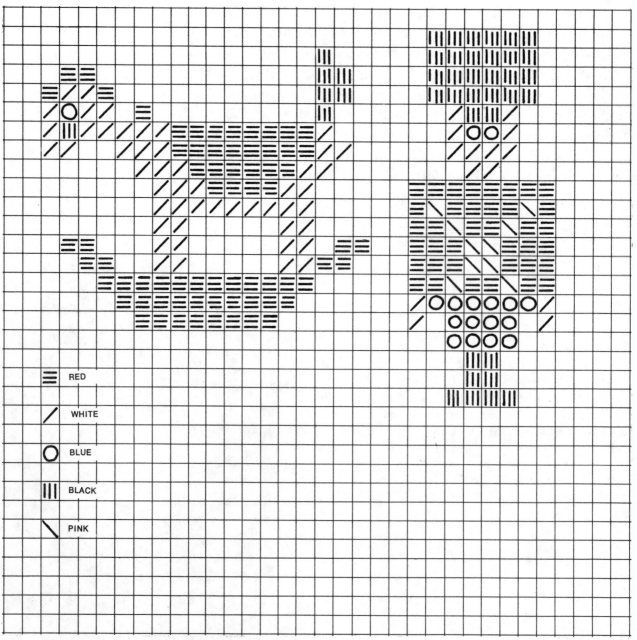

Patterns for petit point figures in brass rings

We used brass rings 1½ inches in diameter. They have a nice little ring at the top in which you can tie gilt ribbon or string for hanging. The two designs shown opposite are sketched on graph paper divided ten squares to the inch, and are twice their actual size. If you are doing the petit point on, say, canvas that is twenty spaces to the inch, you will get approximately the right size—or, since the rings come in any size, perhaps it would be best to do your petit point and then buy rings to fit it. The background of the dog figure is done in green; the soldier is on a background of white; these could be reversed. Get yourself a pad of graph paper, and you will find that you can work out other appropriate designs.

Use Persian needlepoint wool, split so that you're working with only one strand. Do the design first, then fill in the background, but before you start the background, trim the canvas to a circle that will exactly fit the ring, with enough overlap for gluing. Glue securely and allow to dry. Cut a circle of felt exactly the same size, and glue this over the canvas for a finish. Finish the hangings with a red bow at the top.

These are most attractive when worked out in little sunbonnet figures, too, in pastel colors and backgrounds of blue, pink, or yellow.

Red Boots

Everyone is familiar with the little red boots, of course. These are made of red felt cut according to the pattern at right, stitched with tiny hand stitches or glued, then finished with a strip of white felt at top. We sewed a tiny sequined ornament to ours. You will find plenty of tiny toys to go into them; check the catalogues or keep your eyes open in shops.

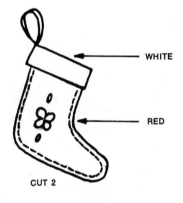

WHITE

RED

CUT 2

Pattern for red boot

Gingerbread House

The gingerbread house which Clothilde Sutton of Cold Spring Harbor, New York, makes for her dollhouse is one that anyone can make (although Mrs. Sutton had to be smart enough to come up with the original idea) with a little patience.

Use thin cardboard, such as that on the backs of writing pads; trace the pattern onto the cardboard; then cut out with a pair of scissors. Mark on the base, as shown by the dotted lines, where the front, back, and sides are to go, and glue them in place. You will conclude that this takes three hands, but with patience you can manage it with

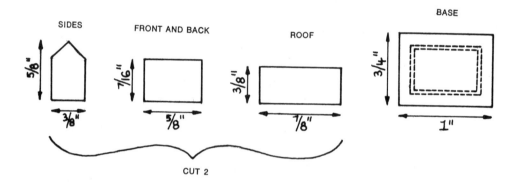

Patterns for gingerbread house

two. Allow to dry, then gently put the roof in place, and glue. Use an emery stick to smooth rough edges and slightly round the edges and corner of the base.

Paint with acrylic paint—yellow oxide and burnt umber mixed make a good gingerbread color. Use the paint quite thick to give a slightly uneven "dough" look. For the white "sugar frosting" use acrylic white paint straight from the tube. A real gingerbread house is glued together with sugar frosting, so put the paint along on all sections that have been glued together. Apply globs along the edges of the roof for an icicle effect. If you wish, paint "sugar" outlines for doors and windows and shingles for the roof. When the "paint" is dry, glue on cake decorations to look like tiny candies. Look for McCormick's "Festive Fixings" and Durkee's "Sequins." With a toothpick, put a dab of Elmer's Glue-All wherever you plan to put a decoration, doing one side at a time. Tweezers will help in placing the "candies."

If you're doing the house for Easter, you might want to elaborate a bit and add a "marshmallow" bunny or a chick. For Christmas, a lollypop tree made on a sliver of toothpick is a pretty decoration. Mrs. Sutton uses Sculpey for modeling decorations and acrylics for all painting.

As a finishing touch, glue the house on a tiny lace-paper doily which has been set on waxed paper. A small doily is easily cut from a large one.

Materials Needed for the Gingerbread House

Small piece thin cardboard
Elmer's Glue-All
Acrylic paints in colors
Tiny decorations such as "Festive Fixings" and "Sequins"
Toothpick
Tweezers
Sculpey
Paper doily

15 Renovating and Housekeeping

The renovating of dollhouses, old or new, is a ticklish proposition. There are dedicated collectors who insist that nothing, absolutely nothing, must be changed in the renovating, since any change will mean that the original thought or idea, the true inspiration of the house, will be lost.

Then, there are other collectors who feel that if a house is to be renovated, it should thoroughly be renovated. Change faded paper, refurbish scratched floors and woodwork, restore a gleam to the outside. I think that most collectors will tolerate this approach if we are sincere about it; the only really objectionable procedure is that in which an insensitive person tears off old Victorian wallpaper and substitutes a modern abstract design, covers lovely old faded woodwork with a hard finish, or tears off fine old silk upholstery, no matter how split and threadbare, in favor of modern material.

Sometimes these atrocities are committed in good faith; for example, I recently spent a whole morning with a collector who had come into possession of a very old dollhouse of only two rooms which were, however, quite large—15 x 15 x 13 inches. The rooms had been papered with a hideous paper of 1900 vintage that she couldn't bear to look at. So, she sprayed the paper with water, let it stand (see p. 85) and, when she pulled it off, found that walls and floors were made of a beautifully grained walnut. The problem? Whether to replace the paper with something of a suitable period that was beautiful or to cover only the floors and leave the walls in the natural wood. We never did come to a conclusion and concluded that it was too serious a problem to decide at one sitting.

When one encounters a truly important house of the kind pictured next, however, there is really no problem; it is a sacred piece of history, and the owner has an obligation, at least in my mind, to try to restore it to its original state or to leave it alone.

This house is now in the possession of Mrs. Fred Thiem of Keokuk, Iowa. It originally belonged to Todd and Mary Harlan Lincoln, who

252

Three views of the Todd and Mary Harlan Lincoln dollhouse, which was recently rediscovered and is about to be renovated. Courtesy of Mrs. Fred Thiem.

gave it to a friend, one Sue Roper, who lived in Mt. Pleasant, Iowa. Ms. Roper married a Dr. Christiansen and they became friends of Mrs. Thiem's sister. The house was turned over to the sister when the Christiansens moved to California and had been stored in her garage for thirty or more years when Mrs. Thiem found it.

Notice that both chimneys and all the windows are gone. A little transom over the door (usually stained glass in Lincoln's time) is missing. The inside is in a deplorable state, but there is enough wallpaper still on the walls to identify it; it is probably not so old as the house, but is generally ugly no matter what its age.

The house was obviously made by an expert. Of grooved wood to represent clapboard, the windows and doors are meticulously cut and shaped. Notice that the two on the right have little arches over the windows but the corresponding ones in windows on the left are missing. These, no doubt, were put in to mark division of the windows into the narrow panes, a fashionable detail of this period. The mansard roof, while coming a bit apart at the seams, is well made, but not detachable, and the large coping gives it a nice finish.

The third photograph, from the back, gives a hint of the wallpaper, and one wonders how even Todd Lincoln's dollhouse family could have endured that narrow hallway.

A few pieces of furniture were found in the house, but all of it is in need of refinishing. One leg was gone from the sofa, and the Thiems have replaced that. The handle was also missing from the little chamber pot, which was carved from wood, and this, too, they have restored.

Since it is generally in such deplorable condition, we agree with Mrs. Thiem in her wish that it not be made to look new. We would, however, love to see some qualified person restore it so far as is possible, so that the children of today may see what the children of many yesterdays ago enjoyed. All of us are lucky that such a treasure fell into such sensitive hands.

The two arch enemies of dollhouses, most collectors agree, are cats and dust. The cats we can keep out—but the dust? Unless one's house is an airtight box it becomes a real problem. One subscriber to *The Dollhouse (and Miniature) News* writes,

Because I hate housework in any dimension, I have my dollhouse chores quite organized. In a shoe box marked "Cleaning Closet" there is stored all the special things to make a cleaning quick and easy, whether just a dust-and-touch-up, or a housecleaning.

The main secrets of easy cleaning are to have the right tools and to keep one's big hands out of the room as much as possible.

Furniture found in the Lincoln dollhouse. Courtesy of Mrs. Fred Thiem.

Two good sources of tools are art and hobby stores and office equipment shops—just don't use the things as intended. The same applies to drug stores.

My basic tools are an assortment of:

- Tweezers to pick up and place tinies.
- Water color brushes, different sizes, all with long handles, for dusting.
- Different pastry and typewriter brushes to brush upholstery walls and carpets.
- Any small brush, not too stiff, with a wire handle. Bend the handle at a 45 degree angle so the brush sticks down like the teeth on a garden rake. This will flick up things on the floor under a piece of furniture where a brush with a straight handle will not reach.
- Many swab sticks (various lengths from drug stores) with plain twisted cotton ends, for applying glass cleaner to permanently set inside windows, wall mirrors, etc. Make a lot of them at a time with different-sized ends in the cotton for different jobs.
- A cotton padded end on a stick, then covered with a fine toweling, for cleaning the glass. Different sizes for different minis. Toweling can be attached with a tightly twisted bit of Twistem. Do not let the Twistem ends remain, or you may knock something over.
- Swab stick with a bit of sponge fastened on with Twistem. This will often remove lint on mini carpets that a brush won't touch.

- A small medicine bottle with glass cleaner liquid, preferably wide-mouthed.
- A straight-sided old peanut butter jar for washing all glass chandeliers and other items which can be immersed. Must be deep enough so the chandelier is in no danger of hitting bottom. To minimize accidents, I pad the insides of the jar with a wash cloth, then fill with detergent solution and dunk the chandelier up and down until clean. I rinse in a wide padded mixing bowl, either using some non-spotting preparation such as is used in dishwashers or rinse thoroughly in distilled water.
- A very fine jeweler's cloth (need only a tiny bit) for a quick polish on a single piece of silver in a room. Much silver polishing is a problem, and a big project.

If your tiny accessories are not fastened down with some harmless adhesive, it is best to do casual dusting with a tool in both hands. Reach in with the end (either one, brush or wood, whichever is most suitable for the object) and hold the piece down on the table or shelf with a little pressure on top, then dust around it with the second watercolor brush in the other hand. The slim blunt end of the watercolor brush is perfect for pushing the miniatures back into place after dusting. If a piece is upset, you will need the long tweezers.

With a little experimenting, you can make a set of "dust mops." It isn't practical to try for a swivel on a single mop, so make several with the mop ends at different angles. These will clean bare or partially bare floors without, for example, moving a loaded dining or kitchen table. Use a piece of wire for the long handle and bend a blunt loop in the business end so no sharp wire can work out through the padding. Pad in any material and size and fasten with the Twistem again. You can even apply Endust and take off the mop ends and wash them if you care to.

No long handle should be so long that you will strike the ceiling if it is used upright or the walls in a small room if used horizontally, but there are no other rules about the length you choose.

One last thought, always keep a bit of Pink Pearl eraser (this is the very best, available at any stationery or office supply store) or art gum for repair in case you hit a painted wall with the end of a brush. Use the art gum as a last resort, since all those crumbs only make more cleaning necessary.

Appendix: List of Suppliers for Craftspeople

(Always check on local hobby or craft stores, art marts, and construction suppliers first. Then check with these specialists.)

A & L Hobbicraft
50 Broadway, Box 7025
Asheville, N.C. 28802

Send $1.00 for catalogue; many varieties of tiles available.

P. S. Andrews Co.
603 So. Main St.
St. Charles, Mo. 63301

Send $2.00 for 180-page catalogue (refunded on the first $12.00 order) which includes all the tools and supplies you'll ever need.

Architectural Model Supplies, Inc.
115D Bellam Blvd.
P.O. Box 3497
San Rafael, Calif. 94902

Everything to finish mini buildings; trees, grass, basswood, paints, surface materials. Send $1.00 for catalogue.

The Bead Game
505 No. Fairfax Ave.
Los Angeles, Calif. 90036

Send 25 cents for catalogue on beads and jewelry findings great for chandeliers.

C. E. Bergeron
123 Laurel Ave.
Bradford, Mass. 01830

Send 50 cents for list and box of samples. All varieties of moldings, etc.

Bob's Arts and Crafts
11880 No. Washington
Northglenn, Colo. 80233

Send for 268-page catalogue ($2.00) DHN, which may be the most complete in the business today.

D. Bosse
2040 Greenwood Dr.
San Carlos, Calif. 94070

SASE and 25 cents for dollhouses, rug patterns, list of other items carried.

The Brookstone Co.
Peterborough, N.H. 03458

Send $1.00 for catalogue of special tools and many other supplies, lots of hard-to-find things valuable to miniaturists.

Cerami Corner, Inc.
607 W. San Gabriel Ave.
Agusa, Calif. 91702

$1.00 for a catalogue which includes decals for ceramics, many other deails.

Chestnut Hill Studio
Box 38
Churchville, N.Y. 14428

Send $1.00 for catalogue that includes doors, windows, and paneling in exquisite detail.

Constantine's 2050 Eastchester Road Bronx, N.Y. 10461	Send 50 cents for complete catalogue of tools, hardware, finishing materials, woods in sizes to $\frac{1}{16}$ inch, veneers to $\frac{1}{28}$ inch.
Craft Creative Kits, Dept. DHN Elmhurst, Ill. 60126	Send $2.00 for catalogue that includes doors, windows, and and houses. Fine line of kits, all sorts.
Craft Midwest Box 42 Northbrook, Ill. 60062	Magazine devoted to craftspeople but not necessarily miniatures. Send $1.50 for sample.
Craftsman Wood Service Co. 2727 South Mary St. Chicago, Ill. 60608	Catalogue as above; everything you'll need in tools, hardware, wood in all thicknesses.
Deft Wood Finishes P.O. Box 3669, Dept. DHN Torrance, Calif. 90510	Send SASE for descriptive, instructive material on wood finishing.
Dollhouse Factory Box 456, 156 Main St. Lebanon, N.J. 08833	Hand-made shingles, leaded windows, light fixtures, many other supplies.
Dollhouse Factory P.O. Box 2232 Sunnyvale, Calif. 94087	Send SASE for list of supplies.
Dollhouses 16460 Wagon Wheel Drive Riverside, Calif. 92506	Send SASE for catalogue of ¼-inch to 1-inch ideas, glass, mirrors, many accessories.
Edabub's Dollhouse R.D. #1, Box 84B Great Barrington, Mass. 01230	Catalogue (50 cents) shows siding, flooring, wainscoting, moldings, and many others.
Elspeth 7404 Helmsdale Road Bethesda, Md. 20034	Original patterns for miniature rooms, now has four rooms, $2.00 each.
Enchanted Toy Shop, Dept. DHN 23812 Lorain Road No. Olmstead, Ohio 44070	Send SASE for complete lists of electric wiring and accessory supplies. Also booklet on wiring.
The Ginger Jar 6133 Wakefield Dr. Sylvania, Ohio 43560	Bricks, many accessories for houses. Send 50 cents for list.
Green Door Studios 517 E. Annapolis St. St. Paul, Minn. 55118	Send 50 cents for list of patterns, accessories, supplies for almost anything.
J. Hermes Box 23 El Monte, Calif. 91734	SASE for list. Wallpapers, glues, some miniature pieces.
Holgate & Reynolds 601 Davis St. Evanston, Ill. 60201	Complete line of architectural scale model plastic surfaces. Send $1.00 for catalogue.
Illinois Hobbycraft 12 So. Fifth St. Geneva, Ill. 60134	Most complete line of electric lamps, fixtures, supplies, and instructions for wiring. Send 25 cents for catalogue.

Jewel Thief
#38 Fashion Square
La Habra, Calif. 90631

Send $1.25 for color list of jewelry findings for making chandeliers, many other things.

Joen Ellen Kanze
26 Palmer Ave.
No. White Plains, N.Y. 10603

Free list. Has dollhouse plans, many accessories, makes dollhouses to order.

The Lilliput Shop
5955 S.W. 179th Ave.
Beaverton, Ore. 97005

Send 50 cents for list; dollhouses, hand-carved furniture, wood and moldings, many supplies.

Lilliput, Unlimited
P.O. Box 450
La Mirada, Calif. 90637

Send 25 cents and SASE for many tools and supplies for electrifying your dollhouse.

Maid of Scandinavia
3244 Raleigh Blvd.
Minneapolis, Minn. 55416

Send $1.00 for catalogue of home-baking supplies that includes nearly fifty pages of craft supplies.

Metal Miniatures
601 Davis St.
Evanston, Ill. 60201

Send 25 cents and SASE for all-inclusive list of metal miniatures of all kinds, door knobs and findings, much more.

Miniature Book Studio
Carol Wenk
P.O. Box 2603
Lakewood, Ohio 44107

Send 25 cents for list. Makes small blank books to fill bookcases. Many printed books also.

The Miniature Mart
883 - 39th Ave.
San Francisco, Calif. 94121

Send $2.00 for a fine catalogue which includes not only great miniatures but hardware findings, doors and moldings, many other things.

Ron T. Muckerman
Rt. 1 Box 154
Beaufort, Mo. 63013

Send 50 cents and SASE for list of box rooms built to order, shipped assembled or in kit form.

C. A. ("Chuck") Newland
2465 E. Commonwealth
Fullerton, Calif. 92631

Send 25 cents and SASE for full list of patterns, woods, and moldings. Newland also builds dollhouses.

Norm Nielsen
6678 So. Clayton St.
Littleton, Colo. 80121

Send $1.50 for catalogue of custom dollhouses, shadow boxes, wood supplies.

Northeastern Scale Models, Inc.
Box 425
Methuen, Mass. 01844

Send $1.00 for list and box of samples; complete stock of moldings, supplies, including windows that go up and down.

Peddler's Shop
883 - 39th Ave.
San Francisco, Calif. 94121

Now combined with The Miniature Mart (which see). Fine wallpapers, metal findings for dollhouse builders. $2.00 for catalogue.

Pickwick Miniatures
P.O. Box 297
Glenview, Ill. 60025

Send $1.00 for list. Includes fireplaces, accessories, very fine flower arrangements, and plants.

Doreen Sinnett Designs
418 Santa Ana Ave.
Newport Beach, Calif. 92660

Papier-mâché shingles, bricks, etc. Wallpapers and a line of dollhouses. Send $1.00 for catalogue.

Talents Unlimited
801 Glenbrook Road
Anchorage, Ky. 40223

Send $2.00 for a most beautiful catalogue which includes tools, wood moldings, miniatures, all the supplies you need.

Art Triplett
412 El Portal Drive
Santa Rosa, Calif. 95401

Shadow boxes, dollhouses to individual order, trunk reproductions, many interesting pieces. Send 50 cents for list.

Village Smithy
Al Atkins
R.D. 5
Hemlock Trail
Carmel, N.Y. 10512

Send $3.00 for catalogue (refunded on first order) that is a work of art. Anything handmade in metal plus carefully researched accessories.

Walther's
4050 No. 34th St.
Milwaukee, Wis. 53216

Send $1.00 for catalogue of miniature-railroad supplies, which lists many items useful in dollhouse-making.

The Workshop
424 No. Broadview
Wichita, Kan. 67208

Really great doors, windows, and miniatures. Beautiful fireplaces, flooring, and moldings. Catalogue $1.00.

Index